DEER VALLEY

THE QUEST FOR EXCELLENCE

BY KRISTEN GOULD CASE

MOUNTAIN SPORTS PRESS

BOULDER, COLORADO USA

Deer Valley: The Quest for Excellence

Published by Mountain Sports Press

Distributed to the book trade by:
PUBLISHERS GROUP WEST

Text © 2003 Kristen Gould Case

Bill Grout, *Editor-in-Chief*
Michelle Klammer Schrantz, *Art Director*
Scott Kronberg, *Photo Editor & Associate Art Director*
Elizabeth Downey, *Associate Art Director*
Christopher Salt, *Production Manager*
Andy Hawk, *Account Manager*

ISBN 0-9724827-0-9
Library of Congress Cataloging-in-Publication Data applied for.

Printed in Canada by Friesens Corporation

Prepress by Westphal West, Boulder, Colorado

A subsidiary of:

929 Pearl Street, Suite 200
Boulder, CO 80302
303-448-7617

To all of the Deer Valley employees,
past and present,
who have worked so hard
to make every day at the resort
seamless and magical
for its guests.

CONTENTS

FOREWORD
The Deer Valley Experience

BY ROGER PENSKE

It begins with the solid base on which the company stands. It includes technical, practical, well-thought-out business practices. It involves participating in market research, buying the best quality equipment and products, having sound marketing and financial plans, and training and empowering resort employees to do their jobs autonomously. The philosophy that guides every decision at Deer Valley is a commitment to excellence, to being the best and to doing things right.

Do the skiers, when they arrive at Deer Valley, really think about any of this? Probably not. But they see the results in the uniformed attendants who invariably greet them with a smile, and in the comfort and beauty of the day lodges. They know that ski resort operations are sound, the chairlifts will be running on time, their ski instructors will be waiting for them in uniform as scheduled, and their children will be well cared for during the day, whether in ski school or at the Children's Center. Guests know that the slopes have been prepared for them and that their meals will be fresh and appetizing.

The end result for the Deer Valley guest is satisfaction. Deer Valley guests come here for the Deer Valley experience. At the end of the day, when their expectations are met, they are satisfied. They want to experience that satisfaction time and again, and so they keep coming back to Deer Valley because their expectations are consistently met.

But the icing on the cake for the guests—the magic that lingers in their minds—is that spark of energy and excitement that they create that makes the resort come to life for them. It comes from their interaction with the mountain, the elements and the Deer Valley people. It begins when they encounter the fresh mountain air, voluminous powder snow, mind-clearing vistas and soothing mountainscapes.

So much is done for the guests at Deer Valley that they needn't worry about details. Lack of worry means they can go out and enjoy the day to the fullest. Call it enchantment, transcending everyday concerns, or suspension of disbelief. Call it what you will. It is the benefit of found time—of a son or daughter opening up in conversation on the chairlift, or of a friend smiling over lunch by the fire. It is the surrender of letting skis succumb to gravity, carving the first turn of the day—or the last.

The Deer Valley experience comes together every day for guests at Deer Valley Resort. That is why it's such a great place to be. We hope that this book will give you an understanding of Deer Valley's footings—its history, philosophy and goals—and the nuts and bolts that make the operation work. We hope it will also give you a taste for its charm, its allure and the people who are its heart and soul. We hope that it will draw you into Deer Valley's quiet elegance and encourage you to discover the Deer Valley experience for yourself, in your own way.

However you get to know Deer Valley, enjoy. That is what it's all about.

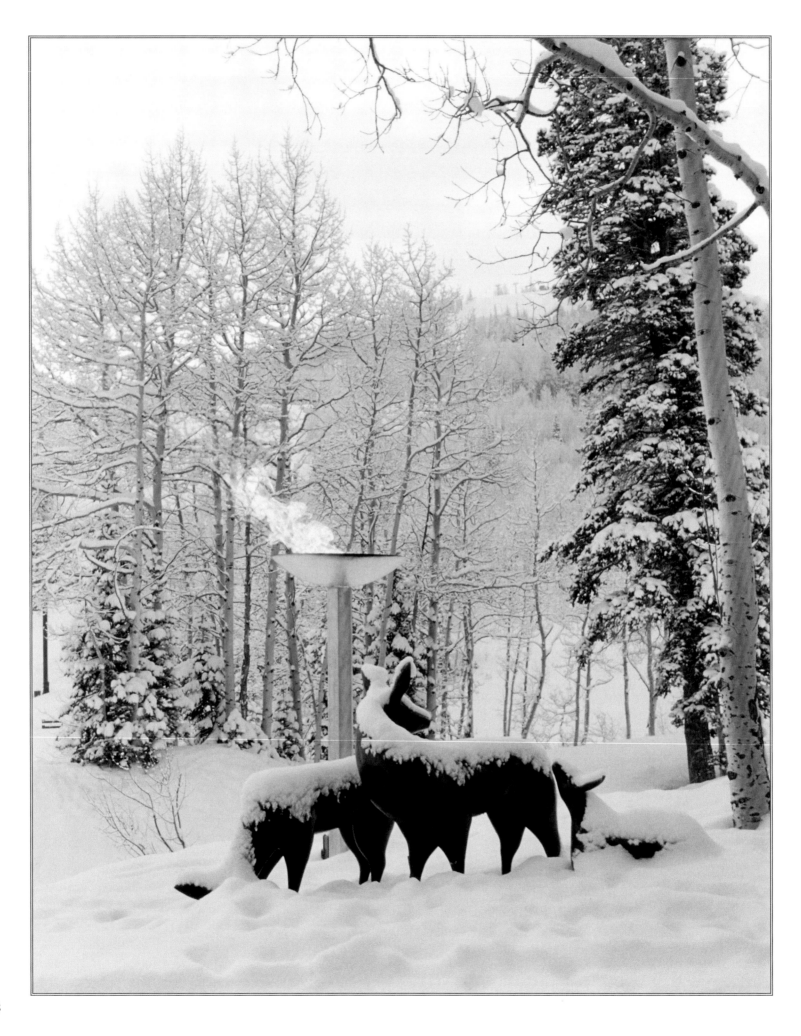

Chapter 1

HISTORY

Sophisticated. Beautifully planned. Upscale. That's how visitors see Deer Valley Resort today. It wasn't always like that. In the late 19th century, the area that was to become Deer Valley was a rough-and-tumble kind of place, a gritty mining camp where noisy, soot-belching ore trains came and went day and night. Over the decades the area was known variously for its thriving red-light district, illegal stills that produced Utah moonshine, a race track, baseball fields and a "pest house" in which unfortunate residents with smallpox and diphtheria were quarantined.

In fact, Park City's rich history began in the area that is now Deer Valley Resort. The first official mining claim in the region, Flagstaff, was here, and lift-served skiing started with the town's very first ski area, Snow Park.

The story began at the start of the Civil War. Volunteer soldiers from California, under the command of Colonel Patrick Connor, were stationed in Salt Lake City to protect the east-west overland mail route from Indian attack and to ensure that Utah Territory would not secede from the Union. Connor, like many working for the U.S. government at the time, was virulently anti-Mormon. He encouraged his soldiers to spend their free time prospecting in the nearby Wasatch Mountains, in the hope that if gold or silver were discovered, the subsequent influx of treasure seekers might "even out" Utah's Mormon-dominated population.

One day in October 1868, three prospecting soldiers were shielding themselves from the wind behind an outcropping on the east side of the Wasatch range. They saw a glinting lump of galena—a sign that silver ore was nearby. They tied a red bandana to a pine pole to mark the spot so they

THIS ELEGANT SETTING OUTSIDE STEIN ERIKSEN LODGE WAS ONCE THE SITE OF PARLEY'S PARK SILVER MINE. DURING LODGE CONSTRUCTION IN 1980, SWIMMING POOL EXCAVATION REVEALED OLD MINE WORKINGS.

THE 1860S VERSION OF WHAT IS NOW SILVER LAKE VILLAGE, MIDMOUNTAIN AT DEER VALLEY.
THE AREA WAS THEN CALLED "LAKE FLAT" AND IS WHERE PARK CITY'S FIRST COMMUNITY OF MINERS WERE
HOUSED IN RUDIMENTARY SHACKS. AN 1870 CENSUS REPORTED 164 RESIDENTS.

would be able to find it later. The peak where they inserted the pole became known as Flagstaff Mountain. (A Deer Valley ski run in that area is called Bandana.)

Their ore samples proved to be loaded with silver, so the soldiers returned in the spring and began mining in earnest. Prospectors formed a mining community around a small lake just northeast of the Flagstaff Mine. Named Lake Flat, the settlement became a hive of activity. An 1870 census counted 164 people living in the area. The spot that is now Silver Lake—the Deer Valley mid-mountain area where you'll find multimillion-dollar lodges, upscale boutiques and the popular tanning and lounging spot known as McHenry's Beach—began as a squatter's village of tents, rickety shacks and log houses.

The late Jim Ivers, a longtime Park City miner, recalled that Lake Flat's inhabitants were mostly Scotsmen, and local historians surmise that they loved the beautiful meadow at Lake Flat because it reminded them of their homeland. As George Thompson and Fraser Buck wrote in their book *Treasure Mountain Home*, "The setting was one of unsurpassed beauty, with its white-barked aspens mirrored on the tiny mountain lake, all outlined by stands of forest-green pines and carpeted with acres of crimson Indian paintbrush and

ABOVE: THE FLAGSTAFF MINE WAS STARTED
IN 1868 ON THE SITE WHERE PARK CITY'S
VERY FIRST SILVER ORE WAS DISCOVERED.
THAT SITE WOULD EVENTUALLY BECOME
PART OF DEER VALLEY RESORT. NOTE THE
MINE TAILINGS PILE. WHEN COVERED WITH
SNOW, OLD TAILINGS PILES MAKE GREAT SKI
LINES. RIGHT: A BIRDS-EYE VIEW OF THE
ONTARIO MINE, CIRCA 1891. THE ONTARIO
WAS THE LONGEST-RUNNING SILVER MINE
OPERATION IN THE UNITED STATES, REAPING
OVER $50 MILLION IN PROFITS.

nodding white columbines. Little wonder the miners who lived there called it 'The Robin's Nest of the Wasatch.'"

Word spread about the silver discovery, and in 1872 mining speculator George Hearst came sniffing around. He rode his horse down an aspen-lined dirt path (today's McHenry ski run) and investigated the doings at the newly opened McHenry Mine. He couldn't get a good look because the mine was flooded with underground water, so he decided to explore elsewhere. He wandered into a little canyon just below the ridge where Stein Eriksen Lodge is now located and saw several men digging a trench at the Ontario claim. Hearst found plenty of ore here and bought the Ontario claim for $27,000. It became the longest-running silver mining operation in the United States, reaping over $50 million in profits and contributing to the enormous Hearst family fortune that helped finance the vast publishing empire built by George Hearst's son, William Randolph Hearst.

Raging underground water hampered operations at all of Park City's mines. More money was spent pumping water from local mines than on all other operating costs combined. Park City miners and engineers pioneered revolutionary solutions to the problem of underground water. Engineers at the Ontario designed the world-famous Cornish Pump, which had two

enormous 20-inch pistons and could pump four million gallons of water a day. Later, miners built drain tunnels. The Keetley Tunnel, which carried water out of the Ontario Mine and was named for the man who designed it, took seven years to complete. It was engineered so precisely that to this day observers can stand at one end and see sunlight coming in the other, three miles away. A third of Park City's drinking water still comes from two other local tunnels, the Judge and the Spiro.

Mining was no easy job. Miners often worked in waist-deep icy water, toiling 10 to 12 hours a day for $3. Working 1,500 feet underground with only candles as a light source (after 1897, carbide lamps became available), the miners cut through Wasatch Mountain rock inch by inch, using hammers and chisels until compressed-air drills were introduced. Later

known as "widowmakers," the new drills kicked up ore dust filled with razor-sharp quartz particles that pierced the miners' lungs, causing them to drown in their own fluids. Thousands died from this silicosis (known as "miner's consumption" or "miner's con"). The Park City Miners Hospital, where most of them died, was built in 1904 and still stands in the town's City Park.

Aside from the Ontario, the most famous mines in the area were the Daly-Judge, the Daly-West and the Park City Consolidated

(Park Con). John Daly, who operated the Daly-West and then the Daly-Judge from 1881 until 1907, saw the value of zinc when no one else did. The Daly-Judge ended up being one of the first zinc producers in the country, and its silver and gold revenues rivaled those of the Ontario.

On July 15, 1902, 34 men were killed in an underground blast at the Daly-West and Ontario mines, the worst mining disaster in Park City history. The explosion occurred in the Daly-West, but poisonous gas spread through a tunnel to the Ontario. That week's headline for

The Park Record (now Utah's oldest continuously published weekly newspaper) read, "Most Appalling Accident. Thirty-Four Lives Lost Through Explosion of a Powder Magazine." Many of the funerals were held on the same day, with a solemn procession down Main Street. The accident prompted an immediate change in state law, mandating that mine explosives be stored above ground.

The Park Con Mine was located just above what is now Snow Park Lodge at Deer Valley's resort base. The Union Pacific and Rio Grande railroads ran a spur line for transporting ore from the Park Con, approximately where Deer Valley's parking lots are today. A horse-racing track and Henry Newell's slaughterhouse were also located near the current resort base. According to *Treasure Mountain Home*, "A straight-away race

ABOVE: THE PARK CON MINE WAS
LOCATED JUST ABOVE THE CURRENT
SNOW PARK LODGE AT DEER
VALLEY'S BASE. UNION PACIFIC AND
RIO GRANDE RAILROADS RAN SPUR
LINES TO TRANSPORT ORE. IN THE
LATE 1930S, THE RAIL LINES WERE
USED TO TRANSPORT SKIERS TO DEER
VALLEY. LEFT: THIS 1891 AERIAL
VIEW, TAKEN FROM THE CRESCENT
TRAMWAY (ON PROPERTY NOW PART
OF PARK CITY MOUNTAIN RESORT)
SHOWS THE RACETRACK THAT ONCE
EXISTED ON THE LAND NEAR DEER
VALLEY RESORT'S BASE AREA.
OPPOSITE: YOU THINK DRIVING IN
THE SNOW CAN BE CHALLENGING
TODAY? THIS LOCOMOTIVE, DESTINED
FOR THE ONTARIO MILL ON ROSSI
HILL'S HIGH LINE TRACK, HAD TO
PUSH MASSIVE AMOUNTS OF UTAH
SNOW AHEAD OF IT AS IT WENT.

track was built under the shadow of Mt. Neff in Deer Valley where the sports wagered on their favorite racers with many a gold piece changing hands."

The railroad also ran up the route of the Ontario Canyon State Highway (Utah Highway 224, known locally as the "Mine Road"), the back way to Deer Valley, to receive ore from the Ontario Mine. Years later, a miner described to Park City historian Sally Elliott what it had been like to live at the base of the mine road during that time: "[The] big old honker engine would come along clearing the track and there'd be so much ice and snow and it would fly so far it would break the windows of my house." According to *Treasure Mountain Home*, Empire Canyon, adjacent to Ontario Canyon, was home to Park City's "pest house" for residents with contagious

diseases. The Judge Zinc Smelter, located near today's Royal Street and In the Trees condos, filled the air with coal smoke. When it rained, a chemical reaction created sulfuric acid, which burned tiny holes in laundry left hanging out to dry—the bane of Park City's early housewives.

Park City got its name during a Fourth of July celebration in 1872, when boarding house owner and polygamist George Snyder hung up a makeshift American flag and declared that the little town would henceforth be called "Parley's Park City," after Parley Pratt, the first

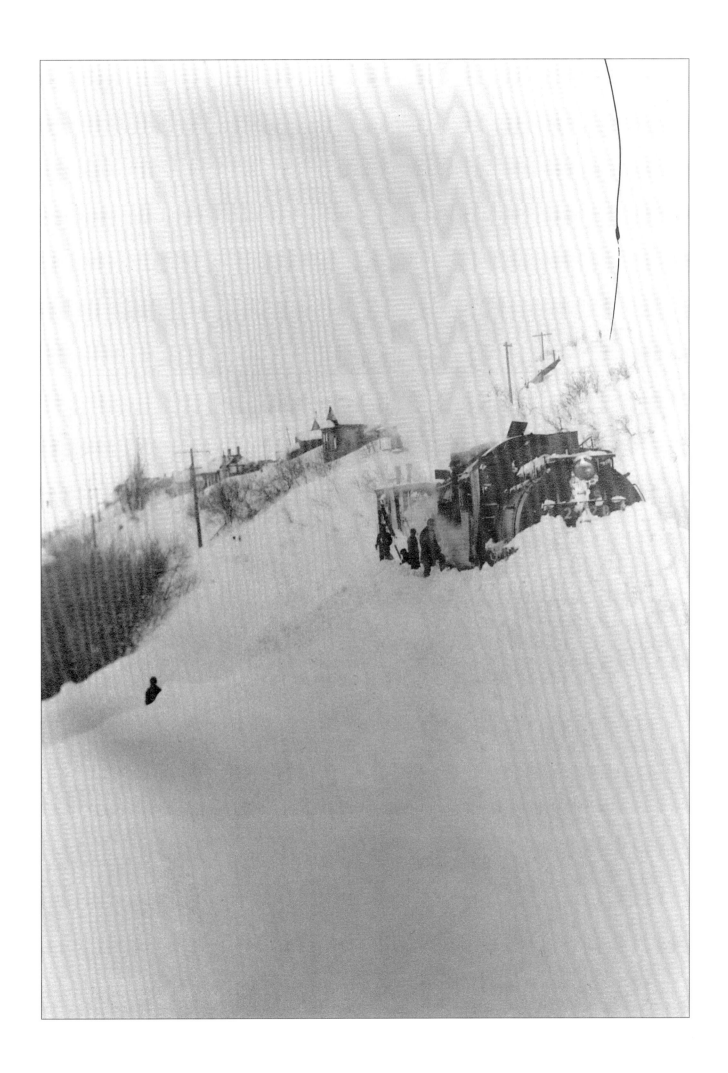

The Deer Valley Difference
Trails with a Past

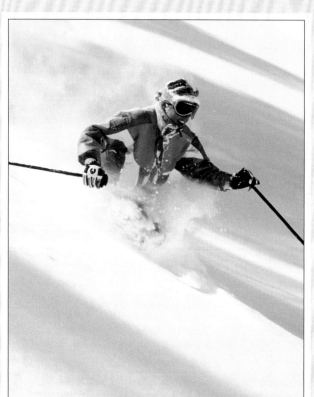

All but a handful of Deer Valley's ski runs are named after mining claims in the area. Most of the names can be found on an 1882 claims map, including McHenry's, Ontario, Grizzly, Trainer, Bonanza, Mayflower, Last Chance, Star Gazer, Tycoon, Hawkeye, Daly, Hidden Splendor, Square Deal and the curiously misspelled Know You Don't. When Edgar Stern created Deer Valley in 1981, he held true to the area's history by using these names. There was one name, however, that he nixed. Park City historian Hal Compton says that "Poor Boy" was one of the mining claims suggested as moniker for a Deer Valley ski run. "There will not be a 'poor boy' at Deer Valley," said Stern emphatically. That was the end of that. ☾

DEER VALLEY RUNS LIKE HAWKEYE (LEFT) AND MAYFLOWER BOWL (BELOW) WERE NAMED AFTER MINING CLAIMS FROM THE 1880S.

THE DEER VALLEY DIFFERENCE
Historical Markers

"It started with an absolute temper tantrum," says Park City historian Sally Elliott. "Sandra Morrison [director of the Park City Historical Society] called me and said, 'Sally! They've torn down the Kearns-Keith Mill!' So the next morning I hiked up there, and sure enough, it was gone! Just obliterated. Without a trace."

The 100-year-old Kearns-Keith Mill had been razed by its owner, United Park City Mines, to avert potential accidents caused by the crumbling structure, reduce the company's exposure to liability and make way for future development. Elliott and Morrison immediately formed the Historic Mines Preservation Committee. "We've been on their [United Park City Mines'] butts ever since. And we'll never get off," laughs Elliott. The committee, fully embraced by the city and county, ski resorts and the historical society, has been in place since 2000. Thanks to grants from the restaurant sales tax, each of the remaining historical sites is spotlighted with a handsome sign that features a paragraph describing the site's significance. Thirteen signs have been erected at Deer Valley Resort so that Deer Valley skiers can honor the past while enjoying the present. ☾

ABOVE: HANDSOME HISTORICAL MARKERS EDUCATE DEER VALLEY SKIERS AS TO THE HISTORY OF THE AREA. RIGHT: THE REMNANTS OF HISTORIC MINE STRUCTURES DOT THE DEER VALLEY LANDSCAPE.

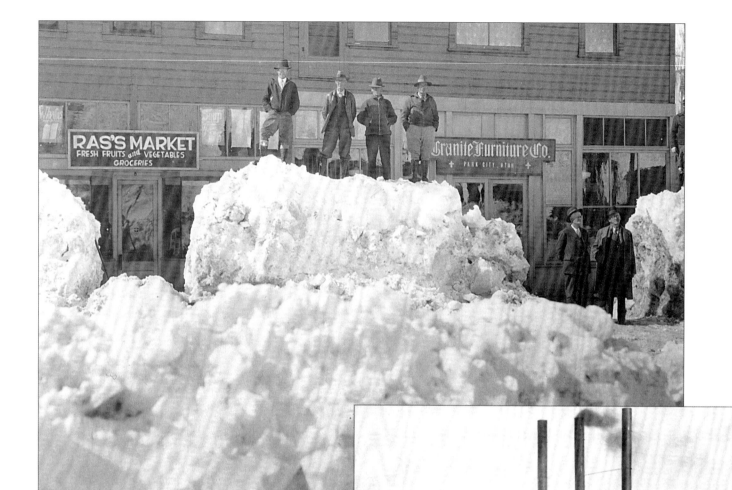

ABOVE: MAIN STREET IN THE 1930S DURING
A HUGE UTAH SNOW YEAR. IT IS SAID THAT
AVALANCHES KILLED MORE MINERS THAN DID
MINING ACCIDENTS IN PARK CITY, BECAUSE
THE MOUNTAINS HAD BEEN DENUDED OF TREES
DUE TO CLEAR-CUTTING. RIGHT: A MINER
OUTSIDE THE DALY-JUDGE MINE IN THE 1920S
SKIS TO WORK. MINERS BEGAN SKIING AS EARLY
AS THE 1890S. MAIL WAS ALSO DELIVERED TO
MINING CAMPS BY POSTMEN ON SKIS.

Mormon explorer to graze livestock in the area, using the word park to mean "a high mountain meadow." "Parley's" was soon dropped from the name. Park City wasn't officially incorporated until March 1884, on the fourth attempt. The state legislature wasn't happy about conferring legitimacy on a town that had become known as "Sin City," but the miners—4,000 strong—prevailed.

Sin City was rowdy. An 1887 article from *The Park Record* stated, "There is altogether too much promiscuous shooting in the streets at night!"

The community comprised a raucous mixture of Irishmen, Scotsmen, Cornishmen, Italians and Scandinavians, as well as Chinese who had originally come to Utah to work on the transcontinental railroad and then took to running laundries and restaurants. Some surmise that the Park City spirit

of acceptance for outsiders is due to this diversity during the town's early days.

Throughout the town's mining heyday, the deep winter snow was considered a nuisance by most residents. But not by the miners of Scandinavian descent. A 1900 census showed 227 residents of Danish, Swedish, Finnish or Norwegian background. Many of them liked to ski on 12-foot skis made from wood floor planks or oak barrel slats. They called the monstrous skis "flip-flops" and used single bamboo sticks as ski poles and brakes. Postmen used skis to deliver mail

ABOVE: PARK CITY'S RED LIGHT
DISTRICT COMPRISED 16 HOUSES ON THE
NORTH SIDE OF WHAT IS NOW DEER
VALLEY DRIVE. A FEW OF THE OLD
HOMES FROM "THE ROW" OR "THE LINE"
STILL STAND TODAY, BUT PROSTITUTION
IN PARK CITY WAS OUTLAWED BY THE
STATE IN 1955. RIGHT: ONE OF THE
MINERS' FAVORITE PASTIMES WAS
BASEBALL. MANY OF THE LARGER MINES
SPORTED THEIR OWN TEAMS. THESE
TWO GENTLEMEN ARE THE CATCHER AND
PITCHER FOR THE ONTARIO MINE
TEAM, CIRCA 1905–1915. THREE BALL
FIELDS WERE ONCE LOCATED NEAR DEER
VALLEY'S PRESENT-DAY BASE AREA.

to the mines, and ski-jumping competitions were held at local jumping hills like Creole and Ecker.

Miners had many other pastimes. Some visited "the row" or "the line" at the mouth of what is now Deer Valley Drive, where 16 brothels harbored "soiled doves" or "fairies of the tenderloin." Prostitution was an important part of the economic health of Park City from the town's early days until 1955, when the state government finally put an end to it. One of the town's most notorious madams was Rachel Urban, or "Mother Urban" (whose name lives

on in the name of a local bar). She was a hugely overweight woman with a limp who carried a parrot on her shoulder and was driven around town in a chauffeured limousine that tilted to one side due to her rotundity. But she and other "leading ladies" also gave donations to support community events and families in need.

Miners also enjoyed drinking in the saloons. In 1910, Main Street's Oak Saloon was robbed by a man some claimed to be Butch Cassidy (even though he was supposed to have been killed years earlier in Bolivia). During Prohibition, many of the side hollows and small canyons that are now part of Deer Valley Resort were favorite spots for illegal whiskey stills.

In addition to indulging in these dubious diversions, the miners enjoyed a more wholesome pursuit: baseball. Each large mine had a team,

THE GREAT FIRE OF 1898 BURNED MORE THAN 200
PARK CITY BUILDINGS IN LESS THAN FOUR HOURS
AND LEFT MORE THAN 500 RESIDENTS HOMELESS.
ABOVE: THE VIEW FROM THE MARSAC MILL SHOWS
OLD TOWN IN FLAMES. LEFT: THE SMOLDERING
AFTERMATH. THE CHIMNEY AT LEFT MARKS THE
REMAINS OF THE CONGREGATIONAL CHURCH ON
PARK AVENUE.

providing a legal and healthy outlet for the miners.

And there was another aspect to the town. Perhaps nothing showed Park City's fortitude better than the aftermath of the Great Fire of 1898. The fire started in a Main Street hotel and burned more than 200 buildings in less than four hours. The fire left more than 500 residents homeless. A local saloon musician reportedly pulled his piano out into the middle of Main Street and sang "A Hot Time in the Old Town Tonight" while the town burned. Local lore says that residents began rebuilding before the smoke had even cleared, and a mere 18 months later, Park City had been almost completely rebuilt. *The Park Record* didn't even skip an issue; its inimitable editor, Sam Raddon, set up a makeshift tent to replace his destroyed office.

Park City's population peaked at 5,000 in 1907. Then, after the stock market crash of 1929, the mining industry went into a decline, and so did the town. In 1930, dropping silver prices caused many of Park City's mines to close, or forced mergers. By the mid 1950s, there were only 200 people employed at the mines, and Park City was listed in a book called *Ghost Towns of the West* (which greatly annoyed the 1,200 people who still lived there).

Local residents began recreational downhill skiing before the 1920s, but the sport didn't become popular until the late 1930s. In 1936,

Horse-drawn wagons transport shoppers up Park City's Main Street in the 1920s. The sight
of pedestrians with skis slung over their shoulders (lower right) was familiar even then. The Great
Depression of 1929 marked the beginning of the end for the Park City mining industry.

the Park City Junior Chamber of Commerce organized a ski train that carried skiers from Salt Lake City to Park City on the old Denver–Rio Grande mining lines. "It would come up loaded with people who had started drinking as soon as they left Salt Lake," recounts historian Sally Elliott. "They'd walk up the hills and ski down." The very first outing drew 500 skiers for the four-hour journey. "People were so anxious to ski that they were climbing out of the windows," recounts Park City native Mel Fletcher. "Quite a few of them were quite inebri-

ated. Some of them didn't even make it off the train, but they all had fun."

Describing that first ski train, a passage from Salt Lake City's *Deseret News* read, "The Salt Lake contingent was joined by 200 additional skiers from Park City at the Deer Valley destination and the steep hillside suddenly looked as though a forest had sprung up by magic, as 700 skiers dotted its surface. And most of the skiers continued to dot the surface and even dent it appreciably through the day, for falls were as the grains of sand on the seashore."

In 1937, a Works Progress Administration (WPA) project created three ski runs, a ski jump, a toboggan course and a warming shelter near meadows that locals called "Deer Valley" or "Frog Valley." Early settlers had used these names due to the large number of deer in the area and the abundance of ponds and marshes that attracted wetland creatures. Some

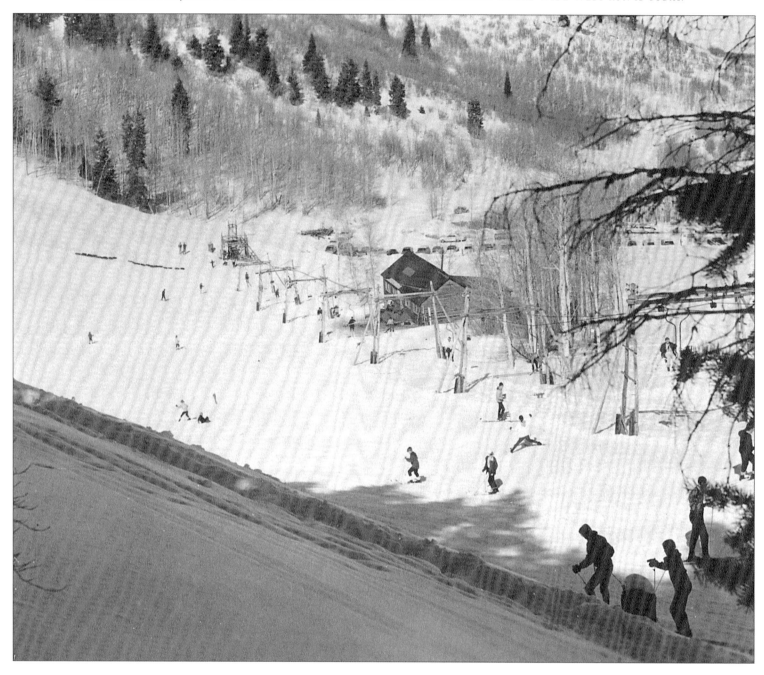

of those ponds still exist around Deer Valley Resort's base area and are enjoyed by fly-fishermen and children sailing toy boats.

World War II put ski action on hold for several years. Interest picked up again in 1946, when locals Bob Burns and Otto Carpenter returned from the war and decided to make use of the old WPA ski runs. They opened Snow Park ski area, borrowing the name of a ski club Mel Fletcher and friends had started. Park City had its first official ski resort.

The 50-member Snow Park Ski Club was organized so that its members "could start traveling as a jump team and get more activity for Otto and Bob's new lifts," recalls Fletcher, who ran the ski school at the area. The locals had another name for the club, though. "We had these red sweaters made," said Fletcher. "[The design] was supposed to be a heart with a ski

trail down through it, so it would depict the 'heart of skiing.' Well, they started calling us the 'broken heart club' because of the big crack going down through the heart."

At one point, Fletcher tried to recruit skiers from Brigham Young University (BYU), renowned for its predominantly Mormon student body. "I went over to Snow Park and showed 'em what a nice little setup we had," says Fletcher. "What befell us then was the fact that we had to go back past the ladies in the red-light district. The visitors were all eyes and ears and

ABOVE: FOUR SKIERS RIP IT UP ON SNOW PARK'S NO DELAY RUN. THE TWO MIDDLE SKIERS ARE MEL FLETCHER, SNOW PARK SKI SCHOOL DIRECTOR (CENTER LEFT) AND BOB BURNS, SNOW PARK FOUNDER (CENTER RIGHT). DEER VALLEY'S SNOW PARK LODGE IS NAMED FOR THIS HISTORIC SKI AREA. LEFT: IN THE SNOW PARK DAYS, THESE SKIERS CAUGHT SOME SUN OUTSIDE THE HAMBURGER SHACK ON THE LOWER MOUNTAIN. TODAY, SKIERS SOAK UP THE SUN'S RAYS AT McHENRY'S BEACH, MIDMOUNTAIN AT DEER VALLEY.

they said, 'Is that where Park City's brothel is?' I said, 'Yes.' 'Well, we can't bring our buses past that!' That was the end of my promotion."

Snow Park's first lift was a 1,400-foot T-bar that hadn't been designed for such steep runs. For the second season, Burns, a machinist at the Judge Mine, and Carpenter, a skilled builder, erected a chairlift powered by a Ford automobile engine. A second chairlift was added in 1949. They built the lift towers from aspen and pine trunks, tied together in a teepee shape. "They got the engine mounted on the

top of the hill," says Fletcher. "The reason is you had to have a counterbalance on the bullwheel to keep the cables taut so you wouldn't have any sag in them. Rather than have to carry all that weight to the top, they put the counterbalance on bottom and the motor on top. During the cold winter, it was started by battery. Since they ran it only on weekends, they were able to bring the battery down and keep it warm. Then they'd have to carry the battery clear to the top. [In] knee-deep snow, it was quite an operation, early in the morning, to get the ski lift going.

"We'd use the [ski school] students every Saturday to sidestep out a teaching area while we were waiting for the lift to go. After they got the lift going, they would transport the gasoline [cans] on the chairs. That was the first thing up those chairs: the gasoline so you could run the motor."

Deer Valley People
Guest Services Assistant Manager Roger Burns

Roger Burns, Deer Valley's guest services assistant manager, has been with Deer Valley for 20 years. Hospitality runs in Roger's family. His grandfather, Bob Burns, and his uncle, Otto Carpenter, founded Park City's original ski resort, Snow Park. Burns and Carpenter loved sharing their enthusiasm for skiing and the beauty of the area. Roger carries on the tradition at Deer Valley.

Roger was only five when Snow Park closed, but he clearly remembers the warm and smoky hamburger shack up the little draw just to skiers' right off Big Stick. "They were the best hamburgers in town." The menu also included soups (made by Roger's grandmother) and candy bars. "Big Hunks were my favorite." Roger's older brother remembers going to Snow Park late on Friday nights with their dad to start up the Ford engines that drove the lifts. Roger also remembers Snow Park's parking lot being where Deer Valley's Wide West ski run is now, and he recalls that "Uncle Otto had a ton of inner tubes" that local kids borrowed for weeknight tubing. After Snow Park closed and before Deer Valley was created, the dirt trails left behind were good places to ride motorbikes. Of the Burns and Carpenter lifts, named after his grandfather and uncle, Roger says, "I don't like to toot my family's horn, but I'm very proud of that."

Roger was a senior in high school when Deer Valley opened in December 1981. "I have vivid memories of skiing the Wasatch lift the first week. It was snowing so hard, we'd ski down, come back up, ski our exact same tracks and not even know it. It was powder face shots all day long. We skied three days straight like that. Then I got a job here, and now I have to work on those [powder] days!"

In fact, says Roger's boss, guest services manager Terry Bouman, "The best powder day is our toughest day. There's nothing worse than getting up here at 7 A.M. and having two feet of snow on the deck at Silver Lake. It takes six of us to shovel it out and get McHenry's Beach dug out and set up. That deck has quadrupled in size since I started here 19 years ago. The ski corrals are busy, too, and [we may be short-staffed because some] always call in with the 'powder flu.'"

Other challenges for the 80-member guest services crew include snow removal on sidewalks and decks; running the parking lots and parking shuttle systems; and managing the information desks, complaints, lost-and-found service, curbside valet, loading zones and ski corrals. The most difficult complaint Roger has ever faced? "One couple was just furious because we didn't have water and cookies at the top of our chairlifts like Vail does." Roger spent an hour with the couple, who started out complaining that he was incompetent and couldn't do his job. But when the conversation was finished, "they filled out a comment card and wrote how wonderful Deer Valley was." The most outrageous request Bouman ever received was being asked to drive a guest back to his lodge—a distance of 150 yards. "I didn't get the full story," he laughs. "I just remember getting a call from ski school, saying, 'Would you please take this man home? He's had a bad day.'" A combination of light snowfall and rapidly rising temperatures can cause chairlift grease to drip. The few times grease has fallen onto a guest's jacket, Roger has picked up the coat from the guest's hotel room, spent about four hours scrubbing and machine-washing it, then delivered it back to the guest either that night or early the next morning. "I've gotten really good at it," he says. "We've only had to buy one coat."

At the resort known for bend-over-backward service and presentation, it's Roger and Terry's department that attends to idiosyncratic details like making sure plastic garbage-can liners don't protrude from carefully designed wooden bins; making sure there are no puddles on resort plazas; coaching ski valets never to accept tips; and dealing with complaints like, "It's snowing." (The official and polite

ABOVE: HAVING TAKEN A SKIING FAMILY'S EQUIPMENT OUT OF THE CAR FOR THEM, THIS SKI VALET NOW STORES SKIS AND POLES ON A CONVENIENT RACK ON THE PLAZA AT DEER VALLEY'S BASE AREA. DEER VALLEY'S SKI VALET SERVICE—A FIRST IN THE INDUSTRY—IS COMPLIMENTARY. RIGHT: AN EVER-PRESENT CREW OF MOUNTAIN HOSTS IS AVAILABLE FOR QUESTIONS, DIRECTIONS OR SUGGESTIONS.

response: "This is a ski resort; there's supposed to be snow," and "No, sorry, we don't refund lift tickets on account of snowfall.")

One of the department's biggest challenges is keeping track of the 3,000-plus pairs of skis that are handled each day at the resort's free ski corrals and racks. Because of the sheer numbers, it is not surprising that skis have gone missing when a guest has grabbed the wrong pair. "Just as a personal challenge, I try to find out what happens to the skis," says Roger. "It's like solving a mystery. Sometimes it takes two or three days to track down the right pair. Recently we had a three-way switch going. One man grabbed the wrong skis off the rack in the morning, skied on them until lunch, then grabbed another pair of skis on his way out of Empire Canyon Lodge. I tracked down a cell phone number for him from the rental shop and rendezvoused with him at the end of the day. He was shocked. He'd had no idea he had someone else's skis." Apparently these unintentional ski-swaps happen on a daily basis. "We have some repeat offenders who do it every year," laughs Roger.

What is the best part of his job? "When people I haven't even had dealings with come up spontaneously and tell me what a wonderful place this is, that they love it and will be back," answers Roger.

"The most satisfaction comes from resolving the guests' problems and making their experience here at Deer Valley something they'll remember," says Terry. "Even when we're having a difficult day, we can always stop and get some perspective by remembering we're in charge of the guest services department for the top-rated ski resort in North America. That means a great deal." ☾

LEFT: SNOW PARK'S OTTO BAHN CHAIRLIFT WAS POWERED BY A FORD AUTOMOBILE ENGINE. BELOW: SNOW PARK'S LIFT TOWERS WERE FASHIONED FROM ASPEN AND PINE TREE TRUNKS.

Local artist Marianne Cone remembers skiing at Snow Park when she was a girl in about 1959. One chair called the Otto Bahn ran up the mountain where the White Owl ski run is now (the 2002 Olympic Winter Games aerials course). There was a beginner chair at the bottom, the Playpen Express, that started near the top of the current Burns chair. Cone says that on one chairlift, your skis never left the ground. "The first time I rode it, I thought, this is pretty cool. Then I turned around to talk to my friend behind me, caught an edge and splat! I was down."

She also remembers that "if you tipped the chair over, the guy at the top had to run to hand-set the brake. I remember going backward, trying to decide whether to jump or not before I hit the bottom. That chair was very cranky and probably a little dangerous." The story goes that the lift towers sometimes fell over, and skiers would have to vacate the chairs to help employees push the towers back up again.

Snow Park operated only on weekends (founders Carpenter and Burns kept their weekday jobs at the mines) and catered mostly to area children. Ski school classes were held Saturday mornings until noon, when a gong was sounded for lunch. Hamburgers, served in a cabin equipped with a wood stove, were 35 cents, and

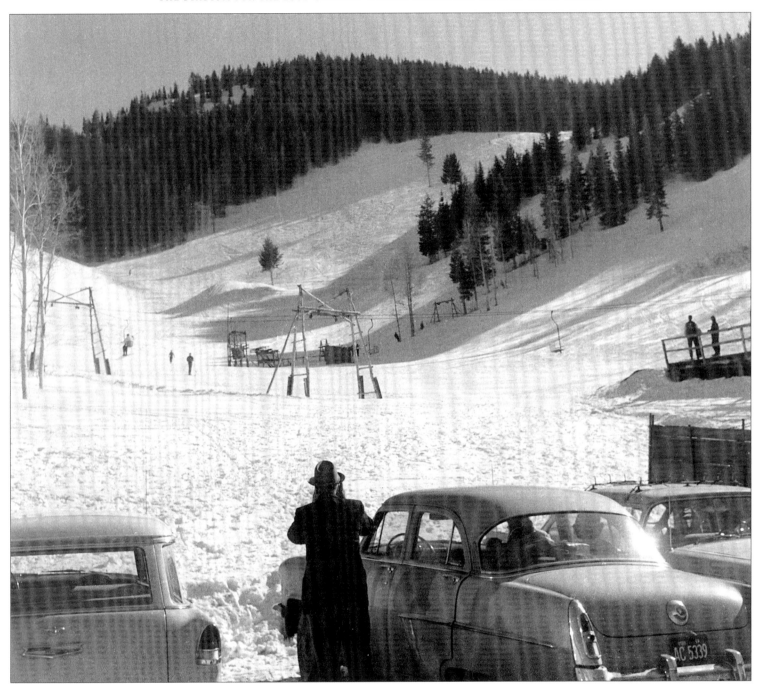

sodas 15 cents. "So, for 50 cents, ski school students could get a half day skiing, have a lesson and lunch," says Fletcher. "Otto charged them a dollar to ski for the rest of the day." (A full-day ticket with a group lesson was $2.50.) Children were carpooled in from Kimball Junction and Coalville—about 60 of them a weekend.

Burns sold his share of Snow Park to Carpenter in 1954 and Carpenter operated the area until 1969, when United Park City Mines—which owned the land on which the ski area operated—declined to renew the lease. By that time competition from the nearby, much larger Treasure Mountain Resort (later called Park City Resort), which had opened in 1963, had become too much for Snow Park.

Deer Valley Resort's current Carpenter and Burns chairlifts are named for Snow Park's founders, and the base lodge is named for the original resort.

After Snow Park closed, the land remained vacant for years, even becoming an unofficial dump for locals who discarded old mattresses and washing machines there. Local resident Destiny Grose recalls, "All I knew was I was never allowed to play with the kids from Deer Valley. That was like the slums."

How perceptions changed in 1981, when Edgar Stern opened Deer Valley Resort.

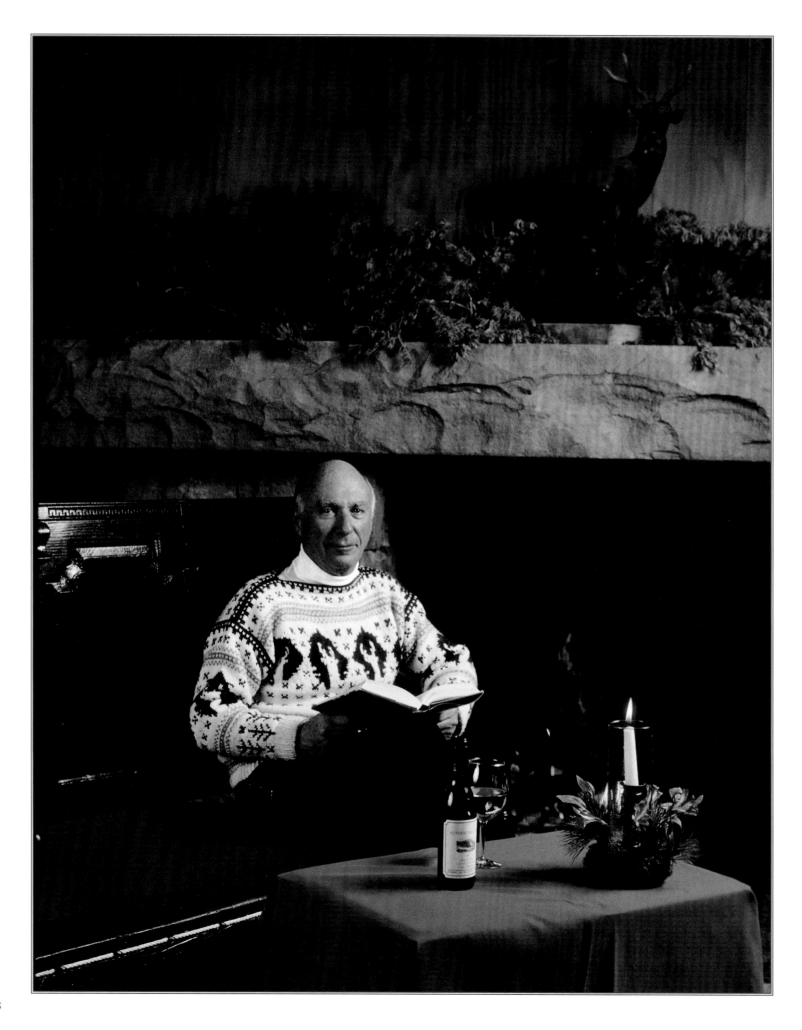

Chapter 2

THE VISIONARY: EDGAR STERN

The history of Deer Valley Resort began with Edgar Bloom Stern Jr. Edgar Stern's unassuming demeanor makes him unrecognizable to most guests as the man who, with the opening of Deer Valley Resort 23 years ago, created a new direction in the operation of a destination ski area. His trend-setting vision made the resort unique. His prior experience made this possible. "Edgar Stern tried to do something that nobody had ever tried before," says Deer Valley's food and beverage director, Julie Wilson. "He was a risk taker. He put his money behind his beliefs, and they blossomed."

Stern's dream was to combine the first-class service and fine dining of a top-quality hotel with one of his lifelong passions—skiing. He realized that dream, building on his extensive experience at Sears, Roebuck & Company, in the world of broadcasting and in the luxury hotel business. Though undeniably driven to succeed, Stern is also a man who simply follows his interests. His skiing nickname, No-Turn Stern, reflects the way in which he pursues those interests—fast, focused and straight down the fall line. Stern's passion for the things that have sparked his imagination, and his innate and wide-ranging curiosity, drove him to quietly accomplish an incredible amount.

Stern was born in 1922 and grew up in New Orleans. He was raised to appreciate quality. His parents, Edgar Stern Sr. and Edith Rosenwald Stern, were prominent in New Orleans in business, philanthropic activities and the arts. Respected philanthropists, they donated their 1942 Classical Revival–style home, Longue Vue, to the city of New Orleans. Today its eight acres of gardens and impressive art and furniture collections delight the public.

EDGAR STERN "AT HOME" IN THE MARIPOSA AT SILVER LAKE LODGE IN 1984, THREE YEARS AFTER THE RESORT OPENED.

Stern attended private schools, including The Hotchkiss School in Connecticut, and the Le Rosey School in Switzerland, where he learned to ski at the winter campus in Gstaad and where his enthusiasm for the sport was born.

Stern has vivid memories of summers spent at his family's White Pine Camp in New York's Adirondacks, once the summer White House of President Calvin Coolidge. "The living room was huge," Stern remembers. "Just spectacular. You could walk into one of the three fireplaces standing up straight." Stern describes his love for the White Pine atmosphere as "almost a religion." It instilled in him an appreciation of time spent in the great outdoors and for homes nestled in the woods.

It was at Harvard where Stern experienced his life's first pivotal shift. "It was

1942," he recounts, "just a month after the attack on Pearl Harbor. An Army officer walked into our physics class and said, 'I want all of you to sign up for the Electronics Training Group.' He didn't say that the course was about radar, because that information was top secret. It changed my college career and accelerated everything."

Stern graduated cum laude from Harvard in 1943, a year earlier than his class of '44 planned. Armed with a B.S. degree in math and sciences, he completed basic Army training and was assigned to the Army Signal Corps. It was

LEFT: EDGAR (ON THE RIGHT) AND
HIS BROTHER PHILIP (LEFT), AT
WHITE PINE CAMP, JUST BACK
FROM OVERSEAS DUTY. ABOVE:
SECOND LIEUTENANT STERN
CORRESPONDED DAILY WITH HIS
FIANCÉE, PAULINE STEWART, WHILE
HE WAS ON OVERSEAS DUTY FOR A
YEAR AND A HALF.

while attending Officer Candidate School in Fort Monmouth, New Jersey, that he met his future wife, Pauline Stewart. A New Jersey native, Pauline remembers that, as a child, she spent "a great deal of time being a tomboy and playing the violin."

It is touching that even today, 60 years later, tears come to Stern's eyes when he tells the story of meeting Pauline. He first saw her through a crowd at an OCS dance. "I took one look at that little face," Stern says, cupping his hands in the air before him as if holding her face, "and knew she was the girl I was going to marry." Their romance flourished, and they were engaged in 1944. Pauline's future mother-in-law nicknamed her Polly, a name she has embraced ever since.

Stern graduated from Officer Candidate School in January 1944 and was subsequently ordered to complete further training at both Harvard and MIT, where he repeated in six months all of the electronics training he had received during his Harvard years. He spent a year and a half on overseas duty, during which time he and Polly continued their courtship with daily correspondence. Edgar accepted his first post-war job upon his return in 1946, working for Offshore Navigation Company, where he used radar equipment in the hunt for underwater and underground petroleum sources.

Edgar and Polly were married in 1947 and they settled in New

ABOVE: PAULINE STEWART IN
1943. THUMBNAILS: EDGAR
AND PAULINE'S COURTSHIP
FLOURISHED OVER A
FOUR-YEAR PERIOD BEFORE
THEY WERE MARRIED.

Orleans, where Stern began his career in earnest. He doesn't attribute his business success to having great vision but rather to seizing opportunities. In some situations, he admits, he entered a business for the wrong reason, but then "everything turned out all right in the end." Such was the case in 1948 when Stern joined his father, Edgar Sr., in founding WDSU Broadcasting Services. Edgar Sr. had made his living as a cotton broker and was a director of Sears, Roebuck & Company, but when he found a local radio station with a TV license, he bought it, plunging his son into the fledgling television market.

"Because I had been trained as a radar repair officer during the war, I was interested in TV from an engineering standpoint. Radar and television are first cousins from a technical standpoint. This is one example of my entering a business for the wrong reason," says Stern. "I didn't know a thing about the business end of it." He would learn fast.

WDSU-TV, the first television station in New Orleans and one of the first in the South, began broadcasting in 1948. It was a challenging era for this brand-new entertainment medium. WDSU-TV made a name for itself by producing daily editorials, in newspaper fashion, that addressed local controversies such as the desegregation of schools in the 1950s, and a documentary that addressed the resur-

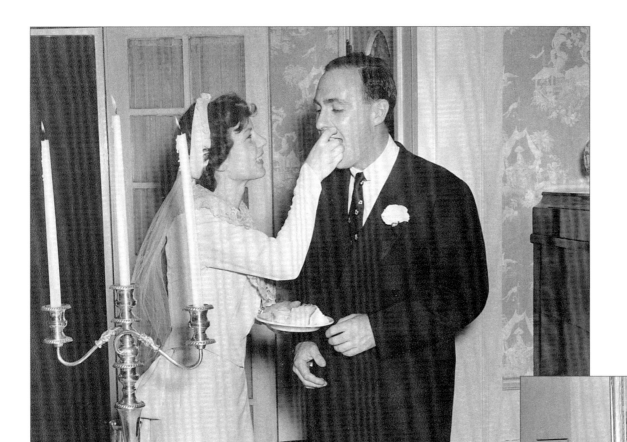

ABOVE: THE STERNS'
FAVORITE WEDDING PICTURE.
RIGHT: EDGAR AND POLLY
WERE MARRIED IN 1947.

gence of the local KKK. Stern received many threats for the opinions expressed on WDSU. His response? "Those were tense and frightening days, so we became the owners of the first of many huge German shepherds," he says.

Under Stern's behind-the-scenes leadership, WDSU earned national recognition for its groundbreaking editorials and for providing the first live coverage of events such as the 1953 Sugar Bowl and local hearings of the Senate's Special Committee on Organized Crime in Interstate Commerce (better known as the Kefauver

Committee). WDSU became known as an originator of television with true journalistic integrity. Between 1966 and 1972, the station was awarded many television journalism awards, including an Emmy and a Peabody.

Edgar and Polly led an active and colorful life. "We were dedicated to having a good time in New Orleans," Stern remembers. "We had lots of good friends there—families growing up together. Lots of swimming and barbecuing, and enjoying Carnival with those friends." Stern was the "float sergeant" of the title float in the Krewe of Rex Mardi Gras parade. He and his float partners began the day at 6 A.M. with a champagne breakfast before the parade.

"You can't live in New Orleans without enjoying good food," says Polly. The Sterns dined frequently at Antoine's, located around the corner from

the WDSU offices and studios, where their favorite waiter, Harold Lemoine, would serve them, as was custom, regardless of where they were seated in the vast restaurant. They enjoyed regional dishes like Antoine's famous soufflé potatoes, oysters Rockefeller, pompano topped with sautéed crabmeat, and Harold's salad.

"The best bartender in town," Stern recalls, "was Arthur Lamazou, who poured drinks at the old Absinthe House, one block from WDSU in the French Quarter. After work we'd all go to 'Mr. Lamazou's office'—that's what we'd tell the secretaries. He made a marvelous martini." Stern's affection for martinis became legendary. He had a specific way he wanted his martinis prepared: "a Beefeater martini, very dry, up, with a twist." Waiters often bungled the order, so at one point Polly had business cards printed

for Edgar with instructions on the preparation of his martinis. He used these cards for years, handing them to servers without a word. Ski writer Fred Smith would later write in a magazine article, "Edgar Stern likes his martinis straight up, cold and dry and his ski slopes straight down, silky and uncluttered." "That will be my epitaph!" Stern jokes.

In the very early days, WDSU operated from cramped quarters in a downtown office building. Then came an opportunity for a 99-year lease on the Brulatour Court, a historic mansion on Royal

Street in the Vieux Carre (French Quarter). WDSU corporate executives and staff moved their offices into the building, where the two top executives enjoyed the spacious quarters of the former ballroom.

"The Brulatour Court building had the character of the old city," recalls Stern, "with a beautiful courtyard." One of Stern's favorite stories revolves around a maid named Birda, "who was funny as hell," he relates. "When there were guided tours of the courtyard, she'd be up there on the balcony cleaning. The guide would say,

'These were the old slave quarters,' and she'd shout down, 'Yeah? Dey still is!'"

WDSU built its radio and television broadcast studios on part of the property adjoining the Brulatour Court—property already owned by Edgar Stern Sr. that was once the site of the old St. Louis Hotel. Edgar Sr. fondly remembered the St. Louis Hotel from his youth. "Dad had an ambition," says Stern. "It was so unlike him because he never liked real estate, but he wanted in the worst way to rebuild the old St. Louis Hotel he had known as a teenager." Thus a consortium of New Orleans businessmen, including Edgar Sr. and Jr., built the luxurious Royal Orleans Hotel on the corner of St. Louis and Royal streets. It was the first new hotel to be built in New Orleans in approximately 50 years, and it was an immediate success. The group went on to build a second luxury hotel, the

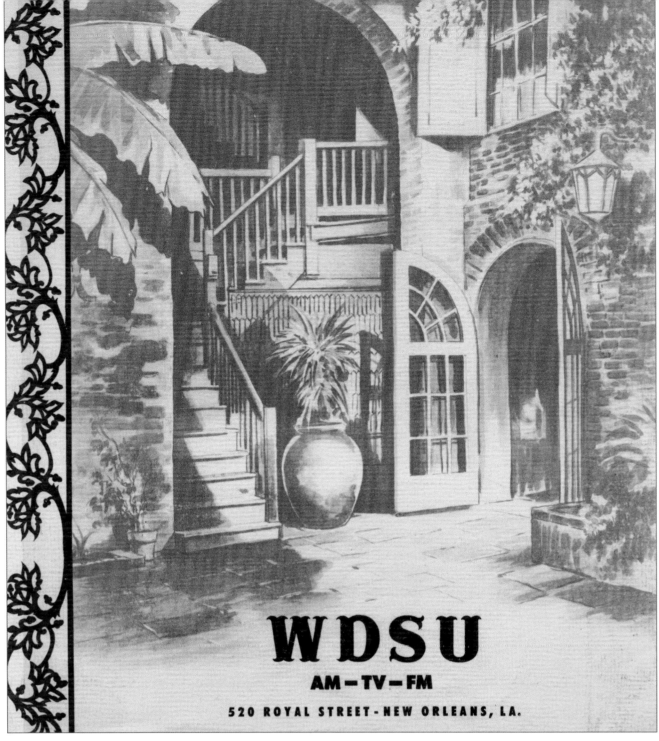

WDSU

AM — TV — FM

520 ROYAL STREET - NEW ORLEANS, LA.

UNDER EDGAR STERN'S LEADERSHIP, WDSU, INITIALLY JUST A RADIO STATION, BECAME THE FIRST TELEVISION STATION IN
NEW ORLEANS, AND ONE OF THE FIRST IN THE SOUTH. AN OLD POSTER DEPICTS THE COURTYARD OF THE BRULATOUR
COURT BUILDING WHERE WDSU HAD ITS OFFICES.

Royal Sonesta Hotel on Bourbon Street.

On ground that had been the first transmitter site for WDSU Radio, the Sterns developed and built Oakwood, New Orleans' first fully air-conditioned shopping mall. In 1962, because the company was expanding into new, non-broadcasting businesses, the Sterns changed its name from WDSU Broadcasting Services to Royal Street Corporation, after the historic location of the company's offices.

Though the Sterns remained involved in ownership of WDSU until 1973, Edgar Stern Jr. had been thinking beyond New Orleans since the late 1950s. During his television career he had served on numerous civic organizations. He was a commissioner of New Orleans Housing Authority in 1955 and later became its vice chairman, a position he held

until 1963. He was also campaign chairman, then president, of the United Fund of New Orleans. However, he became increasingly frustrated by the inability of the civic organizations to produce significant and lasting change. He was disturbed by the city's increasing crime rate. And he yearned for the mountains and skiing.

In 1956, the Sterns had built a small vacation home in Aspen as a refuge from New Orleans' humidity. It was in Aspen in 1961 that Stern became interested in ski area development. "I had

ABOVE: EDGAR STERN'S LIFELONG LOVE OF THE GREAT OUTDOORS STARTED EARLY. RIGHT: EDGAR AND POLLY STERN ENJOYED THE BEST OF BOTH WORLDS: CITY LIFE IN NEW ORLEANS AND COUNTRY LIFE IN ASPEN.

no intention of buying land there," he says. "We'd been out skiing many times, and my ski instructor insisted I see a beautiful ranch just on the way out of Aspen, down the valley, looking back over the mountains. There were a thousand acres of flat land, 500 feet above the valley floor. It was spectacular. And it was for sale."

The Sterns remember walking around the land with Nino and Arthur Trentaz, the two shovel-toting ranchers who owned it. To this day, the Sterns marvel at the Trentaz brothers' skill with irrigation. "Nino was a genius at controlling

the water flow in the irrigation ditches," recounts Polly. "The water for the ranch came through a many-mile-long ditch that had been created by Art and Nino's father, a miner. His hard work was responsible for the fact that the water rights, which were invaluable to the development of the land, were well established." Edgar bought the thousand acres in 1961 and developed Starwood, a residential community with a focus on land planning that kept intact all of the original ranchland meadows, with building allowed only on the surrounding mountainsides. Legendary skier Stein Eriksen and the late singer John Denver became Starwood neighbors and friends of the Sterns. John Denver even wrote a song about Starwood.

In 1958, Stern was invited to serve on the Sears, Roebuck & Company board of directors. His maternal grandfather, Julius Rosenwald, had served

ABOVE: THE VIEW FROM THE TERRACE AT THE STERNS' ASPEN HOME IN STARWOOD, THE SITE OF MANY DINNERS SUPPORTING THE ASPEN MUSIC FESTIVAL. LEFT: THIS PHOTO, WHICH WAS PUBLISHED IN *NATIONAL GEOGRAPHIC*, SHOWS A GATHERING OF ASPENITES AT THE STERNS' HOME.

as chairman of Sears and at one time owned 25 percent of the company. Edgar Sr. had also served on the Sears board. Thus, at age 36, Stern began absorbing business philosophies of Sears that he would later incorporate into his own business enterprises.

Julius Rosenwald had introduced the concept of employee profit sharing at Sears, which became one of the first U.S. companies to embrace the idea. "Profit sharing was important, but personal consideration of people was even more significant," says Stern. "The Sears personnel department created annual morale surveys in which personnel interviews were conducted, similar to what we have at Deer Valley now. They asked very personal questions, such as, 'What do you think of your immediate boss, his boss and his boss?' The employee was supposed to speak out truthfully, without fear of

retribution. I've used this feedback system in every business I've owned, and it's worked out really well." The 36 years he spent on the Sears board also taught Stern the power of promoting from within a company and allowing employees to perform their jobs autonomously. Sears' tendency to allow store managers to "rule their own kingdoms" resonated for Stern. "What I learned from the Sears model contributed to the strong employee morale and retention we have at Deer Valley today," he says.

The Sterns moved to Aspen in 1968. They

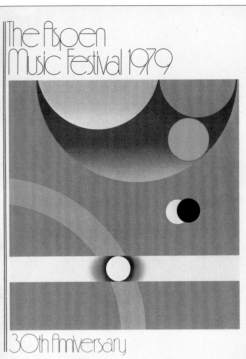

ROCKY MOUNTAIN NEWS PHOTO BY MEL SCHIELTZ

New facility planned at Aspen

Robert Welborn, right, points out a feature of proposed facility announced Wednesday designed to replace the colorful tent used for Aspen Music Festival concerts, while Aspen board chairman, Edgar Stern Jr., looks at the model. chairman, Edgar Stern Jr. looks at the model. The permanent facility will feature a cable net construction widely used around the world. A fund drive will be mounted soon to raise $2 million for the new facility. (See story on Page 59.)

LEFT: THIS *ROCKY MOUNTAIN NEWS* ARTICLE SHOWS EDGAR, THEN BOARD CHAIRMAN OF THE ASPEN MUSIC FESTIVAL, PLANNING THE REDESIGN OF THE FESTIVAL'S COLORFUL TENT. ABOVE: A COPY OF THE ASPEN MUSIC FESTIVAL'S 30TH ANNIVERSARY PROGRAM, FEATURING THE ART OF ASPENITE HERBERT BAYER, A BAUHAUS-TRAINED ARCHITECT AND ARTIST. THE STERNS' SUMMER SOCIAL LIFE REVOLVED AROUND THE FESTIVAL.

lived there for 20 years. They saw the build-out of Starwood and spent their weekends 9,600 feet above it all at Woods Lake, a private community of rustic, aged log cabins. Originally a fishing resort dating back to the late 1880s, Woods Lake is historically recognized as the first fishing resort in the state of Colorado. At Woods Lake the family fished for brook, rainbow and brown trout and enjoyed high-mountain horseback riding. "Neither Edgar nor I proved to be a capable fly fisherman," recalls Polly. "Edgar put flies in everybody's hair and often caught my sweater."

Polly writes of Aspen, "The resurgent community offered not only a picture-book setting for Christmas celebrations and skiing, but also, in summer, a wealth of outdoor experiences, Jeep trails, fine restaurants and the Aspen Music Festival. We could go from the woods to the concert tent. Edgar was invited to serve on the board of directors of the Music Associates of Aspen, eventually becoming chairman of the board." Summer social life revolved around the Music Festival, with the Sterns giving weekly dinner gatherings on the terraces and throughout the house, during which student musicians performed. Some parties were given in honor of the popular entertainers Jack Benny and Danny Kaye, who gave so generously of their time and talents for the benefit of music

THE DEER VALLEY DIFFERENCE
Staying Power

The concepts of extraordinary customer service and employee satisfaction became mainstream business practices for Edgar Stern, and he embedded these concepts into Deer Valley's corporate culture. Stern believes that the employees are the most important part of any business. His employee-friendly philosophy includes these edicts:

- "Pick the right people, pay them properly, give them free rein to do what they do best, and allow them to exercise their own genius."
- "People make the difference in every business. Instill respect among employees at all levels. Give every employee a chance to contribute to the operation of the business, and let each one know how important he or she is to the overall success of the business."
- "Treat the back of the house as well as the front of the house."
- "Promote employees from within the business for advancement."

Though these philosophies are the backbone of Deer Valley culture, Stern credits the resort's president and general manager, Bob Wheaton, with giving them life. "Bob is a person who early on accepted this philosophy with the employees and promoted it with his heart to continue it. It's wonderful to have a dream, but also wonderful to have a person like Bob to make the dream work." As a result, Deer Valley has one of the highest employee retention rates in the ski industry. Forty of Deer Valley's employees have worked there 20 years or more. One hundred sixty-six have been with the company between 10 and 19 years. Almost 300 of the resort's employees have worked at Deer Valley between five and nine years. ☾

DEER VALLEY BOASTS ONE OF THE HIGHEST EMPLOYEE RETENTION RATES IN THE SKI INDUSTRY. EMPLOYEES WHO ARE WELL TAKEN CARE OF ARE HAPPY EMPLOYEES.

JIM NASSIKAS (LEFT) AND STEIN ERIKSEN (RIGHT) PLAYED IMPORTANT ROLES IN MAKING DEER VALLEY WHAT IT IS TODAY.
THEY ARE SHOWN HERE IN 1983 ENJOYING THE MOUNTAIN IN THE COMPANY OF A SKIING COMPANION, OTTO LANG.

organizations. The late John Denver, a friend of the Sterns and a Starwood and Woods Lake neighbor, also performed for the benefit of music organizations, and once taped a television special featuring world-famous violinist Itzak Perlman in the Sterns' living room—an exciting experience for them.

The Sterns' Starwood home overlooked beautiful meadows and their herd of Tennessee walking horses, another passion that had fired Edgar's imagination. He was interested in breeding the horses so as to return them to characteristics they had displayed before being bred as show horses. Though the Sterns eventually donated their horses to Utah State University, they were captivated with riding for many years. "A marvelous rancher I knew said, 'Edgar, you only get one great horse in your lifetime,'" says Stern. "For me, Major was it. I'd close my eyes and hang on. He'd go in his fast-walking gait, almost at the speed of a trot, down these rocky, winding mountain trails. At the end of a riding trip with others, I would unsaddle him, cool him down, put the saddle away, put him away, and sit there and wait 45 minutes for everyone else." Polly remembers it differently. "My horse was Supreme Sensation. She was fast too. She'd try to get ahead of Major." Then there is a silence before Polly delivers the quiet punch line for which she is famous. "So Edgar sold her."

While living in Aspen, Stern had use of a company Grumman Gulfstream I, which was "a good plane for Aspen—those were the days when you could meet a cow on the runway." Having access to a private propjet saved him multiple days' commercial travel to board and business meetings, and allowed him to fly around the country investigating other intriguing business opportunities. One of these opportunities was an old apartment building on Nob Hill in San Francisco.

After the success of the Royal Orleans Hotel, Stern and Jim Nassikas, the renowned hotelier and general manager of the Royal Orleans, fantasized about creating their own luxury hotel. Stan Cohen, a Royal Street employee who was involved with Stern in Mission Hills, a California real estate development, was in frequent contact with Hubert Eller, a San

Francisco real estate consultant. Stern remembers, "Hubert called one day and said, 'Edgar, I've found the most beautiful property in San Francisco. You've got to come out and look at it.' He went to visit and immediately saw the potential. Nassikas followed shortly thereafter and confirmed Edgar's opinion. "We said, 'This has got to be it!'" says Stern.

"It" was the Stanford Court Apartments, an old apartment building on top of Nob Hill. The building occupied the site of the former Leland Stanford mansion that had been

ABOVE: HOTELIER JIM NASSIKAS, WHO
WAS GENERAL MANAGER OF THE ROYAL
ORLEANS HOTEL IN NEW ORLEANS,
WAS PRESIDENT AND MANAGING
PARTNER OF THE STANFORD COURT
FOR 20 YEARS. RIGHT: VALET SERVICE
PROVIDED FOR GUESTS AT THE ELE-
GANT ENTRYWAY TO THE STANFORD
COURT HELPED INSPIRE SKI VALET
SERVICE AT DEER VALLEY.

destroyed by fire following the 1906 earth-
quake, and was across the street from the
famous Fairmont Hotel.

Stern, Nassikas and Royal Street staffers
negotiated a lease agreement with the option
to tear the building down and start over. "But
the more we thought about it, the more we
wanted to keep it," recounts Stern. "The building was a landmark, structurally sound and
earthquake-proof, so we transformed the
apartments into a hotel. It wasn't easy. People
thought we were absolutely crazy. The corri-

dors were narrow. But it had so much charm." The luxurious Stanford
Court Hotel opened in 1972. "We operated for many years there and had
the highest occupancy in San Francisco, at the highest rate—unheard of,"
says Stern. The Stanford Court Hotel enjoyed a reputation for fine and
friendly service.

Precepts of service at the Stanford Court would later be applied at Deer
Valley. "First impressions are of great importance," says Polly. "In the beautiful courtyard entry to the Stanford Court, there was somebody right there
to greet you at your car and take your bags. That eventually translated into
the ski valet service at Deer Valley. And overall the guests' experience at the
Stanford Court was quite relaxed. Service was faultless yet unobtrusive."

Stern became involved in other business ventures. Under his direction,

DEER VALLEY PEOPLE
Jim Nassikas

Like the sourdough starter that he hand-carried to Deer Valley Resort from the kitchens of the Stanford Court Hotel, the foundation from which Deer Valley grew was laid by Jim Nassikas. He was a member of the original executive committee and was the first president of Deer Valley. Nassikas' knowledge of food, wine and service, and his notorious obsession with detail (such as his routine of running his fingers along walls and door frames), left an indelible mark on the way business is done at Deer Valley today.

A New Hampshire native, Nassikas was raised in a family of Greek immigrants whose appreciation for nature's bounty went back generations. His father owned an 80-acre poultry farm outside of Manchester. "I was born amongst the fresh eggs and chickens, and the rich growing seasons of New England," says Nassikas, who often speaks in poetic phrases. "I can remember having a wonderful garden with fresh, fragrant tomatoes, cucumbers and squash. Introduce into that picture a lot of southern Mediterranean cuisine. My grandmother lived with us, and she and my mother were constantly at it in terms of preparing meals. An interest in culinary arts was second nature to me."

Though Nassikas never forgot his roots, his own life took a more sophisticated turn. Nassikas began his college education at the University of New Hampshire, and at the urging of his mother, followed a course of pre-med studies. "Completion of such a curriculum was not to be, for reasons of disinterestedness and a minimal grade-point performance," wrote Nassikas. Instead he was attracted to the School of Hotel Administration, which changed the course of his life. Upon graduating in 1952, Nassikas and his recent bride, Helen, sailed for Switzerland. Nassikas earned his certificates in service and cuisine over a four-year period at the renowned École Hôtelière de la Societé Suisse des Hôteliers, in Lausanne, where former *New York Times* critic Craig Claiborne was a classmate. Also a classmate was Peter Seibert, who went on to found Vail, Colorado, and with whom Nassikas kept in close touch. It was the Swiss, Nassikas says, and their credos such as "A place for everything and everything in its place" that drilled into him "almost a fanaticism" for meticulous attention to detail.

His plan was to settle in New Hampshire. "I was going to come back and run a small 20- to 30-room inn, offering the finest cuisine and wine. The whole fantasy. We're talking about 1956 or '57, when the best-selling wine in America was Lancer's Sparkling Rosé. It was a wide-open field. I was really going to show them. But I was never able to put it together." Instead, Nassikas accepted employment in the purchasing department of the Boston-based Hotel Corporation of America. He worked there for 12 years and was promoted through the ranks. During his tenure Nassikas served as food and beverage manager at some of the country's most prestigious hotels, including The Plaza in New York City and the Mayflower in Washington, D.C. Nassikas met Edgar Stern in 1959 when he consulted on the opening of the Royal Orleans Hotel. He became vice president and general manager of the Royal Orleans in 1965, and in 1968 he directed the construction and opening of the Royal Sonesta Hotel.

Stern took Nassikas to San Francisco to see the old apartment building that would become the Stanford Court Hotel, where Nassikas presided as president and managing partner for 20 years. The Stanford Court achieved great acclaim under Nassikas' management, including earning a *Mobil Travel Guide* Five-Star award for 15 consecutive years, one of only seven city hotels in North America to do so. During his time at Stanford Court, Nassikas received countless accolades and was invited to join some of the world's most prestigious food and wine societies. One of his biggest honors came in 1986, when *International Hotels* magazine

LEFT: NASSIKAS SELECTED MANY OF THE ANTIQUES THAT DECORATE DEER VALLEY RESTAURANTS, SUCH AS THIS ARMOIRE IN THE MARIPOSA. ABOVE: UNDER NASSIKAS' GUIDANCE, DEER VALLEY'S DAY LODGE RESTAURANTS WERE DESIGNED TO BE WELL SIGNED AND WELL LIT, WITH EASY FLOW FOR HUNGRY SKIERS. NOTE THE ANTIQUE ENGLISH CLOCK-TOWER CLOCK FACE ABOVE AND TO THE LEFT OF THE BEVERAGE ISLAND.

named Nassikas Independent Hotelier of the World. In 1979, the Harvard School of Business selected the Stanford Court and Nassikas as the subjects of a celebrated case study that remained a mainstay of the school's curriculum for nearly 10 years.

A skier and snowshoer by the age of five, Nassikas always had skiing in his heart. The day he met Edgar Stern, they talked about skiing and the Sterns' Aspen home. "I conveyed to Edgar at that time that there was no way I wanted to stay with a big corporation. I wanted a ski resort. He said, 'Someday, we will do something.' That was the spark, kept alive for years. One day he said to me, 'Jim, I think we found it.'" Stern had discovered the Park City property.

It was Nassikas who set up Deer Valley's kitchens in the style of those found in fine hotels, with a range line, bakery capabilities, storerooms, dishwashing facilities and everything laid out with traffic patterns in mind. He insisted on uniforms for all staff. One of his greatest joys, he says, was traveling around the country choosing antiques for Deer Valley's day lodges. He selected items that fit his "compatible incongruity" theory. The point was to incorporate things that might at first seem incongruous at a ski area, yet whose compatibility conveyed a feeling that a lot of thought had gone into their selection. Examples are the hefty, individually built chairs used in the lodge "cafeterias," wooden—not folding—tables, and the granite countertops and brass fixtures in the restrooms. Some of his favorite furniture selections include the antique armoires in The Mariposa restaurant, English clock-tower clock faces that grace

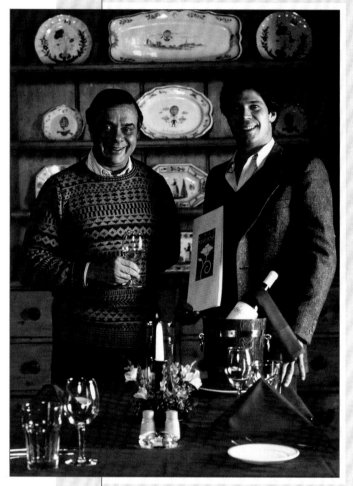

the walls of the Snow Park and Silver Lake lodges, and the deer head mounted in Snow Park Lodge. According to Nassikas, the deer head dates back to the 1800s and was displayed at the city hall in Purchase, New York, before he obtained it from Urban Archaeology in New York City.

Nassikas' attention to detail manifested itself in various ways, such as his insistence that the matchbooks placed in ashtrays (in the days when smoking was allowed inside) be positioned so that the deer in the Deer Valley logo on the cover always faced up the mountain, and his practice of feeling coffee cups and soup tureens with his hand to make sure they'd been adequately preheated. He always used, and still uses, a brown felt-tipped pen for correspondence, and he instructed Deer Valley's first staff to do the same. In Deer Valley's early days, brown typewriter ribbons were installed in all of the resort typewriters. Cindy Williams, who was hired to work in the ticket office and is now Deer Valley's payroll manager, recalls her first day on the job when a 3,000-piece mailing she was metering for postage was recalled by Nassikas because the white address labels didn't match the tan color of the envelopes. The entire mailing had to be redone, with labels dyed to match the envelope color. When he was displeased with something, Nassikas was known to strike his desktop with his hand and declare, "Mediocrity!"

Nassikas showed great warmth and caring for his employees. He is renowned for having known every Deer Valley employee (330 of them in his day) by his or her first name, and for caring not so much about an employee's past history as his or her potential. He says his greatest achievement at Deer Valley was not the award-winning food or dazzling day lodge designs, but an "organizational culture" that allows individuals to follow their passions. He revels in the success of Deer Valley's food and beverage director, Julie Wilson, and that of executive pastry chef, Letty Flatt, who authored her own cookbook.

And he has a sense of humor. The resort's first marketing director, Steve Dering, remembers one day when, stressed out about business, he called Nassikas and launched into a tirade about the problems. After he'd gone on for nearly five minutes, Nassikas said, "I'm fine, Steve. And how are you today?" True to his sense of whimsy, Nassikas was the one who decided to have the eyes in the aforementioned Snow Park Lodge deer head light up for 10 seconds every half hour. "I envisioned a family of eight in conversation at lunch," chuckles Nassikas, "and Mama would look up and say, 'I just saw the eyes light up!' and the others would say, 'Oh, come on!' Though he has opened and operated 17 fine restaurants throughout his career, and perhaps has one of the country's finest palates, he has also been spotted greatly enjoying a Fudgsicle from 7-Eleven.

Nassikas retired in 1996. He was absolutely passionate about his work, he says, but admits that "after 40 years of morning, noon and night, I was ready to be done." He adds that he has "never known happiness like the last 15 years." ☾

Royal Street Corporation also developed the Tipple Inn condominium and the Red Mountain Ranch, both in Aspen. He considered all sorts of other opportunities, including the possible purchase of the New Orleans Saints football team, the Queen Mary ocean liner (with thoughts of turning it into a floating hotel) and Aspen's Hotel Jerome, but rejected them because none seemed financially viable. As one friend puts it, "Edgar's not one to collect toys." If something isn't economically feasible, he's not going to get involved. His business credo includes statements such as: "If you can't go first class, don't make the trip," and "In all things, don't do it unless you do it right." But Stern's business sense is complemented by the soul of an artist, and he has the clarity of mind to imagine what could become a reality, the passion to follow his heart, and a willingness to take risks.

It all came together when Stern first saw Park City, Utah, in 1968. At the invitation of Warren King, a skiing friend and contractor with whom Edgar had worked on several developments, he and Polly visited Park City, looking at the possibility of developing condominiums in a ski area. (By then Aspen had strict zoning controls in place that amounted to a no-growth policy.) Referring to Park City's dilapidated condition at the time, Polly recalls, "We carefully walked down the middle of the streets in Park

VIEWS SUCH AS THIS ON THE ROAD TO PARK CITY FURTHER ENTICED THE STERNS TO "POKE AROUND." IN THE
FOREGROUND IS PARK CITY'S HISTORIC OSGUTHORPE FARM (NOW CALLED THE MCPOLIN FARM.)

City because we were afraid the buildings would fall down on our heads." "But we started poking around," recounts Edgar, pointing to an oversized aerial map of the Wasatch Mountains that he loves to ponder, "and found this," waving at the acres of land that were owned at the time by United Park City Mines Company.

Stern spotted a gold mine where once there had been silver mines. Park City was located just 35 miles from Salt Lake City International Airport, a major stopover on the east-west flyway between New York and San Francisco. During a visit to Park City, Stern learned that plans were already firmly set for construction of the six-lane Interstate 80 through the Wasatch Mountains. The interstate highway would mean a 40-minute drive from the Salt Lake airport to Park City, compared with the five-hour drive (in those days) from

Denver to Aspen. Utah's fine snow was legendary and the mountains were beautiful. Much of the land in the mountains was privately owned by mining companies, and it could be developed without the governmental restrictions often attached to public lands. Stern was enamored. "I thought, 'This has everything!'"

After a few days of exploring, Stern said to Warren King over evening martinis, "Let's buy the whole damn thing!" The whole damn thing was 7,000 acres—land that included the then-struggling Treasure Mountains Ski Area (now

Left: "No-turn Stern" spends as much time on Deer Valley's slopes as possible. Above: Edgar Stern is a very private man, but this rare photograph of Deer Valley's founder was published in a *Town and Country* article touting Deer Valley's allure.

Park City Mountain Resort) and the undeveloped mountains that would later become Deer Valley Resort. A quick study of U.S. Geological Survey contour maps of the area revealed that the surrounding mountains offered the opportunity to build a ski area that could be enthusiastically enjoyed by almost any skier, even those with moderate skills. "My good friend, the former Olympic champion Friedl Pfeifer, had always used the term "the money is in the bunny," says Stern. He accepted the idea embodied in those few words.

After difficult and complicated negotiations with United Park City Mines Company, Treasure Mountain Resort Company was formed by Royal Street Development Company (a subsidiary of Royal Street Corporation), United Park City Mines and Unionamerica, Inc. Treasure Mountain Resort Company purchased the developable land owned by the mining company and leased the surface of the remaining property for the ski area operation. Serendipity was at work for Edgar Stern. He was heading down a path he had hoped to be on—the path to a ski resort of his own.

You may have heard apocryphal stories of men who bought hotels so they would be assured of a room reservation. Edgar Stern is probably the first man to develop a ski resort so he wouldn't have to stand in line for a lift ticket. ❦

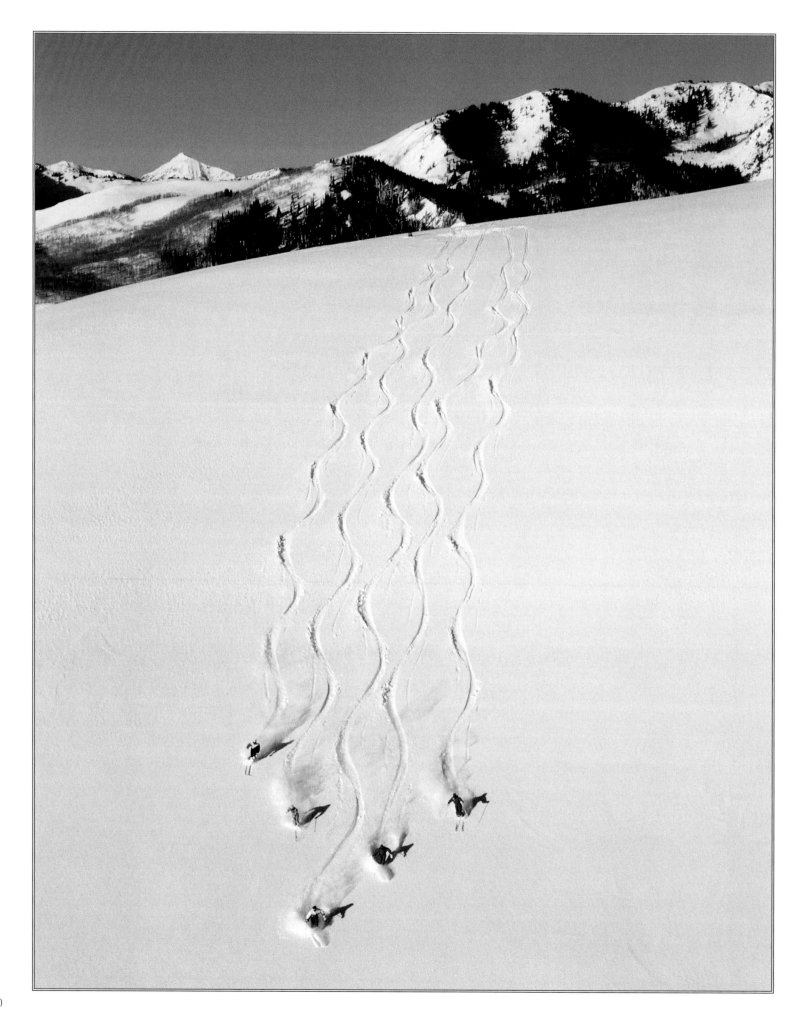

Ralph Waldo Emerson wrote, "To believe your own thought, to believe that what is true for you in your private heart is true for all men—that is genius." Edgar Stern certainly knew what was true for him—he wanted to build the ski resort that he had envisioned. Judging by the success of Deer Valley, his vision has resonated with many.

In 1971 Royal Street Development Company (a subsidiary of Royal Street Corporation) teamed with United Park City Mines Company and Unionamerica, Inc., to form a company called Treasure Mountain Resort Company. That company bought and leased the property on which Treasure Mountain Resort was then operating, along with other property in the Park City area, including the land on which Deer Valley Resort was ultimately built. The name of the company was changed to Greater Park City Company (GPCC) and the name of the resort to Park City Resort. This acquisition was the first step toward Stern's fulfilling his dream of owning a ski resort, but Park City Resort wasn't a completely agreeable fit. "We managed Park City ski area and got our feet wet," explains Stern. "It was a good experience, but the thing was, I didn't like that mountain as well as I liked the rest of the property we had acquired."

During his time at Park City Resort, Stern made many contributions to the community's overall development. Though it's difficult today to imagine a Park City that needed to grow, in 1971 the town was quite run down, with only a handful of restaurants and lodges. Jack Johnson, an engineer on GPCC's design team, wrote, "In 1971, the town ended at what is now a 7-Eleven near the base of Park Avenue. Beyond that point, there were farms

THIS DEER VALLEY POWDER SKIING SHOT WAS FEATURED IN A 1989 PRINT AD FOR THE RESORT.

and little else. [Edgar] and his associates put together a multi-faceted company to take the old silver-mining camp of Park City [and turn it into] a competitive recreational resort community."

Stern convinced his friend from Aspen, ski legend Stein Eriksen, to move to Park City and become Park City Resort's director of skiing. Eriksen's move attracted national attention. Between 1971 and 1975, GPCC built a number of condominium complexes, including Three Kings, Crescent Ridge, Payday, Park Avenue, Homestake, Claimjumper, Marsac Mill Manor and Silver Mill House. It added chairlifts and runs to the ski area and expanded the Park City Golf Course. The company also built the Snow Country apartments as employee housing and developed the Thaynes Canyon and Holiday Ranch subdivisions, as well as the Resort

Center base area. Edgar Stern played a pivotal role in convincing the U.S. Ski Team to move its headquarters to Park City in 1974.

Unfortunately, the economy at the time proved inhospitable to Stern's enterprises. The recession of the 1970s halted hopes for profitable condominium sales. "We were a highly leveraged company," says Bob Wells, vice president of real estate for the Royal Street companies, "and that's an understatement. We needed to create about 100 units of real estate projects a year, at a profit, in order to make our game plan work.

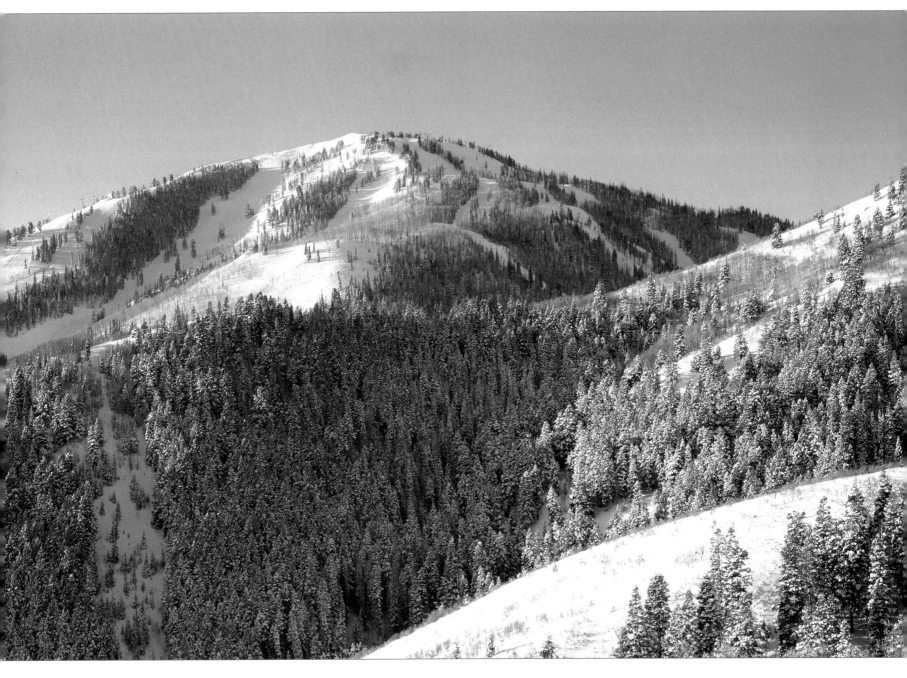

We were a company that was trying to be all things to all people. We were the architects, the builders, the operators of the rental programs and the property management company. In hindsight, at that point in time, we were stretched too thin. We met our goal of producing 100 units a year for that five-year period, but we didn't meet the second half of the bargain: doing it at a profit."

Just as frustrating to Edgar Stern was the fact that he couldn't shape Park City Resort from the ground up, as he'd envisioned. His original plan was to incorporate into Park City Resort the land that would later become Deer Valley Resort. Instead, he decided to sell his interest in GPCC and Park City Resort and focus on the remaining land, "which is what I'd had my eye on all along." GPCC and Park City Resort were sold to Alpine Meadows of Tahoe, controlled by Nick Badami. Royal Street Land Company, also a subsidiary of Royal Street Corporation, acquired the rights to 1,700 acres of private land that was the core area of what was to become Deer Valley Resort. Stern began planning his dream resort.

While interest rates hovered at a ghastly 11 percent, models of the future Deer Valley Resort appeared around town. There was some skepticism. Deer Valley's president and general manager, Bob Wheaton, puts it in

Above: north-facing runs are ideal ski terrain. Right: An early Deer Valley trail map. Note that ski runs had not yet been cut on Flagstaff Mountain.

perspective. "Park Avenue and the road into town were only two lanes. Albertson's grocery store wasn't there. Main Street and Park Avenue were chock full of potholes that could swallow a truck. The town wasn't in the best of shape. To take a town like that and put a first-class resort in it was a pretty unique concept."

"I remember driving up the Guardsman's Pass road," says longtime local Dixie Geisdorf, "and someone telling me the Deer Valley land was going to be developed and they were selling lots for $25,000. I thought, 'My gosh. Nobody's going to buy a piece of the hill right there.'"

"We did start with the intention of our resort being high-quality and high-end, with everything built to very high standards and therefore commanding higher prices. There was some objection to that locally," admits

Stern. Yet he forged ahead, assembling a team of trusted friends and respected co-workers who shared his vision. Brainstorming meetings for the new resort were attended by Edgar and Polly Stern, Joe Cushing, Jim Nassikas, Stein Eriksen and Friedl Pfeifer, among others.

Friedl Pfeifer, a former Austrian Olympic champion and a World War II U.S. Army 10th Mountain Division veteran, contributed ski-area know-how to the planning process. Pfeifer had helped transform Aspen from a mining

FOUNDER EDGAR STERN CREATED NON-INTIMIDATING RUNS FOR THE LESS ADVENTUROUS AND LESS EXPERIENCED SKIER AT DEER VALLEY.

town into a skiing community after the war. "Friedl and I were friends in Aspen," says Stern, "and I always thought that he knew more about skiing than all the people in the Aspen Ski Corporation put together. He knew so much about snow. He pounded it into my head: ski runs have to be north facing, where the sun is low enough so that it doesn't disturb the snow. He always said that was the essence of skiing. So simple. That's the way he was." Fortuitously, the natural topography of Deer Valley allowed north-facing ski runs. "When

we did design Deer Valley's runs on the north-facing slopes and Friedl came to visit, he loved it here. 'Edgar,' he said, 'You got it right!'"

Another of Pfeifer's winning ideas was his now-famous adage, 'the money's in the bunny.' He had applied this principle successfully at Buttermilk Mountain in Colorado. "Friedl introduced this notion of getting down to the bunny skier," Stern explains. "In Aspen, they liked the pictures of guys doing these chutes. Only one out of 100 skiers can do that." "You can't build a clientele if you scare someone away on the very first visit," adds Polly Stern.

Sno Engineering's Joe Cushing spent a year designing Deer Valley's ski runs. Cushing had a real sense for Edgar's vision of skier-friendly runs. "Laying out runs is not easy," says Stern, "but Joe was a wizard at it. He

ABOVE: FOUNDERS EDGAR AND
POLLY STERN TESTED A NUMBER
OF CHAIRLIFT SEATS BEFORE
SELECTING THE MOST COMFORTABLE
FOR DEER VALLEY GUESTS. ALL
DEER VALLEY CHAIRLIFTS FEATURE
PADDED SEATING AND FOOTRESTS.
LEFT: NORTH-FACING SKI SLOPES
HELP PRESERVE SNOW.

knew how to walk on the fall line. He'd tag the trees as he'd go. Every run at Deer Valley is on the fall line. We have very few of those side runs that I don't like."

"I worked directly in the field, flagging runs with Joe, and he was amazing," says Chuck English, who is now Deer Valley's director of mountain operations. "We'd be walking through dense woods of aspen and choke cherry. You couldn't see four feet. Joe had his altimeter and compass in hand and a map folded under his arm. I remember one day we'd just laid the left sideline of Orient Express and were laying the right side of what would be Stein's Way. Joe said, 'Another ten yards or so we'll run into the flag for Orient, and that will be our intersection.' Sure enough, we busted through the weeds, and that blue flag was right there."

Cushing's trails would later win "Trail and Slope Design" awards from *Snow Country* magazine. Cushing recounts a story about Bill Eppley, who cut many of Deer Valley's first runs, and who had also bulldozed many roads for the Starwood development in Aspen. "The natural grade at the top of what is now called Success was 35 percent. This was 10 percent more than I wanted for that green trail. I told Bill Eppley I would give him a case of beer if he could reduce the grade to 30 percent with his dozers, and a case of Scotch if he could get it

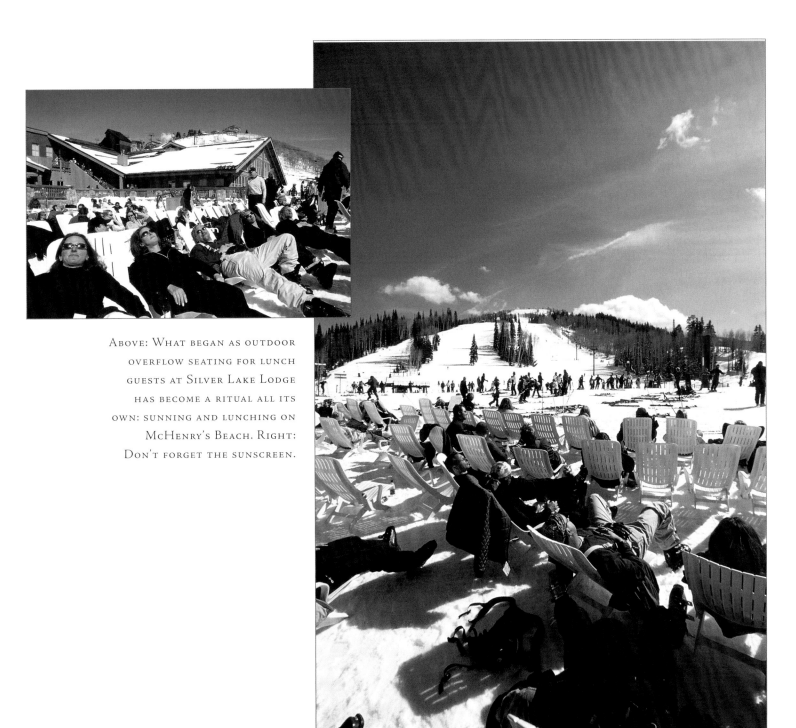

ABOVE: WHAT BEGAN AS OUTDOOR OVERFLOW SEATING FOR LUNCH GUESTS AT SILVER LAKE LODGE HAS BECOME A RITUAL ALL ITS OWN: SUNNING AND LUNCHING ON MCHENRY'S BEACH. RIGHT: DON'T FORGET THE SUNSCREEN.

down to 25 percent. He took home the case of Scotch, much to my delight."

Gil Williams, who is now president of the Royal Street companies, recalls, "I remember hearing lots of stories about people telling Bill, 'You can't take a cat down there, you just can't do that! And he'd say, 'Oh yeah? Watch this!' Then he'd shape it into what became a perfect run. He had a good reputation and won Edgar's respect with his ability."

"Edgar wanted to build the ski resort just the way one would build a high-class hotel, with the finest food, impeccable service and no hassles," recounts Polly Stern. Jim Nassikas, a friend and business associate who had achieved five-star success at numerous hotel properties, including San Francisco's Stanford Court, brought to the table his many years' experience in the hospitality industry, which would prove of enormous value in achieving this goal.

Nassikas, known for his passionate and thorough epistles, wrote on the occasion of Edgar Stern's 80th birthday, "Our mission was to develop a resort that would be better than any which existed. We visited Stowe and Stratton in Vermont; Boyne Mountain in Michigan; Keystone, Copper, Vail, Aspen and Snowmass in Colorado; and Sun Valley in Idaho. All facets of ski operations were studied including destinations and site locations, trail layouts, mountain challenges, grooming techniques, snowmaking,

THE DEER VALLEY DIFFERENCE
Deer Valley Firsts

"Part of what I've learned in my career is to be different," says Deer Valley founder Edgar Stern. "Not to follow the troops. Follow the heart instead." Being different has proven successful at Deer Valley. Here is a list of what Deer Valley staff members believe were "firsts" in the ski industry.

Bolos

While the concept of a hospitality pass (a season pass that is valid not only for the purchaser, but for any guest wearing it) did not originate here, Deer Valley's Hospitality Pass was the first such pass—and still is the only such pass—to be issued in the form of an attractive bolo tie. Though each year's bolo is different in design from that of other years, the focal point is always the famous Deer Valley logo. The Bolo is Deer Valley's only transferable pass.

Ski Valets

One of Deer Valley's signature services is the ski valet team—the men and women in green who approach your car when you arrive in front of Snow Park Lodge, unload your skis for you and place them on ski racks. The ski valet program began several weeks into Deer Valley's first season. "Ski valets are an example of providing a service after observing and listening to the guests' needs," says the resort's president and general manager, Bob Wheaton. "We watched people struggling—walking with their ski gear from the parking lot or even getting it in and out of their cars—and it came to us to have ski valets, like bell staff at a hotel."

Limited Lift Ticket Sales

Deer Valley has always placed a limit on the number of lift tickets sold. It is able to do so because the resort is built on privately owned land. The resort currently limits the number of skiers to 6,000 a day, enabling guests to enjoy ultra-short or nonexistent lift lines, and enough room on the trails to spread out. "The policy gives guests more space and more privacy, and that's what it's all about," says Edgar Stern. The only time the skier limit has an effect on last-minute arrivals is during a busy holiday period when the resort typically sells out. Because of this policy of limiting the number of skiers and the proportionately large number of chairlifts, Deer Valley has the highest per-skier uphill capacity in the country.

Parking Lot Shuttles

When Deer Valley opened in 1981, managers noticed some guests were having difficulty climbing the incline from the parking lots to Snow Park Lodge. A parking shuttle was therefore added. Multiple open-air shuttles run continuously, transporting guests from the six parking lots at the resort's base to Snow Park Lodge, returning them to the lots when they are through for the day.

Federal Expressing Skis

Deer Valley was the first resort to offer to ship ski equipment to and from the resort by Federal Express for those guests who don't want to wrestle with ski bags at the airport.

Grooming 101

Deer Valley's staffers became so committed to grooming techniques that they actually plucked small stones from the pristine slopes during lean snow years or spring thaws, dropping them into a pickle barrel. That practice continues to this day. Resort founder Edgar Stern himself has been known to pick up a stone or two.

State-Licensed Child Care Facility

Deer Valley was the first Utah resort to offer state-licensed child care in its on-site facility. It provides care for children from 2 months to 12 years of age in the ski season, and from 18 months to 12 years of age at Summer Adventure Camp. Deer Valley was the first resort to offer pagers to skiing parents so they could be notified immediately if a problem developed, and the first to provide a separate parking lot for the child care facility, just outside the front door of the Children's Center.

Be Our Guest

Since day one, skiers at Deer Valley have been referred to as "guests." "It's just a different and nicer connotation than saying 'customer' or 'skier,'" says Royal Street President Gil Williams. It is another manifestation of the goal of founders Edgar and Polly Stern to create a ski resort with the best attributes of a fine hotel, where one would always be called a guest.

Back of the House

Just as you'd experience at a fine hotel, resort employees move through a well-designed "back of the house" structure. Employees have their own cafeterias and locker rooms that are separate from the guest facilities. Employee meals are served in "The Spoon" (short for The Silver Spoon), the "Daly Bowl" and "The Grotto." In addition to reasonably priced lunch fare, breakfast pastries are provided to the employees free of charge, as are beverages throughout the day. Elaborate stair and hallway systems in the three day lodges allow employees to remain "behind the scenes" as much as possible.

The Uniform Approach

From the beginning Deer Valley required that almost every resort employee wear a uniform appropriate to his or her job, and it instituted a dress code for employees not required to wear uniforms. Ski instructors are provided with complete uniforms—hats, neck gaiters, turtlenecks, baseball caps and ski suits. Lift attendants, lift ticket sales staff, kitchen staff, restaurant staff and ski valets all wear uniforms. At Aspen, Edgar Stern had discovered, the ski instructors were required to clean their own uniforms. "And they didn't," he bemoans. Deer Valley's Equipment Issue department not only provides the uniforms, but handles all of the laundering as well, ensuring that employees pass the white-glove test. Deer Valley employees who are not required to wear uniforms adhere to a dress and grooming code that reflects the resort's high standards.

Complimentary Ski Check

Deer Valley was the first ski resort to offer complimentary ski check, by the hour or day, or overnight. According to the resort's first marketing director, Steve Dering, "When people have a choice of where to ski each day, and they wake up in the morning and their skis are already at Deer Valley, where do you think they're going to go? It's a win-win situation. It's a lovely amenity for the guest, and in the end, hopefully more profitable for Deer Valley."

Chairlift Foot Rests

Edgar and Polly Stern actually seat-tested a variety of lift chairs before they purchased the lifts in 1980 with which they would open the resort. "I sat in a lot of chairs trying to discern which were the most comfortable," says Polly. Edgar insisted on padded seats and footrests on every single chair at the Resort—even for the short rides—against the advice of the lift company, who didn't think it was necessary. "It was simply a matter of comfort," says Edgar. "I think it's really paid off. It's because of high-end features like that, that we have the high-end reputation." ☾

maintenance and a wide range of hospitality-related components: guest services, food preparation, and dining environments and designs. What became increasingly clear was the dearth of attention devoted to guest oriented hospitality issues. Deer Valley had found its 'raison d'etre.'"

Nassikas' influence became evident. He designed kitchens in the resort's day lodges that could handle full banquet service. He spent countless hours designing menus, kitchen cooking lines and guest traffic areas in the dining rooms. On Deer Valley's opening day, white-toqued chefs served carved roasts at lunch—a level of cuisine simply unheard of at a ski resort before that time. Nassikas also carefully crafted the "look" of Deer Valley, insisting that resort employees, from kitchen staff to ticket takers to lift attendants, wear not only uniforms but a smile. He also insisted that they

learn to anticipate guests' needs before the guests did. Separate employee locker rooms and dining rooms were constructed in areas where employees could move unobtrusively through the "back of the house" without disturbing guest space.

Park City residents had referred to the land near the resort base area as "Frog Valley" since the early 1900s. "Of course we couldn't consider Frog Valley," Polly Stern laughs, "But when Stein and I saw the name 'Deer Valley' we simply knew that was it. Everybody was worried about

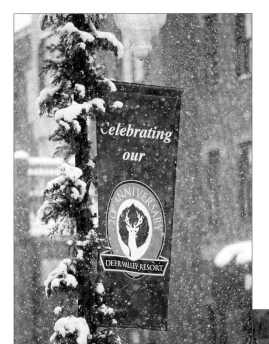

LEFT: WHEN DEER VALLEY CELEBRATED
ITS 20TH ANNIVERSARY, OPENING
WEEKEND FEATURED $20 LIFT TICKETS
AND $20 DINNERS AT THE MARIPOSA.
CURRENT DEER VALLEY MANAGEMENT
HAS DONE A GREAT JOB BRINGING
LOCALS INTO THE FOLD WITH NUMEROUS
LIFT-TICKET AND LODGING PACKAGES
FOR UTAH RESIDENTS. BELOW: DEER
VALLEY FOUNDERS CHOSE COLORS FROM
THE SURROUNDING LANDSCAPE FOR THE
RESORT LOGO.

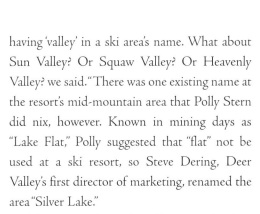

having 'valley' in a ski area's name. What about Sun Valley? Or Squaw Valley? Or Heavenly Valley? we said. "There was one existing name at the resort's mid-mountain area that Polly Stern did nix, however. Known in mining days as "Lake Flat," Polly suggested that "flat" not be used at a ski resort, so Steve Dering, Deer Valley's first director of marketing, renamed the area "Silver Lake."

The resort's logo, the silhouette of a deer head superimposed on an aspen leaf, in Deer Valley's colors—dark green, light green, yellow

and white—appeared throughout the resort on everything from uniforms to cloth napkins to lift towers. "One of the first things that struck me when I came to this area was the colors of the landscape," says Edgar Stern. "The dark green in the logo is for the conifers, the lighter green is the aspen leaves, the yellow is the aspen leaves in autumn, and the white is the snow."

The resort's first two day lodges, Snow Park and Silver Lake, were designed to reflect the National Parks lodge style created by President Franklin D. Roosevelt's WPA in the 1930s. Known as "parkitecture," this style combines native stone, weathered beams with oversized timber columns and broad roof overhangs, all of which combine to form a comfortable, elegant space. Polly Stern, who had studied interior design in New

DEER VALLEY PEOPLE
Co-General Partner Roger Penske

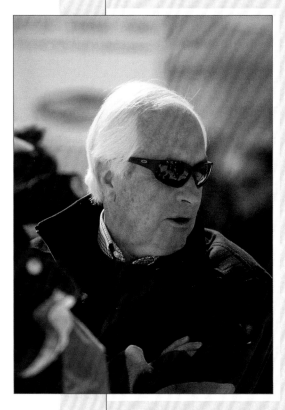

If resort founder Edgar Stern is the heart of Deer Valley, then Roger Penske is its engine. The famed race car driver and automotive magnate came onto the Deer Valley scene in 1987, providing a much-needed financial infusion that helped Deer Valley survive through a challenging economic time.

Penske's wife, Kathy, hails from Utah. While the Penskes were on vacation here, he visited Deer Valley and loved it. "I thought I could make a contribution from a business standpoint. I got to know Edgar at a time when he was looking for potential outside investors. I found that we had the same outlook on the resort, specifically from a quality standpoint. We were on the same track and agreed that we would become co–general partners. From my perspective, we have enjoyed one of the best partnerships that I have experienced in my business career."

"Edgar has great taste and he knows what he wants the resort to feel like," says Chuck English, resort director of mountain operations. "Roger knows the realism of getting there. It's a great combination for us: a great check and balance. Edgar with the vision and Roger with the economics and accounting."

Many will recognize Penske's name from his car-racing days. He was one of racing's most-winning drivers from 1958 to 1965, named *Sports Illustrated* Driver of the Year in 1961.

That was only the beginning of a fast-track career. Penske methodically built Penske Corporation, which includes the nation's largest truck leasing company, Penske Truck Leasing; auto retailing through its Penske Automotive and UnitedAuto dealership groups; and Penske Transportation Components. In addition, Penske Performance owns IRL and NASCAR auto racing teams which hold records in many categories, including the most Indianapolis 500 victories. Penske has served on the board of directors for national companies including General Electric, Home Depot, Delphi, American Express and Philip Morris.

Like Edgar Stern, Penske is known for meticulous attention to detail, unflappable enthusiasm and thorough focus on the things with which he gets personally involved. He's been described as "cool, calculating, never leaving anything to chance" (*The Times Picayune*, 2002), and possessing, "a workaholic schedule, an obsession with detail, a willingness to delegate responsibility, a high tolerance for risk and a flair for seizing opportunities others miss" (*The New York Times*, 1996).

He's been known to show up unannounced at his plants at 2 A.M. to perform vehicle inspections and talk to third-shift factory workers. And to murmur both strategic and emotional encouragements to his race car drivers through their headsets while they're flying down the track at 200 miles an hour. He's also known for insisting on staff collaboration, delegation and teamwork. A credo of his father's, EFFORT EQUALS RESULTS, is well known throughout Penske's nationwide offices.

Penske owns a condominium at Stein Eriksen Lodge and skis about two weeks a year at Deer Valley. "It's a great feeling to be able to talk to guests on the mountain who don't know that I have anything to do with the resort and hear them rave about the Deer Valley experience," he says. "Success is in the details. And Deer Valley's strength in this area is great. Consider, for example, the overall commitment to guest services."

Does he see a similarity between car racing and being part owner of a ski resort? "In motor sports, you must provide a world-class guest experience to about 150,000 people on a weekend, and you don't have a chance to practice. You have to be able to perform and do it right the first time. That is exactly the type of execution that is required to ensure our guests' experience at Deer Valley."

ROGER PENSKE OWNS A CONDOMINIUM AT STEIN ERIKSEN LODGE. VIEWS LIKE THIS
OF EMPIRE CANYON ARE CLOSE BY.

Penske says that delegating is how he runs his own business. "You cannot have a worldwide business without trusting your senior people. I am an advocate of promoting from within. That is what we have done at Deer Valley. Bob Wheaton and his key managers all came up through the organization. That continuity has given us the edge over other resorts."

Penske's focus at Deer Valley has in fact been the human capital. "You have to have the best cars and drivers to win in Indianapolis. In order to have the best resort, you not only need the best runs but, most importantly, you have to have the best people—from the general manager to the people who concierge your skis, to the ski school, to the people who make and serve the great food. All of these things are key to our success."

"I'm really impressed with Roger Penske from a lot of different standpoints," says Bob Wheaton, resort president and general manager. "When I first met him, he scared the hell out of me," Wheaton laughs. "He has a sense of presence that's substantial. He is an amazing businessman and an amazing individual. It's something to watch. It really is. His grasp of any kind of industry is just amazing. He's the epitome of the quick study. He has a memory that's unbelievable. When he first came in, he was looking through a packet of numbers, everything from depreciation to daily income statements from ski programs. Out of seven or eight pages of Excel spread sheets, there was one number that wasn't right. He said, 'So what's up with this?' I thought, 'Oh God.'" Nearly 20 years later, however, Wheaton says that Penske "is very comfortable with the decisions made on the ground here and the direction that the resort is going."

Penske learned to ski in Vermont during his college years. And though he's a self-described highly competitive person, skiing is a way for Penske to unwind. Does he have a favorite run at Deer Valley? "I don't have a favorite," he says. "They're all great." ☾

BELOW: SNOW PARK LODGE WELCOMED DEER VALLEY GUESTS ON OPENING DAY, DECEMBER 26, 1981. LEFT: THE YEAR DEER VALLEY OPENED (1981) WAS ONE OF THE HEAVIEST UTAH SNOW YEARS IN RECENT HISTORY.

York, lobbied for the look, saying, "The timeless, historic feel of those lodges is classic. They fit their natural surroundings and never go out of style." The Sterns took planners on what staffers called "Great Lodges of the West" tours, visiting Mt. Hood's Timberline Lodge and Yosemite's Awahanee, among others, so that the team could borrow stylistic ideas from the classics.

Bob Wheaton remembers "as clearly as yesterday" meeting the Sterns for the first time during lodge construction in September 1980. "The sheetrock wasn't up yet and you could still see through the walls. There were probably 150 tradesmen working in the space, from masons to electricians. Edgar and Polly came through and were very unassuming, just kind of looking around. They were very real people, genuinely interested in the construction and in what I was going to be doing as building maintenance manager. That was

the first real indication that this was going to be a special place. You certainly got that feeling when you looked at the buildings and the plans, but when you met Edgar and Polly, you realized that there were genuine people behind this, not some big company that was in it for bottom-line dollars alone."

Construction of the lodges had to be complete by Christmas week of 1981. Crews worked feverishly around the clock to finish on time. Despite the time constraints, quality was not compromised. The lodges boasted flooring of

Alaskan cedar and flagstone, western red cedar paneling, oversized Oregon timbers, and granite sinks and countertops in the restrooms. The lodges look as good today as they did in the inaugural season, and they have set the standard for the elegant private homes that have since been built in the Deer Valley area. The only casualties were the original tile roofs, which didn't hold up to their first Utah winter and had to be replaced.

While plans were made and construction was underway, Stein Eriksen, Edgar and Polly Stern, Jim Nassikas and Steve Dering spent a considerable amount of time over the course of two winters on the mountain at Deer Valley, hosting private snowcat ski tours for specially invited groups of journalists, celebrities, ski industry pioneers and potential real estate investors. During the tours, the groups skied several already-cut runs. Models of the future lodges were displayed and delicious lunches were served in a log cabin above Silver Lake. Then-newspaper editor and city councilman Jan Wilking recalls, "Those lunches were by far the best meals you could get in Park City at the time. They flamed Steak Diane tableside. And it was the best-stocked bar in town." Pam Prince, Barbara Martin (now Kemp) and Jill Barnhardt, who did business as "Sno-Job Catering," cooked up the impressive fare without running water or electricity. "I don't know how

they did it," says Steve Dering. "They'd have fondue and wine waiting on the cabin deck when we arrived from the snowcat skiing, and then we'd go inside and have a sit-down luncheon and a full bar. Every day."

Not only was the lunch delicious, the skiing was the crème de la crème. Imagine skiing Deer Valley runs with only a handful of other enthusiasts! Joe Cushing wrote, "Edgar, Stacy [Standley, former mayor of Aspen, Colorado and an employee of Sno Engineering] and I skied about 15 inches of unbroken champagne powder on the front side of Flagstaff. I cannot remember if I was paid for that day, but I hope not, for my conscience's sake."

"We skied on two runs initially," recounts Polly Stern. "They were simply called 'Run 1' and 'Run 2' [now known as Birdseye and Wizard]. During

the promotional season of 1979–80, with many more runs cut, Deer Valley inaugurated a second snowcat tour for paying customers. "It was probably the best [skiing] I've ever done in Park City," says Jan Wilking. "They'd groom it at night and then get six or eight inches of powder on top." Park City local Dave Ringelberg rented one of the snowcats for a friend's birthday on March 4, 1980. The experience was so memorable that the same group has held an annual Deer Valley ski day on March 4th ever since. "We broke the record that day by making 18

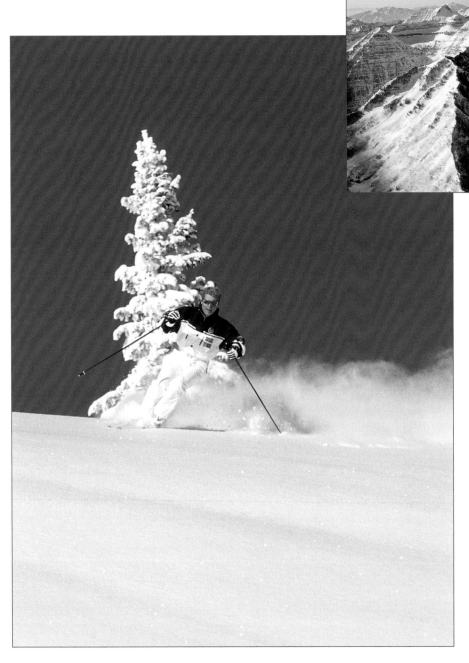

LEFT: STEIN ERIKSEN'S SUAVE SKI
STYLE AND GREGARIOUS PERSONALITY
BROUGHT INTERNATIONAL ATTENTION
TO DEER VALLEY. HE'S BEEN DEER
VALLEY'S DIRECTOR OF SKIING SINCE
THE RESORT OPENED IN 1981. ABOVE:
GUESTS CAN ADMIRE A VIEW OF MT.
TIMPANOGOS FROM STEIN'S FAVORITE
RUN, STEIN'S WAY.

runs," he says. "They had to force us to stop for lunch. The powder was unbelievable. I remember we were all standing at the bottom where Sultan lift is now, waiting for the cat to come back. The sun broke through the clouds, and there was Stein with his group from the other snowcat, skiing the untracked powder. We all started yelling at the top of our lungs, 'Stein! Stein! Stein!' I'll never forget that day."

Occasionally Stein got swept up in his own enthusiasm, standing atop Bald Mountain, waving his arms wide and exclaiming, "And see this? All of it is ours—as far as you can see!" He'd point to thousands of acres, out past Mt. Timpanogos and the Uinta mountains and even into Wyoming. "We could never stop him from doing that," chuckles Edgar, shaking his head.

Deer Valley's pre-opening marketing campaign was unique. Only a few print advertisements were placed in ski publications—lifestyle ads, depicting briefcases, elegant table settings and other high-end paraphernalia, with a snapshot of Stein and a message that read, "Remember that special place we've been searching for? I've found it…Deer Valley!" The ad did not feature skiing, trees or snow. "We didn't have anything to show yet," says Steve Dering. "And emphasizing the lifestyle approach was in line with the hospitality-driven mentality of the resort." The next ad campaign, much in the same vein, showed the Deer Valley

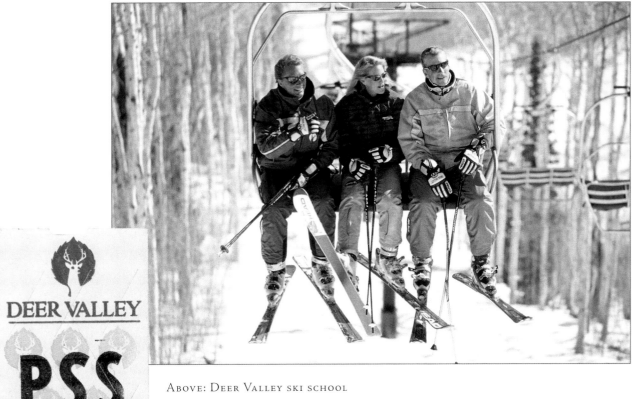

ABOVE: DEER VALLEY SKI SCHOOL
UNIFORMS HAVE CHANGED EVERY
FEW YEARS, BUT THEY'RE ALWAYS A
SHADE OF GREEN, DEER VALLEY'S
TRADEMARK COLOR. LEFT: POLLY
STERN STILL HAS A LIFT TICKET
FROM DEER VALLEY'S OPENING DAY
IN 1981. AS A SURPRISE, EDGAR
STERN HAD THE TICKETS IMPRINTED
WITH POLLY'S INITIALS.

logo and read simply, "Unspoiled. Uncrowded. Uncommonly civilized."

What sold Deer Valley, though, were certainly those years of public relations tours, the intriguing vision and the product itself. Steve Dering says, "One of the ski writers told me, 'Everybody says they're going to be the best. You're the only guys who demonstrated it. Everything you've done from the time you contacted us to the time you dropped us back at the airport was first class, like you said it was going to be.' So even with a primitive cabin, we were

able to deliver that Deer Valley experience from day one. It was very powerful and many positive articles were written about Deer Valley before it even opened."

Deer Valley Resort opened on December 26, 1981. "We were supposed to open on December 12, but we had no snow that year," says Stern. "Then it started snowing on Christmas Eve. And it snowed and it snowed and it snowed. It was unbelievable. The only problem was, we had promised these groomed runs—the Deer Valley corduroy—and we had so much powder we couldn't keep up with the grooming. But few seemed to mind."

The resort opened with five chairlifts, 35 ski runs on Bald Eagle and Bald Mountains, two day lodges (Snow Park and Silver Lake), 200 employees and a $20 lift ticket. Was there a big party to celebrate the opening? "No,"

DEER VALLEY PEOPLE
Resort President and General Manager Bob Wheaton

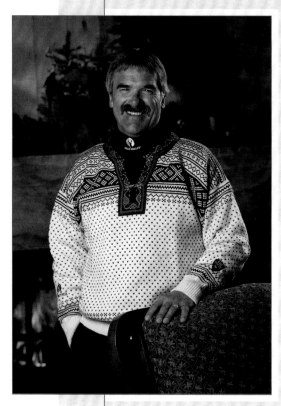

If Bob Wheaton weren't in the ski resort business, he'd be a rancher or a military pilot. Those are his fantasy careers, and they perfectly reveal the yin and yang that make this man so centered: feet on the ground and head in the sky. In his 23 years at Deer Valley, Wheaton has proven that a down-to-earth guy can artfully manage one of the country's most elegant ski resorts.

Wheaton has a voice like a lullaby and a demeanor more like that of a teddy bear than a corporate taskmaster. "There are no ivory towers at Deer Valley," he says, showing up for work every day in a lift-operator uniform and working from a windowless office tucked away in Snow Park Lodge. He's on the mountain daily, riding the chairs so he can chat with guests, refilling tissue boxes in the lift mazes or stopping to assist skiers who need help with the trail map.

"It became apparent pretty soon that Bob is a gem," says resort founder Edgar Stern. "He knows every detail of what goes on here. And he's done a lot to keep Deer Valley's image down to earth, because he's so approachable."

Being an avid outdoorsman keeps Wheaton grounded. He's a hunter, a fly-fisherman and a horse enthusiast who believes in the adage that "the best thing for the inside of a person is the outside of a horse." Wheaton has formed close bonds with Deer Valley and Park City. By creating specially priced lift ticket packages for locals, and by representing Deer Valley on the boards of numerous community non-profit organizations, Wheaton is credited with bringing locals into the fold of what in the beginning was perceived as a resort for wealthy visitors.

"Bob makes you feel like you're the most important person on earth," says Kym Meehan, a World Cup course volunteer. "During events, he comes out to the venue every day and addresses everyone by first name, thanking them for their time." "Bob Wheaton is the biggest asset this company has," says guest services manager Terry Bouman. "He's always willing to jump in and help wherever it's needed. If there's a line at the ski corral, he's in there putting skis away. Often new employees are shocked when they find out that the guy bussing tables during a busy lunch hour is the general manager."

Sometimes Wheaton's friendly nature draws too much attention. Several years ago, while skiing with First Lady Hillary Clinton and her daughter, Chelsea, so many locals greeted Bob in the lift maze that a Secret Service agent finally whispered to Wheaton, "You're really drawing a crowd. You'd better peel off."

A Michigan native, Wheaton became a ski instructor at the age of 15, and later the ski school director, at Mount Holly. He moved to Utah with his wife, Marion, in 1979 and taught skiing for one year at Park City Resort before joining Deer Valley. His favorite part of the job? "First, the skiing," he says. "And next would be…skiing. And third would be…skiing."

Though he's received many awards—"Rotary Professional Citizen of the Year" and "Intermountain Ski Areas Association Outstanding Contribution Award," to name just two—his favorite place to be is the back of the house. "I really enjoy that. The maintenance shop is one of the hubs of the resort. I spend a lot of time there. There's a lot of fun, guy stuff. The best toys I get to play with are snowcats, loaders and bulldozers," he says, his trademark quiet smile widening under a beefy moustache.

Wheaton comes by his fascination with machinery honestly. With a college degree in electrical, structural and mechanical engineering, his first job at Deer Valley was building maintenance manager. He had applied for four other jobs—trail crew, equipment operator, ski school director and ski school supervisor—but didn't get them. He was offered a position as a ski instructor, but he never worked at that job because the building maintenance manager position came open, and after interviewing "with about 40 people," he

BOB WHEATON SAYS THE BEST PART OF HIS JOB IS THE SKIING. HAVING WORKED AT DEER VALLEY SINCE ITS
INCEPTION, HE KNOWS THE RESORT'S MOUNTAINS LIKE THE BACK OF HIS HAND.

was hired. Though he longed to spend time outdoors, Wheaton took the job, he says, because "it was year-round, and because of the economy at that time [1980]. Summertime employment was grim at best. And I thought Deer Valley was going to be something unique in the ski industry." He worked his way through the Deer Valley ranks to vehicle maintenance and operations manager. From there he became director of ski operations, and in 1988 he took over as general manager of the resort. "President" was added to his title in 1999.

Wheaton was asked to sit on several military and civilian committees planning security for the 2002 Olympic Winter Games. It gave him the chance to tour air bases and go on C-135 refueling missions. He even got to fly an F-16 himself, he'll tell you with child-like reverence, saying, "One of my favorite things was banking turns in and out of clouds at five or six g's. Then we went supersonic over the west desert. At only 1,000 feet off the deck, seeing the mountains whiz by like falling dominos was a definite kick."

It's the ability to appreciate the big picture that makes Wheaton an award-winning manager. He fully embraces Deer Valley's corporate culture, and exhibits its fundamentals with daily staff mentoring. "We have a three-circle model on which all of our decisions are based: Take care of the guest, take care of Deer Valley, and take care of each other. Those circles are all interrelated." Lauded as a role model for business managers, Wheaton is frequently invited to speak at career seminars. He says Deer Valley staff members are loyal because they feel a lot of personal return. "People feel like they make a substantial personal contribution on a daily basis. Plus, it's a really nice place to spend your day. There are great facilities. We try to set each individual up to succeed every day," whether with free breakfast pastries, uniforms that keep them safe and comfortable, or the equipment, training and communication tools they need to perform a task. "Job descriptions and expectations are clearly defined, and regular review processes and improvement teams keep communications open throughout every level of the company."

Wheaton's nuts-and-bolts personality doesn't allow him to get caught up in what some might consider the "glamorous" part of his job—occasionally skiing with movie stars and political leaders. And he has his mom, who still asks him when he's going to "get a real job," to keep him grounded. There's nothing better, he says, than "being out in the big office. You just go out and ride the chair with a guest. It really lifts your spirits." ☾

laughs Polly. "We were too busy for a party."

There was talk that the new resort was to be a "members only" club for the rich and famous. "That was only a rumor," explains Gil Williams, who began working for Deer Valley Resort in 1985. "We did try to sell ski tickets by reservation only. Edgar didn't want the resort to be overcrowded like he'd experienced in Aspen, and since it was on private and not public land, we could control the number of people allowed to access it. The perception, however, ended up being that it was tough to get a lift ticket at Deer Valley. It soon became obvious that we'd scared people away. We quickly corrected that during the first year."

There was a plan for the resort to build its own overnight lodge, Deer Valley Inn. At the time lodging was scarce in Park City. "We pre-sold

units for Deer Valley Inn," says Gil Williams, "but the securities laws required an SEC filing. It slowed us down and cost more money. Eventually it was decided it wasn't going to work. We dropped the whole idea." To this day Deer Valley Resort doesn't own any of the luxury overnight lodging that surrounds the resort. Edgar Stern decided to sell land and let others build the lodges. "It's proven to be very successful," Edgar says. "You just can't do everything."

John Guay, now director of skier services,

WHEN DEER VALLEY FIRST OPENED,
SNOW PARK LODGE HAD NO SPACE FOR
A SKI SCHOOL OFFICE. DEER VALLEY'S
FIRST SKI SCHOOL DIRECTOR, SAL
RAIO, COMMANDEERED A SMALL SPACE
IN THE LODGE FOR AN OFFICE. LEFT:
SKI SCHOOL OFFERS LESSONS FOR
CHILDREN AS YOUNG AS THREE.

was one of Deer Valley's first employees. He came to Deer Valley in 1981 from what was then called Park West ski area (now The Canyons). "The hardest thing for ski instructors working at Deer Valley in the early days was that the rest of the industry was loose in terms of customer service issues. Deer Valley had a dress code, guest-space-versus-employee-space rules, and restricted ski privileges. If you were on the clock, you weren't allowed to ski unless you were actually teaching. You didn't just go take a few runs between lessons. Very

few people came to apply that first season because they were scared off by the rumors of how strict it was."

There was a learning curve for Deer Valley, too. Though ski instructors looked fabulous the first year on the hill, sporting green and yellow stretch pants and reversible sweaters, they sadly discovered that the outfits were all fashion and no function. "Those uniforms were like sponges," laughs Chuck English. "And that first year it snowed for about 60 days straight." Instructors could only wear black ski boots and gloves. If an instructor's favorite ski boots happened to be orange, they couldn't be worn with the uniform. Applying hotel philosophies to a snow environment was Edgar's vision, and uniform presentation was an important part of that. But there had to be some adjustments. "Things started out rigid

and then loosened up as we all learned what was classy yet practical in an outdoor arena," says John Guay.

Despite dazzling press reviews that lauded the resort's grooming and accessibility and its upscale food and service, the sales of real estate parcels, which had gone well at first, came to an abrupt halt because the economy had entered a recession and the market had dropped. By 1985 the resort had mountains of debt. "I can remember coming up to a payroll week at that time with definite fear that we weren't going to be able to scrape together enough cash to make it," says Gil Williams, "[but] something came through in the nick of time and we met that payroll." Williams admits that his fear was not that he'd be out of a job if the company went under, but that he'd be the first person ever working for Edgar

Stern to miss a payroll. "We were borrowing money from a New Orleans bank with Edgar's personal guarantees, which is something no businessman wants to do; but Edgar did it to carry us through those years."

"Trammel Crow, the strongest real estate company in the country at the time, had offered to buy the resort," recounts Bob Wheaton. "There were signed papers. They had their guy sitting at this desk. And then Edgar had the chutzpah to stand up and say, 'No. We're not going to do this. That's not what

DEER VALLEY'S ABUNDANCE OF GROOMED RUNS ARE WONDERFUL FOR PRACTICING
ONE'S CARVING TECHNIQUES.

I had in mind when I started this company. We're going to hunker down.'"

"I can't tell you how deserving Edgar Stern is of taking all the glory," says Jim Nassikas, "for the way he stood by Deer Valley. He didn't need headaches like that. But he was so intent on wanting to do something special, he held on. Through all the ups and downs." In 1987 Roger Penske, who was a frequent Deer Valley skier and owned a condominium at Stein Eriksen Lodge, learned that Deer Valley was looking for investors. He invited the Sterns to a cocktail party where he told Edgar he'd be interested in getting involved. Penske became a part owner and co–general partner that year.

When the real estate market improved in 1987, sales of real estate parcels in the Evergreen and Bald Eagle communities took off. Stern and Penske each bought homesites to get things going. Deer Valley was able to pay off its debt in full by 1993. From that year on, Deer Valley has operated in the black, reinvesting profits into snowmaking, grooming and lodges.

In 2001, the readers of SKI magazine named Deer Valley Resort the #1 ski resort in North America, an honor that usually went to much larger resorts. Stern had a pin designed specifically for the employees to wear after the award was announced: the Deer Valley name and logo backed by a large number "1."

MUCH OF THE FUNDING FOR DEER VALLEY CAME FROM SELLING PARCELS OF LAND NEAR ITS BASE TO LODGING DEVELOPERS. TASTEFUL CONDOMINIUMS, TOWNHOMES AND LODGES GET A FRONT-SEAT VIEW OF SNOW CONDITIONS ON DEER VALLEY'S BALD EAGLE AND BALD MOUNTAINS.

That was by no means the end of the story, however. Edgar Stern's passion for Deer Valley Resort remains strong. He and Polly split their time between their home on a small island off the coast of Washington—where Stern likes to watch the Orca whales from his deck "swimming in unison like the Rockettes"—and a condominium in Silver Lake Village. The Sterns continue to give the benefit of their experience to resort management. Sea scallops were taken off the menu at The Mariposa this year because Edgar did not think they were sweet enough. "If we can't get something to meet Mr. Stern's expectations," says Deer Valley's food and beverage director, Julie Wilson, "it's gone." Polly Stern, who is an officer and director of the Royal Street companies, contributes her expertise to Deer Valley's food and beverage operation, building design and marketing decisions. Edgar Stern continues to oversee the big

picture. Is there any better way to do it than from his favorite ski runs?

At 81, "No-Turn Stern" skis down his mountains remarkably well, often in the company of much younger people. He savors every minute of it, especially a little tree shot staffers unofficially call "Edgar's Alley." While he eats a bowl of soup for lunch, employees thank him for providing them such a great place to work. They receive shy but appreciative smiles in return.

Though the Sterns have created what many call the country's most luxurious ski area, their

down-to-earth attitude adds to its staying power. "I don't like the words 'pamper' or 'prestigious' used in reference to Deer Valley," Edgar says. "It makes it sound like you have to be carried down the mountain or something," Polly adds. "My biggest concern," says Edgar, "is that we've gotten such a great reputation and we can't afford to lose it. We have to keep everything absolutely superb. I would never want to hear people say, 'Deer Valley was great, but it's gone downhill.' Never."

The Sterns' vigilance and enthusiasm for fresh strategies is visible even to the newest of observers. After a lunch at Silver Lake restaurant, Polly stands and murmurs, "It's missing a branch," referring to the decorative garland on the mantle over a large stone fireplace. Upon inspection, one can see that, indeed, one end of the arrangement is about a foot shorter than the other. Though many would miss such detail, Polly doesn't. On the way out of the lodge, she stops to straighten a throw pillow on the leather couch in the foyer. Edgar notices a loose section of wooden banister on the stairs leading out of the building. No words need be said. You can bet that the minute he gets back to the company's Silver Lake Village office, his staff will be on the phone to the building maintenance department and the banister will be firmly back in place before the evening's dinner guests arrive.

A dream come true. Edgar Stern's dream.

77

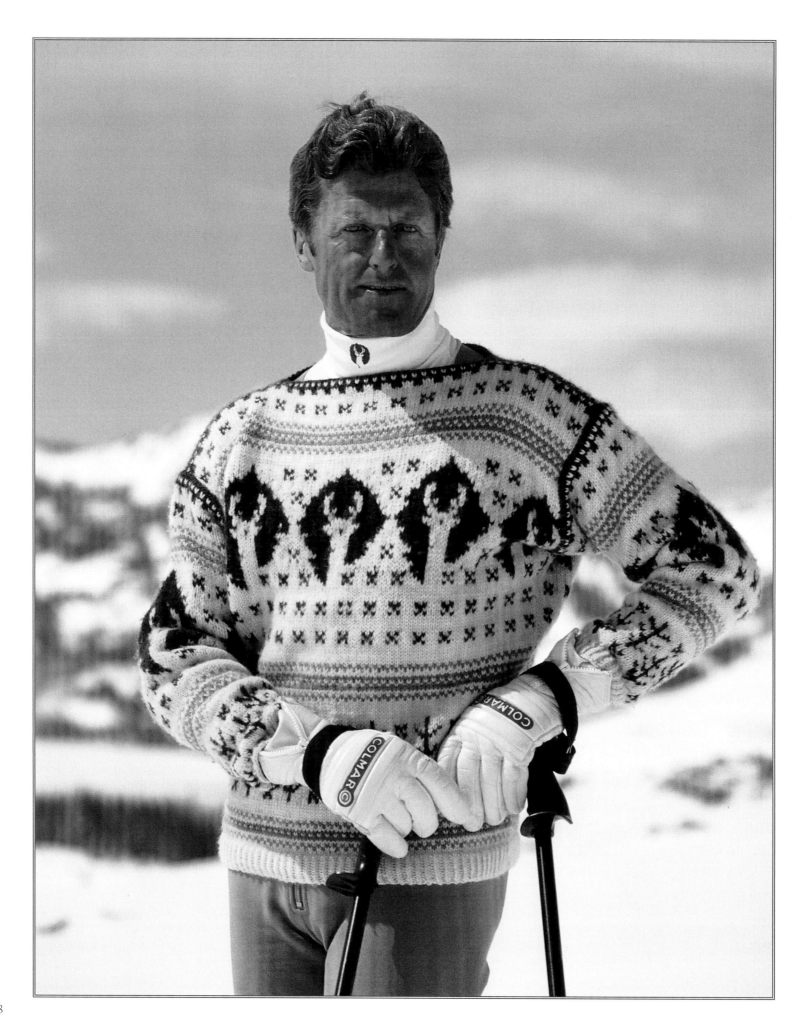

Chapter 4

THE STAR: STEIN ERIKSEN

There are two things you can always count on when you ski with Stein Eriksen. First, no matter who you are, he'll ski faster than you do—guaranteed. With his arms out dramatically, he'll swoop down the trail in wide, carving turns, and before you know it he'll be down at the chairlift. Stein does not like to be kept waiting. "We are burning daylight," he'll say, his lilting Norwegian accent as rhythmic as his perfectly orchestrated GS turns.

The second thing you can count on is this: While he's leaving you in his perfect tracks, he will look really good doing it. Like the slopes at Deer Valley, Stein is always impeccably groomed. He wears a spotless Bogner ski suit, and his silver hair glimmers in the Utah sun like the helmet of a Norse god. He never wears a hat. "My friends who are going bald ask me why I have so much hair and why I never wear the hat," he chuckles. "I tell them it's because one must let the hair breathe." Stein's pride in his appearance is legendary. For his 75th birthday, friends gave him a box of combs.

What is it like spending the day with Stein? Say you're sitting in one of Deer Valley's wood-beamed lodges, with its floor-to-ceiling windows framing views of snow-covered aspens outside. Stein goes to get steaming cups of hot chocolate for both of you. All eyes are on him as he crosses the room. Men and women alike turn their heads as he walks by.

An attractive middle-aged woman approaches your table. "Excuse me, Mr. Eriksen. I'm sorry to interrupt, but I just had to introduce myself. My mother took a ski lesson from you 25 years ago and hasn't stopped talking about it since."

STEIN WEARS A HAND-KNIT DEER VALLEY SWEATER CRAFTED BY HIS MOTHER, BITTEN. AT ONE POINT BITTEN RAN A COTTAGE INDUSTRY PRODUCING SKI SWEATERS AND EMPLOYING 200 WOMEN.

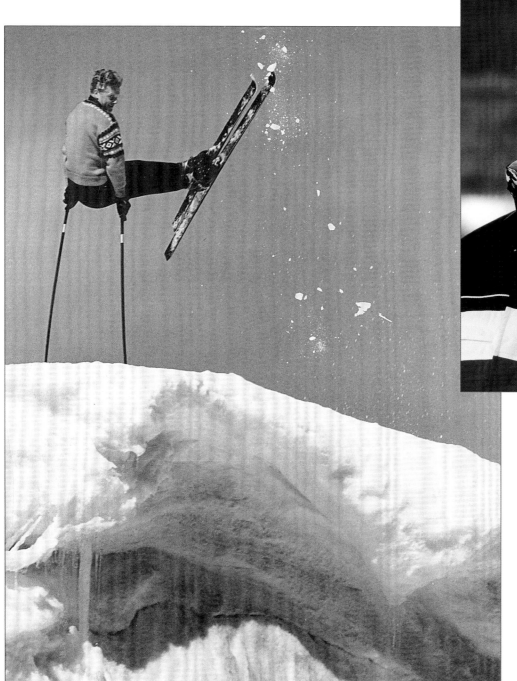

LEFT: STEIN'S PARENTS WORRIED WHEN HE WAS A CHILD THAT HIS BODY WAS TOO SKINNY, SO THEY ENROLLED HIM IN GYMNASTICS. ABOVE: STEIN WEARING A BOGNER SKI SUIT. WILLY BOGNER WAS A CLOSE FRIEND OF THE ERIKSEN FAMILY. BOGNER HAS BEEN STEIN'S EXCLUSIVE SKIWEAR SPONSOR FOR MORE THAN 50 YEARS. OPPOSITE: STEIN SKIS FRESH POWDER AT DEER VALLEY. HE FIRST LEARNED TO SKI POWDER AT SUN VALLEY IN 1952–53.

Stein is on his feet, listening attentively, his hand on the speaker's arm, his blue eyes focused on hers, an ever-widening smile coming over his face. "Ah," he says, "and tell me, does she still ski?" He's disappointed to hear that she's no longer able to, but he quickly moves on to chat with her about this visit to Deer Valley. Before she leaves, he says, "You be sure to give your mother a hello and a hug from me, young lady. I will give you the hug to pass on to your mother." He takes the ski-booted woman in his arms and delivers a long embrace. As she floats away, Stein turns with a wink and says, "I've learned a few tricks over the years."

As Deer Valley's director of skiing, Stein skis with corporate groups, special guests, ski clinics, VIPs and friends. He chats with guests on the chairlifts, asking them what they think of Deer Valley and how they like their skis. He overflows with enthusiasm for Deer Valley and the joy of skiing, and his job fits him as elegantly as his ski suits.

"I love to ski Stein's Way and Tycoon," he says, "but there are a limited number of people skiing those runs. I like to be where the people are. I'm not too egoistic about my skiing…." he laughs. "Of course, it is kind of an ego boost to know that people would like to see me ski. The day they don't ask for me, I will say, 'What have I done wrong now?'"

Stein skis from 10 A.M. until about 1 P.M. each

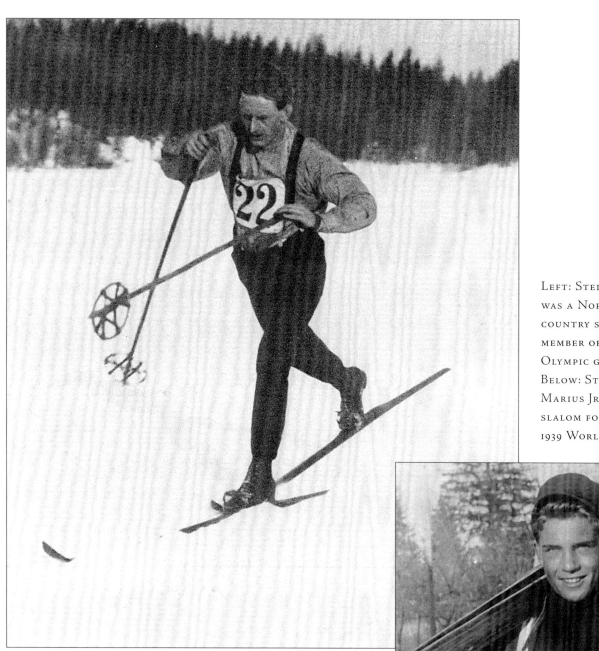

day, and then heads into the Stein Eriksen Lodge (known to most simply as "Stein's"), where he enjoys a lunch of Norwegian foods like gravlax or herring, or a cup of soup. He poses for pictures with children in baggy ski pants, or with groups of women giggling like schoolgirls, their companions standing back, shaking their heads and grinning with a mixture of amusement and respect.

Stein is passionate about life. Like a child, he gushes about new shaped skis, delighting in how easily they turn. He doesn't hide his enthusiasm for Norwegian cakes. His favorite—what Deer Valley bakers have come to call "Stein's cake"—is a decadent concoction of marzipan, almonds and rich raspberry filling. "You see, Americans make their cakes with lots of batter and not very many goodies," he explains. "The Norwegians, we make our cakes with a little batter and lots of goodies."

Stein is a good cook, specializing in Norwegian dishes. He enjoys aquavit with a beer chaser as much as champagne and caviar. He likes to savor a good Riesling over a fondue lunch. On New Year's Eve, he strolls around the dining rooms at Stein's, skoaling guests and singing Norwegian drinking songs. (He has a good voice.) And there's always a glimmer in his eye when he talks about what skiing 100 days a year does for him. "You wonder why people have a love affair with this mountain? How could they not? Look at these views. Look at

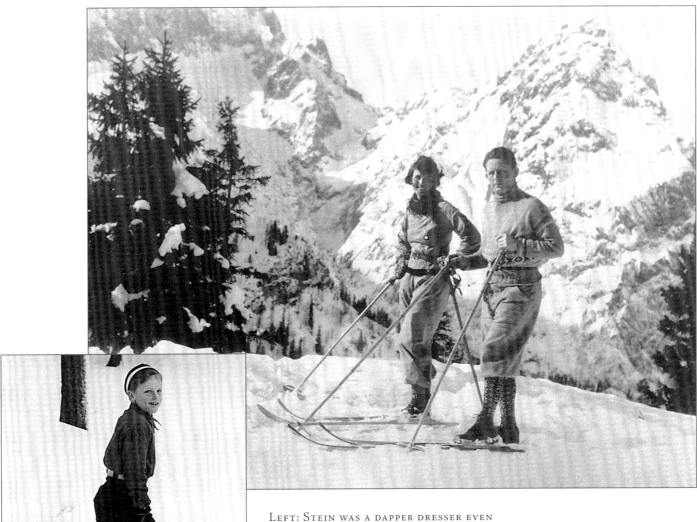

Left: Stein was a dapper dresser even in his youth. Above: Marius and Bitten Eriksen were introduced to alpine skiing by Hannes Schneider and Willy Bogner during this 1930 trip to San Anton, Austria.

the beauty. I would miss it a lot if I didn't have it around me every day. It's part of me."

Stein credits his vigor to his parents and what he depicts as a winter-wonderland Norwegian childhood. Marius and Birgit ("Bitten") Eriksen were avid cross-country skiers, and they raised their sons, Marius Jr. and Stein, to be not only skiers but gentlemen—civilized, educated, sensitive and good sportsmen. Stein remembers skiing in powdery snow around his modest home near the legendary Holmenkollen ski jump, scaring up rabbits, fox and birds and leaving cross-country ski tracks in the powder behind him. He remembers putting his mittens to dry on nails beside the fireplace before stepping into a sauna. (His father told him that to be a great skier, you must take a hot sauna bath several times a week.) Marius was a cross-country ski champion himself and a member of Norway's 1912 Olympic gymnastics team. Marius thought Stein's body was too skinny, so he enrolled him in gymnastics. That was the foundation for Stein's famous flips on skis. Bitten began a cottage industry that produced ski sweaters. She was the first president of the women's ski club in Oslo. Marius regularly tinkered with skis and bindings in the basement. His tinkering evolved into a ski factory, where he produced cross-country skis and eventually the steel-edged, laminated alpine skis called "Eriksen Streamlines" that were among the best-selling skis in Europe during the '30s and '40s and were also exported to the United States.

Stein Eriksen Lodge

The five-diamond Stein Eriksen Lodge was built on a dare. "Edgar Stern and I were walking the property [that would] soon be Deer Valley, looking for a convention-center site," says Stein. "We walked through aspens on the ridge where Stein's Lodge is now, and Edgar said it was too small. Then I said, 'Hey, stop for a second. How about the Stein Eriksen Lodge here? We're going to be working

together for a few years, so, eh, what do you think about that?' Edgar didn't say anything. He walked a few more steps, stopped and said, 'If you're serious about it, why not? But it has to be on the condition that nobody sits on it for 10 years. I want things to happen. If you get construction going within a year, it's a deal.' That was 1980. The lodge opened Christmas of 1982. All on a handshake from Edgar."

A crew of local businessmen that included Rob Morris, Paul Dougan and Rick Prince made it happen, with Stein consulting on design and style, making sure the lodge had Norwegian touches like hand-carved cabinetry and large stone fireplaces. Stein is not the owner, but he is definitely a presence at the lodge. He lunches there almost daily, chatting with guests and sampling butternut squash soup with truffle mascarpone, or wild-game chili with buffalo, venison and boar. His shimmering collection of awards—including silver trophies, plaques and his Olympic and World Championships medals—sits in the lobby trophy case. His wife's boutique, Bjorn Stova, exhibits a mannequin with Stein's "suit du jour," a duplicate of the Bogner outfit Stein will be sporting that day. This provides guests a better chance of spotting Stein on the hill, and of course the opportunity to purchase a part of the fantasy for themselves.

As the model for elegant Deer Valley lodges, Stein's recently underwent a major renovation, adding a spa, a conference center and more living units (the total now stands at 59 suites and 111 deluxe and luxury rooms). The lodge has won all the awards—the *Wine Spectator* Award of Excellence, DiRoNA and Zagat awards for the restaurants; the *Condé Nast Traveler* best-of list; *Mobil Travel Guide's* Four-Star award—you name it.

TOP LEFT: OPENED IN 1982, STEIN ERIKSEN LODGE UNDERWENT A MAJOR RENOVATION IN 2002 THAT INCLUDED THIS STUNNING ENTRY. LEFT: THE FLOOR-TO-CEILING FIREPLACE IN THE STEIN ERIKSEN LODGE LOBBY IS ONE OF 145 FIREPLACES IN THE LODGE.

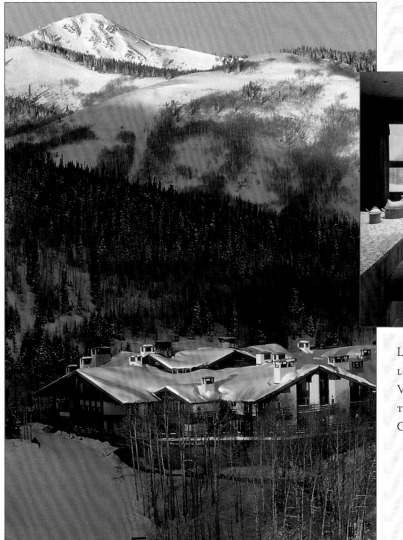

LEFT: STEIN ERIKSEN LODGE IS
LOCATED MIDMOUNTAIN AT DEER
VALLEY WITH BALD MOUNTAIN IN
THE BACKGROUND. ABOVE: THE
GRAND SUITE SLEEPS EIGHT GUESTS.

At Stein Eriksen Lodge, housekeepers back gently out of the room so their footprints won't be left on freshly vacuumed carpets, and the *TV Guide* is wrapped in a hunter-green leather cover. The only sommelier in the state of Utah is on staff at Stein's. The silverware and glasses are hand-buffed by wait staff before each meal, and French-press coffees are served in the lobby near backgammon tables, before a floor-to-ceiling fireplace. Near the footbaths in the spa waiting area, curtained and pillowed reading nooks conjure images from *The Arabian Nights*. Piñon-pine smoke curls from 145 fireplaces, and sidewalks linking the rooms to the main lodge are heated and perpetually snow-free. Guests return from dinner to find that the rich fabric curtains have been drawn, the lights dimmed, and chocolates (wrapped to look like Stein's 1952 Olympic medals) laid out on the pillow. A thick, soft insignia robe is on the bed, and logoed slippers rest on a white floor cloth. A guest might never leave the room if it weren't for the blue sky and sunshine and groomed runs beckoning like waves of ribbon candy just outside the window.

The Glitretind restaurant, known to locals as "The Glit," is a special-occasion restaurant, a favorite for the skiers' buffet lunch (be hungry), or for Sunday brunch, with live jazz and a huge spread. Many Park City restaurant chefs and managers were trained in the kitchens at Stein's, in everything from place settings to baby lettuces to fine-wine tasting. The Troll Hallen bar is one of the coziest in town. You can sit on the leather couch in front of the roaring fire and watch the stars over the aspen trees.

Stein's is the only lodge in Utah—and one of only two ski resort lodges in the country—to win the AAA's Five-Diamond award.☾

LEFT: A YOUNG WILLY BOGNER WAS WELCOMED INTO THE ERIKSEN FAMILY AFTER BEING INVITED TO BREAKFAST AT THEIR HOME AND BRINGING HIS OWN BREAD. BOGNER BECAME AN HONORARY OLDER BROTHER TO THE ERIKSEN BOYS. ABOVE: MARIUS JR. ESCAPED NAZI-OCCUPIED NORWAY DURING WORLD WAR II AND BECAME A SPITFIRE PILOT FOR THE BRITISH ROYAL AIR FORCE. THE SWASTIKAS ON HIS AIRPLANE ARE A TALLY OF HIS NAZI "KILLS." OPPOSITE: THE START OF STEIN'S GOLD-MEDAL RUN DURING THE 1954 WORLD CHAMPIONSHIPS AT ÅRE, SWEDEN.

"I saw the way my mother and father lived their lives," says Stein. "They were always full of good humor and pep, and they had such a happy life because of the surroundings we lived in. We manufactured skis and had a sports shop. Everybody was so up all the time. Friends who came to the house were athletes, full of joy and fun, so I think I inherited that from my parents."

Stein was a solid cross-country skier. Although ski jumping was never his forte, he did jump from the age of five until around 16, often practicing with brother Marius at night on candlelit jumps they built themselves. "The jumping wasn't that much fun for me," laughs Stein, "because all of my friends could beat me." In 1930, Willy Bogner, the German ski clothing manufacturer, and Hannes Schneider, the Austrian ski instruction pioneer, introduced the Eriksens to alpine skiing during a family trip to St. Anton, Austria. Marius

began producing alpine skis, and Stein started skiing on them. He had found his niche.

In 1940, just as Stein and his brother were beginning to excel in slalom (Marius Jr. competed in the 1939 World Championships), the Nazis invaded Norway, beginning a five-year occupation. They prohibited ski competitions unless Nazi youth group members were guaranteed racing spots. As a show of defiance, Norwegian athletes like Stein chose not to compete at all, but they trained secretly whenever possible.

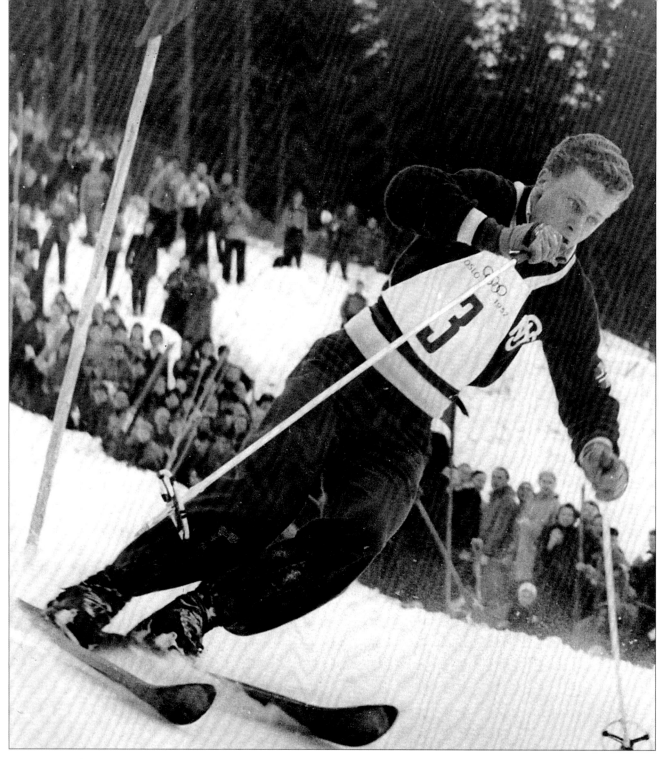

"I was 12 and Marius was 17 when World War II started," says Stein. "Marius fled from Norway to England in a fisherman's boat with the Germans [in pursuit]. Twice [Marius and his companions] had to turn around because of a storm. The third time they made it to England. If they hadn't, the Germans would have been waiting for them to come back. It was like some surrealistic fairy tale," Stein recalls. Marius went on to fly for Britain's Royal Air Force as a Spitfire pilot, gaining hero status for shooting down so many German planes. He was eventually shot down himself, and was imprisoned until the war ended. He received the St. Olaf's medal and the American Silver Star, among other medals.

"I think the war implanted in those of us who were young skiers a sense of responsibility to Norway," wrote Stein in his book, *Come Ski With Me*. "Somehow we developed the drive to go before the world when international competition was again possible and bring our country back to the position it had held before the war. Marius had been thwarted by the war. I felt that he and I should carry on together. In 1947 he became the Norwegian slalom champion, and in 1948 we both made the Norwegian Olympian Team. It was my parents' proudest moment."

Stein's best finish in the '48 Games was a 29th in slalom, but he persevered, traveling to America in 1949 to prepare for the 1950 World Championships in Aspen, Colorado. Still unknown in the ski world, he rode the bus from

RIGHT: Stein's 1952 Olympic medals, gold
in the first-ever Olympic giant slalom
event and silver in slalom, are on
display in the Stein Eriksen Lodge
lobby. Below: This near-fall during the
1952 Olympic giant slalom almost cost
Stein the race. Miraculously, he
recovered and went on to win the event.

Connecticut to Denver, stayed in a dollar-a-night hotel, trained hard and won the bronze medal in slalom. This marked the beginning of international attention for Stein. In 1952 he hit his stride, proving to the world that the Norwegians were "back" by winning the gold medal in the first Olympic giant slalom race and the silver medal in slalom on his home turf at the Oslo Olympics.

Not surprisingly, winning those Olympic medals was the highlight of Stein's career. "I won the gold medal in giant slalom at Norefjell while the opening ceremonies were going on in

Oslo, 90 miles away. So it was announced during the ceremonies that I had won gold for Norway. That was a big deal. The awards were given the next night. Everything was dark, and the only light in the arena was on me and the two Austrians next to me on the podium. To see thousands of people sitting around the stadium….[It was] the first time since before the war that a Scandinavian had won….When they played the national anthem and I saw the spotlight on the Norwegian flag rising to the top of the flagpole….I don't think that can really be described. The emotion was so strong and the tears were so big. It was unbelievable."

Those 1952 Games almost ended differently for Stein. During the giant slalom, his skis momentarily lost their grip and he nearly crashed, right at the gate where his mother was standing. Stein's father had died in 1950, and

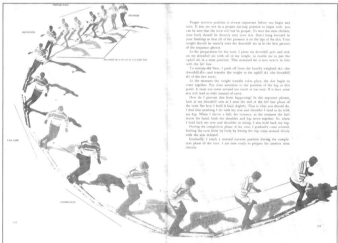

OPPOSITE: STEIN'S EXAGGERATED "REVERSE-SHOULDER" TECHNIQUE WAS UNMISTAKABLE. ABOVE: THE TROPHY CASE AT STEIN ERIKSEN LODGE DISPLAYS STEIN'S IMPRESSIVE COLLECTION OF AWARDS. STEIN WAS THE FIRST ALPINE SKIER EVER TO WIN THREE GOLD MEDALS AT A WORLD CHAMPIONSHIPS EVENT (IN 1954). LEFT: STEIN WROTE MANY INSTRUCTIONAL ARTICLES IN NUMEROUS MAGAZINES INCLUDING *SKIING* AND *SPORTS ILLUSTRATED*. HE DEMONSTRATES THE PERFECT STEM CHRISTIE TURN IN HIS OWN BOOK, *COME SKI WITH ME*.

Bitten had attended the Olympic event reluctantly, since she didn't think she could leave the ski shop. As the story goes, when Stein faltered, Bitten assumed he had missed the gate, and thinking her presence had jinxed him, threw herself down on the snow and cried, "I knew I shouldn't have come; I knew it." That's when a photographer tapped her on the shoulder, saying, "Mrs. Eriksen. He did it. Stein has won the gold medal for Norway!" Bitten became so excited that she skied down the restricted side of the racecourse, then ripped her ski pants in the process of giving Stein an exuberant hug.

Stein's signature skiing style would become legendary. He became a leading exponent of the "reverse-shoulder" ski technique that slowly replaced the traditional Arlberg style. He started performing his "Stein Flip," the first skier to perform layout somersaults on skis. "During the war, I had seen some Norwegians doing somersaults on skis. My friends and I weren't to be outdone. We built kickers, and though we had lots of falls, by the end of the day we were landing [the flips]. The layout part just came naturally from our gymnastics training." Over the years Stein made thousands of flips without accident.

After the Olympics, Sun Valley founder Averill Harriman invited Stein to ski at Sun Valley as a guest instructor during the 1952–53 season. Accustomed to icy racecourses, Stein was greeted by two feet of powder on

DURING HIS LONG CAREER STEIN
PERFORMED MORE THAN 1,000 OF
HIS SIGNATURE LAYOUT FLIPS
WITHOUT ACCIDENT. SOME HAVE
CALLED STEIN THE "FATHER OF
FREESTYLE SKIING."

his first day at the resort. He couldn't make a turn, and eventually suffered an embarrassing fall, prompting one of the American ski instructors to ask, "Are you really Stein Eriksen?" Stein learned to ski deep powder that winter, and then returned to Åre, Sweden, where he won three gold medals at the 1954 World Championships—in slalom, giant slalom and combined—history's first alpine skier to score triple gold at a World Championships event.

Stein had his credentials, and at 28, it was time for him to get a job.

He nearly became ski ambassador for Argentine dictator Juan Peron, but Peron had to flee the country before Stein was officially hired. His first job was in neighboring Chile instead, running the ski school at Portillo in 1955 and 1956. He then returned to the United States, worked as a sales representative for lifetime friend Willy Bogner during the off-seasons ("62 customers and a station wagon full of samples") and established himself by lending his name, his skills or both to ski schools and ski shops across the country. Wherever Stein worked, his fame and glamour brought publicity and a boost in business. He worked at Boyne Mountain, Michigan, from 1954 to 1956, then moved on to Heavenly Valley, California, where his salary increased and a sports shop was thrown into the deal. In 1958 Stein moved to Aspen Highlands, Colorado, where his contract called for him to perform a flip every Sunday at noon. When

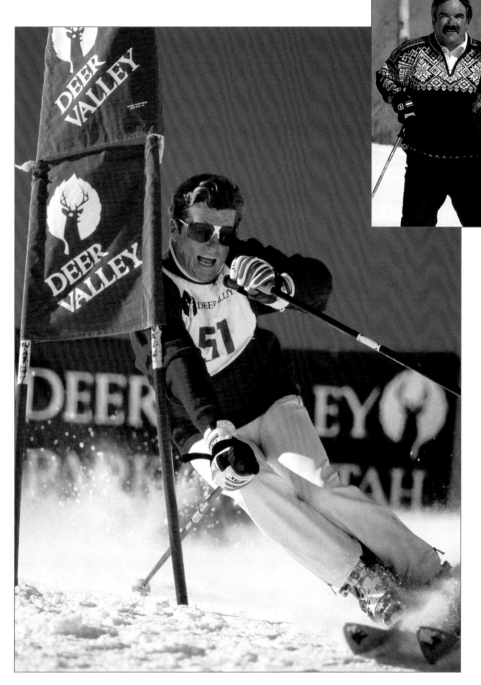

Stein accepted a job at Sugarbush, Vermont, in 1961, *SKI* Magazine described his move as "one of skiing's most discussed post-Olympic events." He worked at Snowmass, Colorado, from 1966 to 1969, and that is where he met Edgar Stern.

When Stern bought Park City Resort in 1971, he lured Stein there, and Stein was the director of skiing from 1972 to 1977. When Stern built Deer Valley Resort, Stein happily followed.

Of his career in the ski industry, Stein says, "the most important thing for me was, of course, the foundation that I established with my medals. That was kind of my education. Then [I moved] around to different places to take advantage of different opportunities, but it wasn't until I shook hands with Edgar Stern that I knew I had a relationship that was binding. My whole career at Deer Valley was based on a handshake. Just recently we drew up a contract on paper because Edgar wanted me to have retirement benefits. My ties are so close to Edgar and Polly—there are no better people in the world. I have everything. I would probably have ended up doing a similar job someplace else, but it isn't just the skiing, it's the people that you're associated with."

Stein's job at Deer Valley will be his last. "I have an agreement with Deer Valley that I can retire anytime I want to," he says, "as long as I don't go to Sun Valley and try to start a new career!" He chuckles.

DEER VALLEY PEOPLE
Ambassador of Skiing Heidi Voelker

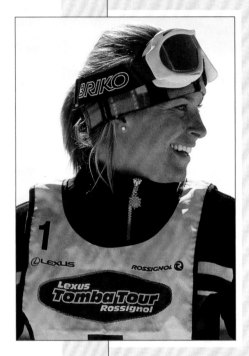

What do ski racers do when they retire? "I dropped 20 pounds of thigh," laughs Deer Valley's ambassador of skiing, Heidi Voelker. "When I was competing, I used to wear size-8 pants. They were the only ones that fit over my legs. But then they'd be too long, so I'd look like some kind of rapper. I don't have that problem anymore. And I don't mind it!"

The five-foot three-inch, 110-pound Voelker wears a fur-collared black turtleneck, her blonde hair corralled in a ponytail, highlighting eyes as green as Caribbean waters. She has the all-American good looks of a cheerleader, and she's tough. Her drive is seen in the way she gesticulates as she talks, her hand chopping back and forth in the air, much like the rhythm of a ski racer handling gates.

She is well-known for being a worrier, a sweet friend, funny and meticulously organized. "Being organized was my way of assessing goals and prioritizing when I was traveling with the U.S. Ski Team and living out of a duffel bag," she says. "It was my way of having a sense of structure." Voelker would ask, "Who's been messin' with my stuff?" if a ski team roommate had pulled one pair of socks from her neatly stacked pile. Since leaving the team, she's been known to rearrange friends' refrigerators when they are not looking. "It bugs me when the Tupperware's just thrown in and not stacked."

A Pittsfield, Massachusetts, native, Voelker began ski racing at tiny Bousquet ski area, where her two older brothers and sister were regularly pulled into the manager's office for skiing too fast. Voelker competed on the U.S. Ski Team from 1985 to 1997 with career highlights that included Junior Alpine Skier of the Year (1988), National Giant Slalom Champion (1995) and National GS bronze medalist (1997). She had six top-10 World Cup finishes. She was a three-time World Championships team member and three-time Olympian.

One of her life's disappointments was not bringing home an Olympic medal. "It didn't happen for me," she says. "I was very competitive. And even though I'd get in the gate and go start to finish down the course as fast as I possibly could, sometimes I'd worry too much about the future and not focus on the task at hand. I'd be thinking, 'Okay, I'm at Nationals, and if I don't ski well here, they won't name me to the team next year....' That was my biggest hang-up, and it interfered with my results."

Perspective, time and the birth of her son, Lucas (whom she calls her real gold medal), have softened the blow. "I've learned not to dwell on things that really don't matter in the long run. Not winning a medal was tough at the time, but now I look back and say, 'Okay, I was part of three Olympics, one of only four racers selected, and I was pointed at as a possible medalist. I know if I'd had my day, I could have been one, too.'"

Freedom from competition is surprisingly enjoyable for Voelker. "After putting everything into ski racing for 12 years, it was nerve-wracking thinking, 'I'm not going to wake up and go to the gym anymore. Will I miss it?' But I never looked back. From the moment I got to Deer Valley I was welcomed with open arms. I always joke with people that if I'd known it was going to be this good, I would have stopped ski racing a lot earlier."

Voelker approached Deer Valley in 1994 about being sponsored, "even though they already had Stein," and the resort was so pleased with the idea that they sealed a deal in a week. Voelker wore the Deer Valley logo on her headband for the last three years of her competitive career, and once she retired, became a full-time ambassador. Like her mentor, Stein, she skis with corporate groups, women's clinics, VIPs and the like. "I think I'm a better skier now and enjoy it more than when I was competing," she says, "because I get to ski on all conditions—powder, groomed, crud. And I don't have to ski in the rain anymore." She tells a story about becoming so lost to freeskiing euphoria one day that she had to be hauled off the hill

HEIDI KNOWS WHERE TO FIND POWDER AT DEER VALLEY—AND HOW TO SKI IT. SHE SAYS SHE ENJOYS SKIING
EVEN MORE NOW THAT SHE'S RETIRED FROM THE U.S. SKI TEAM.

on a snowmobile because she missed the last chair to the lower mountain.

Friends say her sweet nature makes her the type who would do anything for them, yet her competitive nature isn't altogether left by the wayside. She is "the most determined shopper I know," says one girlfriend. On a recent girls' weekend in Las Vegas, shopping with Heidi was "like a death march," the friend remembers. "Half of the group gave up trying to keep up with her and went to the pool for cocktails."

A ski model for her sponsors, Völkl, Tecnica and Marker, Voelker is an eye-catcher just standing around, but a head-turner on the hill, raising the "Ski Like a Girl" bar to new heights. "It's so funny to have Heidi's clients come in and say, 'I had no idea,'" says a staffer from the resort marketing department. Here comes this cute little blonde thing, is what the men are thinking, and then they're blown away by what an incredible skier she is. She out-skis everyone on the mountain."

It all comes naturally to Voelker. "Everyone has their own idea of what gets their mind clean. For me, it's skiing. It's outdoors, in beautiful surroundings, with the fresh air. It's just calming for me." She says that being able to work in the sport that has been part of her life since she was two is a blessing. "I have a unique position here. I'm very fortunate. My main goal is to share with other people the love and fun that skiing's provided me."

So what's it like being Stein's "apprentice"? "Working with Stein, you take what you can from him. He has golden attributes, not only on snow but as a person. He remembers everybody. When he works or skis with somebody, he takes it to heart. To look at how he skis at his age—he wouldn't keep doing it or be as good anymore if it wasn't in his heart as much as it is. I learn a lot from him. I'm not the female Stein. He's the rock star." ☾

Opposite: Stein and his wife, Françoise, in their living room, dressed in traditional Norwegian garb. Stein has known three generations of Norwegian kings and was knighted in 1997. Left: Stein's home overlooking the Park City golf course features his family crest depicted in stained glass. Above: The wall of fame at Stein's home features a pair of his father's "Eriksen Streamline" skis and a photo of Stein with Argentine dictator Juan Peron.

Stein was knighted by the king of Norway in 1997. Other kudos have included the Pioneer Award from the Intermountain Ski Areas Association in 1998 and an annual "Stein Eriksen Day," established by the governor of Utah on the 50th anniversary of Stein's 1952 Olympic medals. To commemorate the occasion, Deer Valley unveiled a bronze statue of Stein in front of Snow Park Lodge. Stein is a National Ski Hall of Fame inductee, and in addition to penning his autobiography, he has written many instructional articles in national ski and sports publications. He has been featured in countless ski movies and television programs over the years. His good looks (nobody has bluer eyes), bold charisma, and of course his always-impressive skiing, catapulted him to star status long ago. Like Bono or Madonna, he is known worldwide simply by his first name (Norwegian for "rock").

Stein wraps up his day at Deer Valley by 2:30 P.M. and heads to his home near the Park City golf course. The house is comfortably adorned with vintage photographs of his family, ski memorabilia, Norwegian costumes and an antique sleigh. It has high ceilings of stucco, huge wooden beams and a built-in flower box along the length of a picture window.

Stein has learned to balance his ultra-public persona with quiet time at home. He has five grown children, Ava, Anja, Julianna, Stein Jr. and Bjorn. He

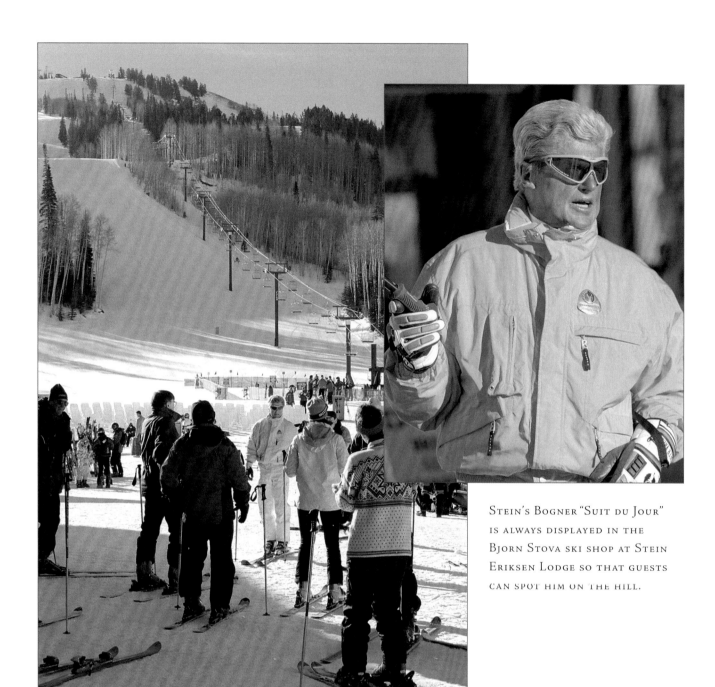

lives with his wife, Françoise, and their son, Bjorn, who is a college student. Once regulars on the party circuit, these days Stein and Françoise spend quiet evenings at home with Bjorn, playing cards and enjoying dinner and sometimes a little television before an early turn-in. Stein gets up around 6 A.M. to make breakfast in bed for Françoise, something he has been doing almost since the day they met 22 years ago. "That was the biggest mistake I ever made." Stein laughs but adds that Françoise is the "best wife I've ever had."

A native of Le Havre, France, Françoise left home at 14 to find a better life. She lived in Los Angeles for 10 years, married twice and made her way as a model, Playboy bunny and owner of an antiques shop. "When Stein came along, zat was eet," she says. Was it love at first sight? "It happened pretty quickly," says Stein. "Look at this," he says, showing old modeling pictures of

Françoise wearing mini dresses, go-go boots, extravagant eyeliner and a swept-back '70s blonde ponytail. "I didn't go into it blindly."

Stein and Françoise met at a party in California. "Oh, I noticed her," says Stein. Françoise's then-current husband was invited to be the fourth in a doubles tennis match with Stein during the party, but he declined, saying he wanted to watch football instead. "That was his big mistake," says Stein. "A month later I moved to Park City," says Françoise. "Yah," laughs Stein, "in a moving van so big that it couldn't turn

around in the cul-de-sac!" "When it's right, you know it," says Françoise.

"Françoise does her own thing," says Stein. "She has a lot of creative interests that are very expensive," he adds with a grin. Joking aside, Françoise is a hard worker who owns and operates seven upscale clothing boutiques, including the Bjorn Stova in the Stein Eriksen Lodge and ski rental shops at Stein Eriksen Lodge and The Chateaux at Silver Lake. She coordinated the interior design of their Park City home and their beloved log home in Montana, where they spend much of the sum-

mer fly-fishing the Madison River and enjoying their children and grandchildren and their dogs. "It's never boring," says Françoise. "All the dogs are called Bamse (pronounced BUM-say), which is a nickname for bear," says Stein. "Bamse 1, Bamse 2 and so on. Bjorn, our son, carries the real name for bear."

Before you know him better, you might think Stein is showing off when he strolls by a crowd with his proud bearing. But anyone who knows Stein the man, as opposed to Stein the icon, knows he is sincere to the core. Stein himself still laughs about the blunder he once made on live television. His English was not quite as smooth as it is now, so when he looked into the camera he said, "Hello, I am Stein Eriksen. Happy for you to meet me." Though many of Stein's Deer Valley coworkers hadn't been born when he was making ski history, they know about—and respect him—for his past achievements. And

99

they enjoy his presence and personality today, never missing a chance to yell, "Good morning, Stein!" from chairlifts. "It's great to see Stein ski and to see people get so excited about seeing Stein," says Deer Valley's 30-something ski patrol manager, Steve Graff. "Just watching him ski to this day, you can see why there's so much buzz about the guy. Stein's got it goin' on."

After 70 years of skiing, Stein still works on it every day. "I like to test my ability and my skis and to make myself absolutely honest about my approaching and finishing of a turn.

It's easy to favor one side. I don't want to cheat. I think about making as identical turns to both sides as possible. I like to do that because once you have the turns identical, and you know you're doing the right thing, then you get full satisfaction out of your day. But if you screw up a little bit on one side, then you say, 'Ah, God, I'd better have one more run.'"

So Stein will hit the slopes again tomorrow, and the day after that, his presence elevating someone's daily life with a bit of pageantry, style, excitement, glamour and poise. You may catch a glimpse of Stein flying down the mountain like a shooting star streaking across the night sky, but you have to be quick.

"Look!" a Deer Valley guest will say to his friends. "That's Stein Eriksen! Follow him!"

Of course, they won't catch him.

101

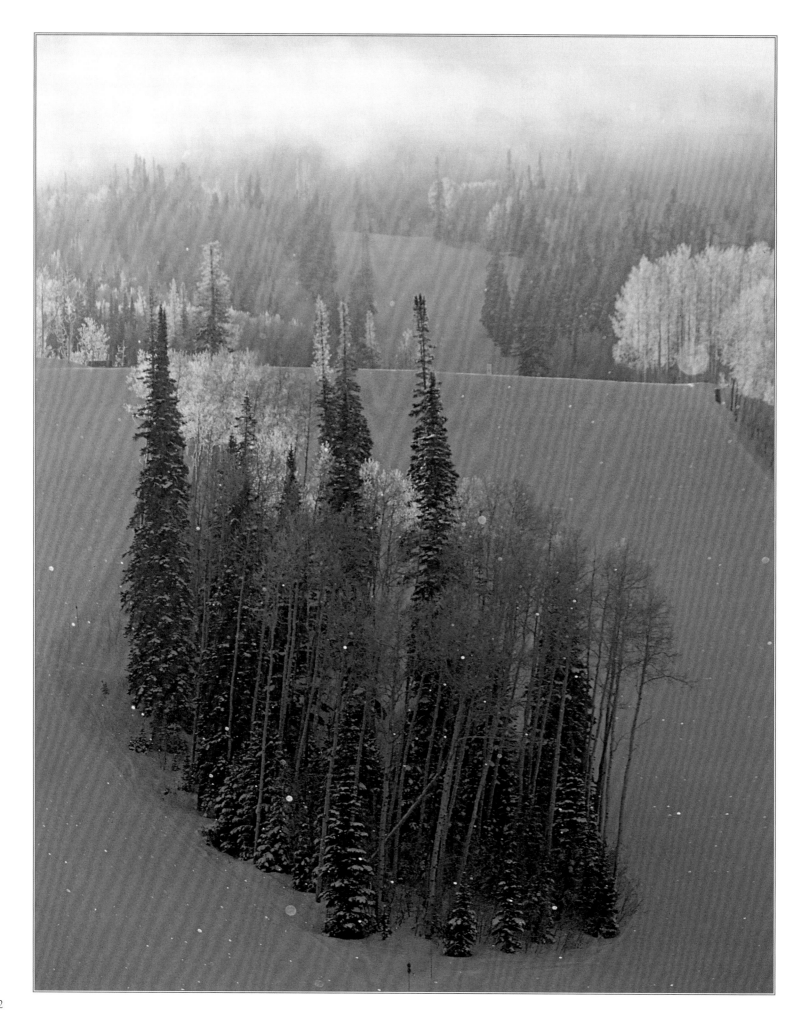

Chapter 5

THE MOUNTAIN

I t is 6 A.M. on a Wednesday. The weathered wood railing on my back deck is piled high with fresh powder that has fallen overnight. From under my warm down comforter I take a quick peek out the bedroom window and make an executive decision. Work can wait a few hours. I'm heading to Deer Valley, where, as my ski instructor friend Maca Leontic says, there are always lines. She doesn't mean lift lines—there aren't any. She means the lines of untracked powder that remain for days after a storm.

Since Deer Valley opened in 1981 it has gained notoriety for its velvety groomed runs, but few people know that Deer Valley is also a powder haven. Deer Valley's terrain is not craggy like Alta's or Jackson Hole's. It is not built on the scale of a Vail or Whistler. Deer Valley is 1,750 acres of quiet beauty. "Bigger is not always better" is a motto that founder Edgar Stern embraced when he created this resort. Lift ticket sales are limited to 6,000 each day, so there are no restive crowds waiting to enter a black-diamond bowl on a powder day. Deer Valley's 19 lifts have a combined uphill capacity of 40,700 skiers per hour, the highest in the country. I don't remember ever waiting in a lift line in my 17 years of skiing at Deer Valley.

And the views? They make me think of something Edward Abbey wrote: "Sit quietly for a while and contemplate the precious stillness." From the top of the Sultan lift you can see the Heber Valley's patchwork of farm fields and Utah's most striking silhouette, Mount Timpanogos, the "sleeping Indian maiden" that looms over Robert Redford's Sundance ski area. Below you is the Jordanelle Reservoir, which was created by damming the trout-filled

EARLY MORNING SUNLIGHT CASTS A LUMINOUS GLOW ON DEER VALLEY'S BIRDSEYE AND NABOB RUNS. BALD MOUNTAIN IS IN THE BACKGROUND.

DAWN ON MOUNT TIMPANOGOS, AS SEEN FROM BALD MOUNTAIN. SOME SAY MOUNT TIMPANOGOS IS SHAPED LIKE A SLEEPING INDIAN MAIDEN.

Provo River and flooding land once occupied by farms, mountain biking trails and pool tables at the Buck Snort Bar. The reservoir gives a sparkling Tahoe-esque feel to the mountainscape.

Looking west from the top of Empire Express lift or the Sunset run, you can see spectacular vistas of the backcountry between Park City and Big Cottonwood Canyon, home to Brighton and Solitude ski areas. You can also see neighboring Park City Mountain Resort and some of Park City's highest peaks, like 10-420, named for its elevation. These views are available to skiers of all abilities. There is a green or blue run off each lift, so even those still making wedge turns can reach a summit comfortably and snap a portrait with a backdrop of snowy peaks and bluebird skies.

During the 2002 Winter Games, Olympic security planners put a radar/air traffic control station atop Deer Valley's 9,400-foot Bald Mountain. From this commanding view they were able to monitor the air space over all of Park City, Soldier Hollow (the cross-country skiing venue a few towns over), and even Snowbasin's downhill course, more than 60 miles away.

Deer Valley boasts prolific wildlife. Animal tracks meander through the snow like beads on a necklace. The mountain is a major migration thoroughfare for elk. An entire elk herd winters near the resort's Mayflower area, where their

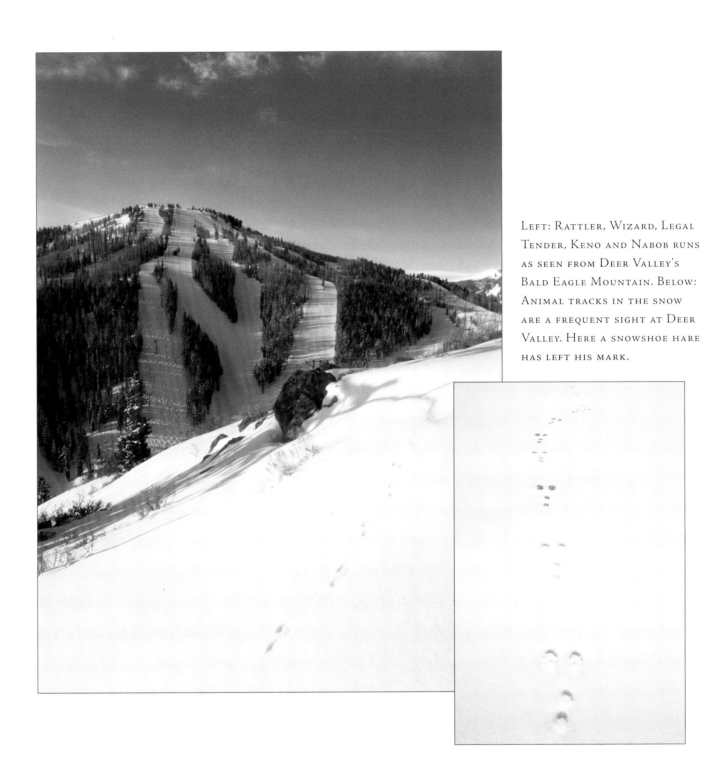

LEFT: RATTLER, WIZARD, LEGAL
TENDER, KENO AND NABOB RUNS
AS SEEN FROM DEER VALLEY'S
BALD EAGLE MOUNTAIN. BELOW:
ANIMAL TRACKS IN THE SNOW
ARE A FREQUENT SIGHT AT DEER
VALLEY. HERE A SNOWSHOE HARE
HAS LEFT HIS MARK.

sleeping places appear as ovals of crushed sage-brush in the snow. Snowcat drivers sometimes spot coyotes in their headlights. Mule deer abound. An occasional six-inch-wide mountain lion print has been found in the snow. Even a black bear was sighted one summer, sniffing around the mid-mountain maintenance shop. At dusk, employees on snowmobiles have spotted great horned owls. There are bald eagles and golden eagles, a summertime flock of turkey vultures and mountain bluebirds. Porcupines sit in the trees, looking like birds' nests until they move.

Moose sightings on ski runs are not uncommon. Employees joke that the 25-million-gallon Bald Mountain snowmaking pond was almost renamed "Dead Moose Lake" when a moose, trying to get a drink, slipped into the pond and couldn't climb the plastic liner to get out. Four employees jumped into the pond and, four hours later, managed to wrestle the exhausted animal to shore. "We put a fence up around the pond after that," says Chuck English, Director of Mountain Operations.

Deer Valley Resort's terrain is rich with history. Thirteen historical markers posted throughout the resort describe the mines from which hundreds of millions of dollars in silver and other minerals were extracted and where 1,200 miles of underground tunnels remain. From Empire Canyon Lodge you can see the towers of the Daly-West mine, where an entire crew

105

of miners died in 1902 when a powder magazine exploded. One of my favorite little shots on the mountain is a short, steep pitch in Empire Canyon off the Solace run. It is built on a mine tailings dump that is nothing but a pile of rock in summer, but the perfect place to catch voluminous snow and to practice pointing your skis straight down the fall line in winter.

A limber pine, estimated to be 300 years old, stands like an ancient man in the middle of Emerald ski run on Bald Mountain. Photos of this area taken in the early 1900s show just this single tree standing. Miners had clear-cut the entire mountain, using the lumber to shore up mine shafts or to fuel boilers that pumped water out of the mines. No one knows why this one tree wasn't cut down; perhaps it made a shady lunch spot for loggers. Its trunk at the base is too large to get your arms around, and the wind

swirling around it never sucks snow into its tree well. Employees call this pine the "magic tree."

Because of the clear-cutting done by the miners, virtually all of the trees you see at Deer Valley are second growth. Nevertheless, Deer Valley's born-again forests are beautiful—a mix of Douglas fir and white fir, big-toothed maple, box elder, river birch, Engelman spruce and pine, interspersed with elderberry, choke cherry, mountain mahogany, redosier dogwood and mountain willow. They are amazingly lush despite the dry soil. Gambel oak (also called

"scrub oak") and aspen are the most abundant. These are unique species: An entire forest of oak or aspen can be made up of a single organism with one root system. Similarly, Deer Valley Resort comprises five mountains connected by a single vision.

Though each mountain has a distinct character, it is the purposefully designed runs, most of which face north and follow the fall line, that tie it all together. As expressed by Chris Sprecher, who has been a ski instructor at Deer Valley for 15 years, "It's like somebody put a bowling ball at the top of the mountain and rolled it down. Wherever that bowling ball went, they cut a trail. When you get to the bottom of a run, there's a lift right there to take you back up. There are no long runouts or side hills to traverse."

"You can have the greatest mountain in the world," says Stein Eriksen,

director of skiing, "but if you don't have the right exposure, you have no mountain. Our north-facing runs make all the difference."

"Ego skiing on hero snow." That's a pretty good description of most of Deer Valley's 65 miles of trails and 88 runs. Heidi Voelker, Deer Valley's ambassador of skiing, says that during her years on the U.S. Ski Team she spent time on the mountain at Deer Valley when she needed a confidence-builder. "I'd come free-ski here if I was down, to get my confidence back, to make sure I still had it. It's hard not to feel

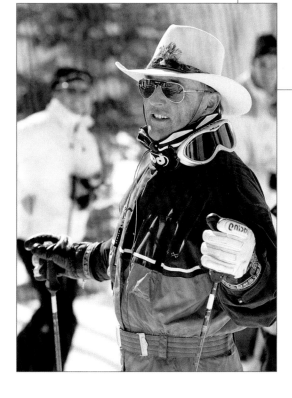

good here. The conditions just allow that."

A perennial medal winner in the grooming category of *SKI* magazine's ranking of North American ski resorts, Deer Valley is justly famous for its "corduroy." Skiers love it not just because it makes skiing easier and more predictable, but because it encourages "carving," or learning to use the sidecut of the ski. "If you don't have a powder day, you may as well have corduroy," says Deer Valley skier Ann Grady. "You can always work on your carving at Deer Valley."

In a 1997 *SKIING* Magazine article about Deer Valley, Olympic medalist Billy Kidd wrote, "I've [skied] the chutes of Val D'Isere and Portillo, but to me a more interesting challenge is racing, and the key to racing is carving. When you carve the perfect turn on a well-groomed slope with enough speed to barely withstand the centrifugal force, you get hooked on the weightlessness that follows a split-second later. Deer Valley has the ideal trails for making a perfect turn: wide, well-groomed, blue-square runs with very few people on them. It's one of the best places to snap into a pair of super-sidecut skis, put them on edge, look out at the scenery, and carve effortlessly like [Alberto] Tomba."

Not all groomed runs are easy, however. Many of Deer Valley's intermediate runs, particularly its double-blues, would be black diamond runs at some other resorts. "Our runs are quite steep," says Deer Valley instructor

THE DEER VALLEY DIFFERENCE
Days (and Nights) of Guns and Hoses

It is 1 A.M., and there is a blizzard of activity at Deer Valley's maintenance shop. Fourteen members of the snowmaking crew are coming off a 12-hour shift, and another team is arriving to take their places. In the glow of car and snowmobile headlights, figures scurry about looking like elves at Santa's workshop. These elves produce quality snow for Deer Valley skiers.

Making snow is a simple process, says snowmaking supervisor Scott Enos. "Snow is made by breaking water into small particles, throwing them into the air and letting them freeze. But there are an infinite number of variables, and they're always conspiring against us." Those variables include temperature, humidity, solar radiation and altitude. "You want to talk about the science of making snow, we'll be here all day," says Enos. "But it's an art too."

ABOVE: DEER VALLEY USES MORE THAN 200 SNOW GUNS THAT PUMP 3,000 GALLONS OF WATER A MINUTE.

The snowmaker's palette results in a variety of snow types, from wet durable" crystals in early season when it is important to lay down a long-lasting base, to lighter "maintenance" snow later in the season to augment Mother Nature's contributions. "The snowmaker's artistry comes in when he's hooking the snow guns up. He's got the temperature, has to anticipate what the wind's going to do and know what type of snow we're making that night. He stands right under the plume of snow coming from the nozzle and watches how the snow bounces off his sleeve to see if he has it right."

It's been rumored that Deer Valley's groomed runs are particularly velvety because snowmakers here blow smaller particles than those at other resorts. In fact, the resort just invests money in the finest equipment and hires good people for the job. "We're the insurance for the resort," says Enos. "We're able to guarantee an opening date and a quality snow surface."

"Snowmaking is expensive," continues Enos. "We call ourselves the 'revenue depletion department.' But it's a necessary evil." When Enos began working at Deer Valley 14 years ago, the resort owned 16 snow guns, two pumps and two air compressors. Today the resort

DEER VALLEY SNOWMAKERS ARE USUALLY FINISHED MAKING SNOW FOR THE SEASON BY THE END OF JANUARY.

boasts 114 fan guns, 90 air/water guns and three pump houses that pump up to 3,000 gallons of water a minute. More than 30 miles of underground air and water pipes run from the top of Empire to the bottom of the Deer Crest gondola. One thousand hydrants are scattered around the resort's 1,750 acres, spaced about every 300 feet. Last winter, Enos' crew converted 166 million gallons of water to snow. They made snow for 60 days straight.

"Snowmakers are a curious bunch," Enos says. "You either love this job or you hate it. If you're in between, you're not going to make it. Occasionally someone walks up at 2:30 in the morning and says, 'This job sucks,' and you never see them again. That happens."

Enos interviews each snowmaker candidate personally. He looks for people who are independent and full of wanderlust, who seek adventure, have heavy-equipment experience and aren't afraid to work outside. The right answers to the question "What do you do for fun?" are skiing, boating, motorcycling and snowmobile riding. (On average, a Deer Valley snowmaker will ride 75 miles on a snowmobile each shift.) "If they like adrenaline sports, they're probably going to enjoy messing with a snow gun in the middle of the night on a steep, icy pitch. And if you're a farmer, you're mine. Farmers are used to being around heavy equipment and don't punch a clock. Snowmaking's not about, 'Oh, the whistle blew, time to take a break.' You work until the job's done."

The snowmaker demographic has changed over the years, from young men looking for free ski passes to middle-aged snowmaking professionals who return each season, about half of them married with families. The 2002–03 team included three women and 17 snowmakers from Australia or New Zealand who made snow all winter at Deer Valley and then went home for winter in the Southern Hemisphere. "They're kind of crazy," says Enos. "I can't imagine going from winter to winter, but they're so talented."

GROOMING OF DEER VALLEY'S RUNS BEGINS WITH LARGE PILES OF DRY SNOW. DEER VALLEY'S 16 SNOWCATS THEN DISTRIBUTE THE SNOW EVENLY.

Maturity is a good thing when it comes to working the most dangerous job on the mountain. Hazards include air and water being forced through two-inch hoses at pressures up to 1,000 pounds per square inch, driving snowmobiles in extreme conditions and standing in three inches of water while plugging fan guns into 480-volt power sources.

The snowmakers are known affectionately to each other as "toads" because of the green uniforms they used to wear. (Now their uniforms are black.) The shop features a "Toad Wall of Shame," where a bulletin board displays burst hoses that look like exploded firework casings and the twisted remains of a snowmobile windshield with a hand-scrawled sign above it that reads, NAUGHTY TOAD. Fortunately, there hasn't been a serious snowmaking accident in Deer Valley's 23-year history. "You can't let your guard down," admonishes Enos, "especially on a 12-hour shift when you're tired."

Quality people make quality snow, says Enos. "We have the best computerized guns and automated systems, and I could make snow from [the comfort of] my office, but it's the crew that makes our snow as good as it is. We strive to manually check every snow gun on the mountain once an hour."

"Our guys work hard," says Enos. "They love winter. Most of them ski every day, even after a 12-hour shift. This job is never boring. Plus you get to walk around under a full moon on a calm night without a boss breathing down your neck. I tell my crew, 'Enjoy what you're doing. Get your work done. Then get out there and watch the sunrise.'" ☾

ABOVE: DEER VALLEY'S SNOWCAT
DRIVERS ENJOY SOME OF THE
PRETTIEST VIEWS OF PARK CITY IN
THE EARLY EVENING HOURS. RIGHT:
THIS BOMBADIER SNOWCAT WEIGHS
17,000 POUNDS AND WIELDS A
16-FOOT-WIDE, 12-WAY BLADE.

Dave Staley, "but the grooming is so immaculate, guests actually ski terrain they'd otherwise avoid." Ski instructor Cheryl Fox says, "Many of our ski school staff have skied the mighty mountains of the West, but they will tell you that they became good skiers at Deer Valley. Because of the steep, groomed runs, your turns have to be accurate if you're going to do it right. You can fudge a bit in powder or crud, but the groomed runs here separate the good from the really good."

In Deer Valley's early days the preponder-ance of groomed runs, or "groomers," caused image problems for the resort. Deer Valley was sometimes referred to as "Bambi Basin" because of its gentle slopes. When the resort opened in 1981 on Bald Eagle and Bald Mountains, the majority of trails were classified "green" or "blue" and meandered through luxury home sites. Bald Mountain trails offered a few black diamonds—steep and bumpy runs like Rattler and Grizzly, and steep and groomed runs like Reward and Perseverance Bowl. Wizard run (which has since been given gentler contours) had a nosedive pitch. Ruins of Pompeii, with its 38-degree slope, was—and still is—one of the most challenging runs on the mountain, its shady face and concave shape always cradling good snow. But the overarching image was still that of a mountain that was "soft."

Opinions changed when Mayflower chair was installed on Bald

113

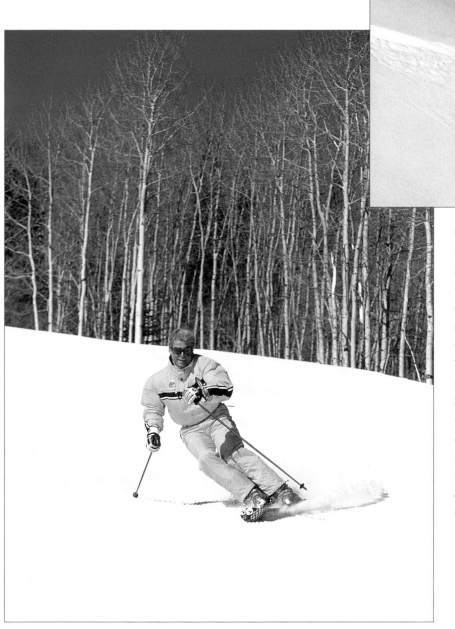

OPPOSITE: DEER VALLEY WAS ONCE
REFERRED TO AS "BAMBI BASIN," BUT
PUBLIC PERCEPTION OF DEER VALLEY'S
TERRAIN HAS CHANGED DRAMATICALLY
OVER THE YEARS. WITH THE ADDITION
OF THE MAYFLOWER AND EMPIRE
CANYON AREAS, THERE IS PLENTY OF
"STEEP AND DEEP" FOR THOSE WHO
DESIRE IT. LEFT: DIRECTOR OF SKIING
STEIN ERIKSEN SAYS THAT STEIN'S WAY
WOULD MAKE THE QUINTESSENTIAL
GIANT SLALOM COURSE. ABOVE: TAILINGS
PILES FROM PARK CITY'S HISTORIC
MINING DAYS PROVIDE WONDERFULLY
OPEN PITCHES FOR SKIING, FOR STEIN
(PICTURED HERE), OR FOR YOU.

Mountain in 1984. Mayflower serves eight black-diamond runs plus the Mayflower Bowl and chutes. Mayflower Bowl and Morning Star hoard powder. Runs like Narrow Gauge, Fortune Teller and Paradise work you, especially in the spring when the bumps are soft and endless—like a shorter version of Jackson Hole's Hobacks. And there's rarely anybody over there. Skiers venture over to Stein's Way to check out the spectacular southwestern view, but most of them cut back to Perseverance Bowl and the

Sultan chair, missing Mayflower's black-diamond allure.

It is not an accident that Stein's Way is named for Deer Valley's director of skiing. It is Stein Eriksen's favorite trail. When Edgar Stern proposed that Stein name a run after himself, Stein chose the run then known as "Hawkeye," because it had "the longest vertical and more variations than most runs." On a tour of Stein's Way one day, Stein waxed enthusiastic about the possibilities for his favorite trail: "It would make a beautiful GS course for an international race…. I see the blue gate there, the red there, then the blue…." The vision got to be too much, and he took off down his namesake run.

The "Bambi Basin" image finally disappeared with the opening of Empire Canyon in 1998. Empire Canyon added 600 acres of "European-style" terrain that included three bowls—Lady Morgan, Empire and

By the time the sun rises over Jupiter Peak, some lucky and ambitious skiers have already left lovely figure eights on Lady Morgan Bowl. (Note: this photo was taken before the Empire chairlift was installed. These skiers earned their untracked powder with a hike.)

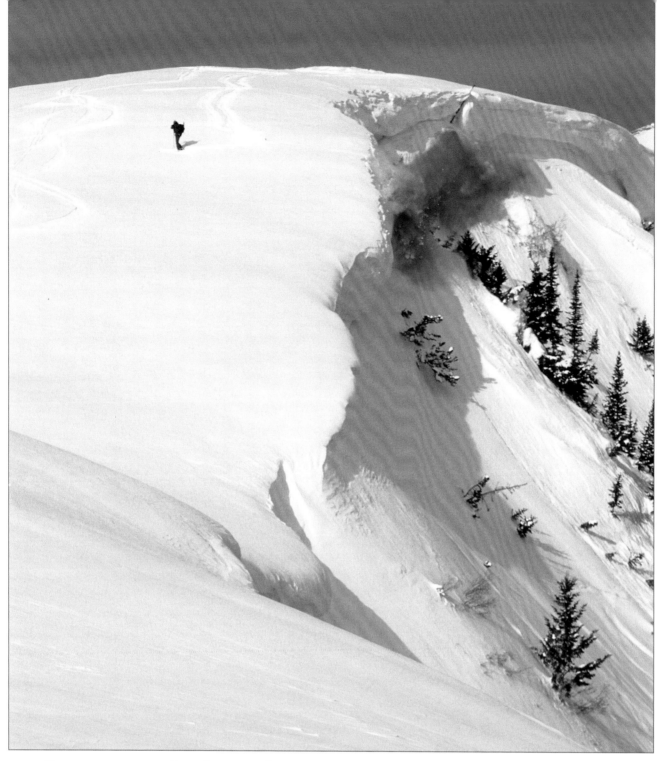

THE CORNICES ON THE DALY CHUTES IN EMPIRE CAN GROW TWO FEET AN HOUR ON A WINDY DAY. THIS SKI PATROLLER HAS JUST SET A BLAST (SEE DARK SMOKE UPPER RIGHT) TO TRIGGER A SLIDE SO THAT SKIERS CAN ENJOY THE AREA SAFELY.

Daly—and six cornice-laden chutes. "You have the cornice there, and from the chair you can see what look like miniature people peeking over it in the distance," says Heidi Voelker. "People didn't used to have that image of Deer Valley. But we do have that kind of terrain, if you want it."

"The reality," says Chuck English, "is that most guests here don't ski that type of terrain, but they like to think it's there if they could." Deer Valley even published an "experts only" trail map when Empire Canyon opened, outlining the Empire and Mayflower areas, Ontario Bowl, and the gladed skiing throughout the resort. The map enhanced the resort's appeal to adrenaline seekers, but it upset some of the locals. "I was so mad when that trail map came out," says longtime Deer Valley skier Arthur Apostolakos. "It showed all the tree shots!"

Anyone who insists that Deer Valley's terrain is easy has only to hang his or her ski tips over the lip of one of the Daly chutes. Ski patrollers say that when the wind blows off Bonanza Flats, the Daly cornices can grow two feet an hour. But when you do find your way over the edge and through one of the chutes, you'll be able to enjoy deep pockets of powder in the widening gullies.

With Empire Canyon have come new worries for Deer Valley. Park City Mountain Resort (PCMR) and Deer Valley Resort are like two brothers who have outgrown their

shared bedroom. The expansions at Deer Valley and PCMR have placed them elbow to elbow. From the top of Empire Express lift, it is only a stone's throw to PCMR's McConkey's Bowl. Between the two resorts, and beside Deer Valley's Supreme run, is a roped-off area 100 feet wide. Deer Valley's ski patrol calls this area the "DMZ," and it is far too tempting for some skiers to resist.

One brilliant spring day I stood with Deer Valley's ski patrol manager, Steve Graff, near the DMZ. Steve pointed out the three flagged ropes marking Deer Valley's boundary. Lo and behold, as he was explaining that despite the markings some people still claim they don't see the closure, two skiers ducked under the ropes and dashed toward PCMR's terrain. Graff chased them down, and using his trauma shears, clipped their Deer Valley lift tickets and sent them on their way. Their adventure would prove expensive. They had accessed Deer Valley via the Jordanelle Gondola, leaving their car parked on Highway 40—a $50 cab ride from PCMR. Graff had radioed his counterparts at PCMR so their patrol could be waiting for the border-jumpers when they got to a PCMR chairlift without a ticket. (Incidentally, for any law-breaking skier whose attitude is rebellious rather than apologetic, resort officials can invoke Summit County Ordinance #91: Trespassing.)

DEER VALLEY PEOPLE
Director of Mountain Operations Chuck English

Chuck English forgot to turn his company radio off last night. Sitting on the nightstand next to his bed, it started squawking at 1:30 A.M. with a snowcat driver announcing he was "winching the upper face of Tycoon." Before this rude awakening, English had been dreaming of surfing the big ones at Santa Cruz like the old days, floating among a school of dolphins or watching a sea otter float by. He still loves the simplicity of surfing. "It's just a surfboard, a bar of wax and your trunks," he says, "and an energy flowing through water that creates this thing for you to ride."

These days, and indeed for all of his 22 years at Deer Valley where he is director of mountain operations, English has been riding a much more complex wave. After nine years working as a patroller at Alta ("snow so deep and so light you had to time your turns so you could breathe"), he joined Deer Valley in its 1981 inaugural season. "[The person interviewing me for the job] asked why an Alta patroller would want to come here. I was honest and told him my wife and I wanted to start a family someplace that had schools and gas stations. He said, 'You're hired,' on the spot."

English wears two radios and a cell phone, making him look like a gunfighter in a vintage Western. He is the nerve center for the resort, especially the parts of it that guests don't see. "People take it for granted, [little knowing] how much goes into having the operation ready for the first customer at 9:00 A.M."

By that time the snowcats have to be off the mountain, snowguns re-wrapped with padding, rope lines flagged and tightened. Every night lift line mazes have to be taken down, and after the snow beneath them is groomed smooth, they have to be put back up. In the morning, all 19 chairlifts have to be running right on time. "Because of that guy who says, 'my watch says that the lifts should be open now,' we don't depend on any one clock to give us accurate time. We open the lifts five minutes early—just to be sure."

English's list of duties is so long that to remember them all he has to keep the list on a piece of paper taped to his office wall. He oversees ski patrol, lift operations, lift maintenance, vehicle maintenance, building maintenance, slope grooming, slope maintenance, snowmaking, snow removal, the mountain host/hostess program, the race department, mountain biking, guest services and grounds maintenance. Four-hundred fifty employees and eight department heads report to him.

Up at 6:00 A.M., English listens to snow grooming and snowmaking reports first, and checks on the local weather and the snow reports from other ski areas. He is at his desk by 7:00 and on the mountain by 9:00, when he begins a day of "management by skiing around." He rides the chair lifts with guests, conducting informal surveys, checks rope lines, times lift lines, and tests new traffic management patterns by placing orange cones in the snow at the top of a lift then standing back and watching how guests move through them.

"It's important for me to be in those spaces to get a feel for what the guest is seeing and feeling." It is also important for his staff to see him out there. "I wear a lift operator's uniform out on the hill, but it's a little difficult to be incognito from the staff. I'm sure there's an APB when I'm out," he chuckles. "The patrol has a code, Charlie Sierra Poppa, that means 'Chuck's Special Project.' Then there's Bravo Sierra Poppa. That's a 'Bob Special Project'" [referring to Bob Wheaton, Deer Valley's president and general manager]. Those have higher priority than mine."

True to his surfing roots, English enjoys snowboarding. "My son said, 'Dad, I want to take a snowboard lesson, and I want you to take one too.' My son hated it. I loved it." Since Deer Valley prohibits snowboarding, English rides his board at other resorts on

CHUCK ENGLISH HAS BEEN WORKING IN THE SKI INDUSTRY FOR 31 YEARS: NINE AT ALTA AND THE LAST 22 AT DEER VALLEY. HE SPENDS THE MAJORITY OF HIS DAYS ON THE HILL, SUPERVISING 450 EMPLOYEES.

his days off. "A lot of the reason I snowboard is to have a better overall feeling of what happens at other ski resorts," says English. "As a new snowboarder, you're put in the same position as a beginner skier. When was the last time you approached the top terminal of a lift and your heart started pounding because you were afraid the ramp might be too steep? Snowboarding does that for me. It makes me understand what our beginner guests might be feeling. And it gets me to other resorts to see what's going on."

English's favorite memories on the mountain include skiing with his daughter on Wizard when she was three, snow falling on golden aspens in the fall, and working Christmases on the mountain. "There's this special spirit on Christmas Day, even though it's sad for some employees because they're away from home, maybe for the first time. But it's my favorite day on the mountain." He has other memories, too, like the day it rained so hard there was a lake 18 inches deep at the bottom of Wasatch Lift. "The chairs were coming down and making a wake!" laughs English. They closed the lift. English has had his share of ski-related injuries, plus five surgeries resulting from a ruptured disk and a blown-out knee. The day he blew out his ACL, he called the ski patrol himself. "I was lying there on my back and just spoke into my radio chest pack: 'Middle-aged guy with knee injury on Persie.'"

Though Deer Valley—and English's responsibilities here—have grown in 22 years, things are still simple. "There's a culture here, a way of doing things, a way of being," says English. "When you understand Deer Valley's philosophy, there's no doubt in your mind where you're going. It's quality of service. You say, okay, how do we fix this? Well, you can jury rig it, or you can do it right, the Deer Valley way. It's our core position. The first thing I look at is what's the most reasonable and prudent thing to do from a guest-safety point of view. But then the solution has to have that component of the Deer Valley way. It has to be good looking, neat, tight, posts symmetrically spaced—those little details that the guest probably won't catch. There are thousands of details on this mountain."

Since he now lives 800 miles from the nearest ocean, English does his communing with nature in the mountains. "There's no better way to enjoy the winter environment," he says. "My favorite time on the mountain is when it's snowing. Really hard. You have your goggles on, your hat, your neck gaiter pulled up to your nose, these big flakes coming down and there's an inch or two of snow on your lap as you ride the chair. It's perfect. I can't imagine being anywhere else." ☾

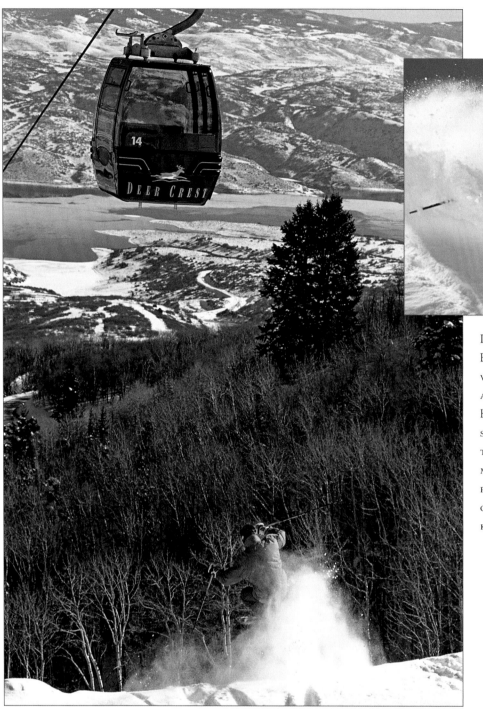

LEFT: THE MILE-LONG JORDANELLE
EXPRESS GONDOLA OFFERS FANTASTIC
VIEWS OF THE JORDANELLE RESERVOIR
AND PROVIDES DIRECT ACCESS FROM
HIGHWAY 40 TO DEER VALLEY'S SKI
SLOPES. ABOVE: THE EIGHT RUNS ON
THE DEER CREST PORTION OF THE
MOUNTAIN CAN BE A GREAT PLACE TO
FIND UNDISTURBED SNOW WHILE
OTHER SKIERS HEAD FOR THE BETTER-
KNOWN POWDER STASHES.

Deer Valley's ways may be hard for some who are used to the European custom of crossing boundaries, but "there are so many issues—snow-boarding being the least of them," says Steve Graff. The trespassers sporting snowboards become obvious rather quickly (snowboards are allowed at PCMR but not at Deer Valley.) One trespasser sheepishly admitted to Graff, "I didn't really know I'd crossed the border until I got down to Deer Valley's lift and everyone was pointing at my snowboard. Oops."

But back to my favorite subject: powder. Deer Valley has plenty of powder that lasts for days after a storm. The phrase "no friends on a powder day" doesn't apply at Deer Valley. There is enough powder skiing for everyone who wants it that way, and those guests can enjoy the uncrowded conditions that are the standard throughout Deer Valley.

"I have a rule: No hiking anymore," says Heidi Voelker. "You can get great powder in Empire, Ontario or Mayflower Bowls just doing multiple rotations on the lifts without exhausting yourself."

"Deer Valley attracts so many skiers who like groomers," says skier Laura Griffiths, who often sports a snow-covered pigtail sticking out from under her hat. "So it leaves lots of powder for those of us who like it. And since there are no snowboards brushing it off in big scoops, there's always hidden powder."

THE MAYFLOWER CHAIR, WITH JORDANELLE RESERVOIR AS BACKDROP. DEER VALLEY'S 19 CHAIRLIFTS GIVE IT ONE OF THE HIGHEST HOURLY UPHILL SKIER CAPACITIES IN THE COUNTRY.

"Sometimes powder is not just about steep," says instructor Maca Leontic. "Sometimes it's just about powder. It can be nice and mellow, but powder up to your knees is still powder up to your knees. Granted, it's nice to jump off a cornice and into a really steep chute sometimes, but those aren't the only places that are fun."

Other fun places include the pocket of gentle intermediate runs served by Flagstaff Mountain's Red Cloud and Northside chairs, and even out-of-the-way spots like Deer Crest, otherwise known as Little Baldy Peak (7,950 feet), the latest mountain to be developed at Deer Valley Resort.

To take full advantage of its proximity to Deer Valley, the developers of Deer Crest, a high-end residential community, built a leather-seated, mile-long gondola and eight Deer Valley ski runs that are mostly intermediate and even less frenzied than the rest of the uncrowded Deer Valley runs. The gondola provides a connection between Deer Valley and Highway 40 that enables skiing guests coming from the direction of Heber, Provo and Sundance to cut 15 miles' driving time and access the resort from Highway 40. The views from the gondola of Jordanelle Reservoir and the surrounding communities are intoxicating. With the continued growth of Deer Crest and the other communities surrounding the Jordanelle, the gondola has a busy future in store.

How Utah Keeps its Powder Dry

For years the Utah ski industry has used the slogan "The Greatest Snow on Earth," even fighting a court battle with Ringling Bros. and Barnum & Bailey Circus ("The Greatest Show on Earth") to keep the right to use it. You see it on T-shirts, coffee mugs, even Utah license plates.

The slogan is not just marketing hype. Skiers the world over sing the praises of Utah's white stuff. It is light, dry and prolific, sometimes so deep it seems bottomless, giving rise to myths about never-ending face shots or the need to use a snorkel to breathe when skiing.

Barstool lore aside, there is a scientific reason for the incredible lightness of Utah snowflakes. Winter trade winds push clouds full of moisture east from the Pacific Ocean, across California and Nevada, to Utah. As the clouds move across the desert, the heat bakes

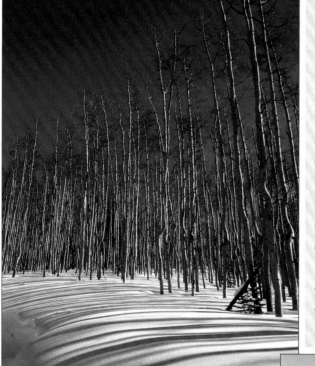

out much of their moisture. When the clouds meet Utah's Wasatch range, any remaining moisture rapidly cools and condenses, and precipitation hits Utah ski resorts with a vengeance, dropping between 350 and 500 inches of light, dry snow a year.

Another factor in the depth and quality of Utah snow is the "lake effect." Dan Pope, the chief meteorologist at Salt Lake City Channel 4, explains it this way: "Often the Great Salt Lake is much warmer than the cold air following a cold front. The lake releases water into the air that rises into clouds of snow, producing squalls on its eastern banks. These squalls contain some of the world's lightest, fluffiest and most powdery snow ever produced. And it falls in feet, not inches, on our Wasatch mountains."

As clouds draw moisture up from the Great Salt Lake, they refortify themselves for several days in the surrounding mountains. Skiers often experience the one-two punch of successive storms dropping precious powder onto the slopes of Utah's mountain resorts day after day.

During the best powder storms, the snow is so light you can clear it off your car's windshield just by breathing on it. There are deep powder stashes to be found amid the trees and hidden gullies for days after a storm. That's not science. That's heaven. ☾

ABOVE: ON AVERAGE, DEER VALLEY RECEIVES 350 INCHES OF SNOW PER SEASON. MUCH OF IT REMAINS FOR DAYS IN THE RESORT'S ABUNDANT ASPEN GROVES. RIGHT: THIS VIEW OF THE RESORT ILLUSTRATES JUST HOW FAR SKIERS CAN SEE FROM DEER VALLEY'S PEAKS.

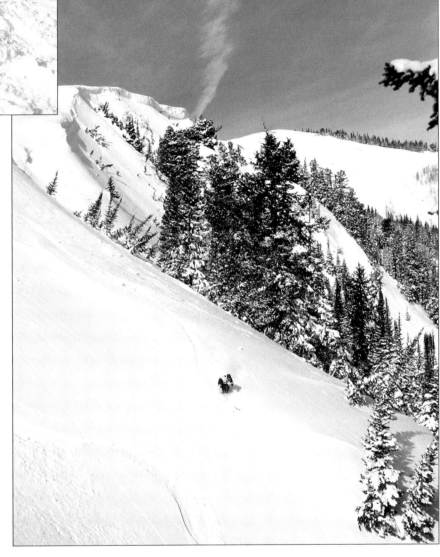

ABOVE: WHEN UTAH STORMS DUMP TWO TO FOUR FEET OF SNOW AT ONCE, THAT MEANS A LOT OF DIGGING FOR SKI PATROL, PICTURED HERE, EXCAVATING THE SKI PATROL BUILDING AT THE TOP OF EMPIRE. RIGHT: THIS LUCKY SKIER WAS THE SECOND ONE DOWN THE DALY CHUTES ON A WINTER MORNING.

The powder falls everywhere at Deer Valley, surprising skiers with untracked shots even on intermediate runs. "There's nothing better than standing at the top of Wasatch chairlift and looking down Legal Tender the morning after a foot of snow has fallen on the freshly groomed run. That's really, really good. There are no obstacles," says instructor Chris Sprecher.

John Guay, who is Deer Valley's director of skier services and has been with the company 23 years, recalls his favorite powder day at Deer Valley. It was a post-season day in the early 1990s that a lot of year-round employees will remember. "We'd been shut down for a couple of weeks. It snowed and snowed and snowed. Bob Wheaton [Deer Valley's president and general manager] gave everybody a call and said to meet him at Silver Lake at 1:00 P.M. He put us in a snow-cat, took us to Sultan and we skied untracked powder for three hours. The moguls were gone. Four feet of snow had covered everything. There was nobody there but us."

"Powder is a blessing and a curse for us," says a shovel-wielding ski patroller who is waist-deep in snow. "It's great because we all love to ski it, but it also means a lot of work for us, doing avalanche control to make sure it's safe. Fences, ropes and 'slow' signs need to be dug out and raised up. In Utah, you get storms of two to four feet at a time. That adds up to a lot of

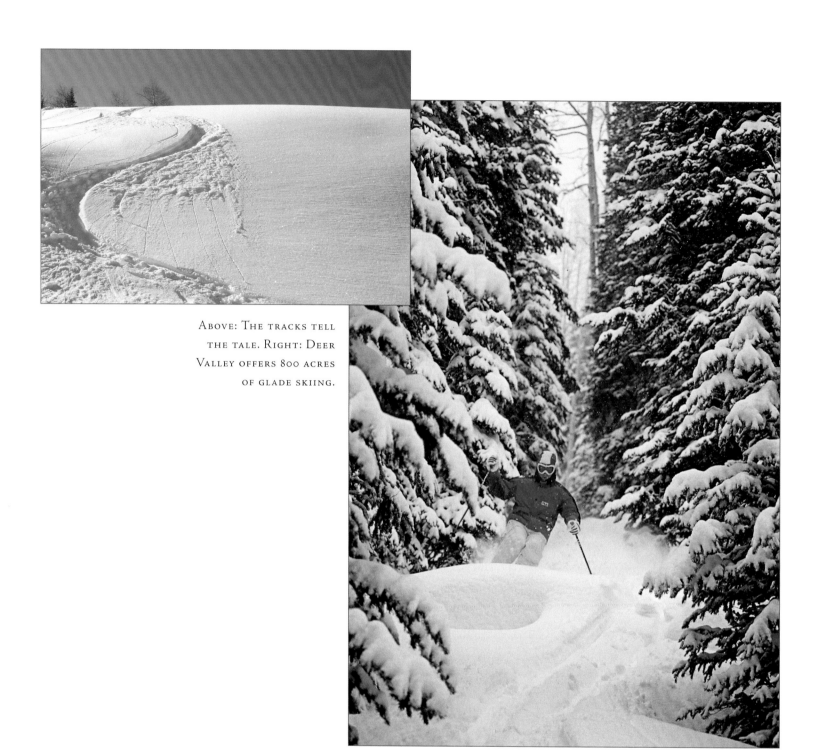

ABOVE: THE TRACKS TELL
THE TALE. RIGHT: DEER
VALLEY OFFERS 800 ACRES
OF GLADE SKIING.

digging." He adds, "Patrollers don't get as much untracked powder as you might think," and then he waxes poetic about the time there was a three-foot storm and he went on a "reconnaissance mission" to Mayflower Bowl before it opened for the season.

A lot of Deer Valley powder is tucked away in 800 acres of glades—places like Sunset Trees, Triangle Trees (between Reward and Tycoon), Evergreen Trees, Ontario Bowl, and Black Forest. "When I first started working here after being at Snowbird with big, open bowls," says Steve Graff, "these guys at Deer Valley would ski through the trees so fast! It was like, Yikes, what are you doing? Now I'm used to it."

Even Deer Valley's youngest guests are taught to explore the trees. One of the most popular children's runs is Enchanted Forest, a winding, gladed area dotted with wooden cutouts of smiling animals; and then there is Dragon Tails (not on the trail map) off Lucky Jack, a winding whoop-de-doo of a trail perfect for younger knees. My six- and nine-year-old sons have come out of their Saturday lessons knowing where to find tree shots I've never heard of. My youngest could say "untracked powder" before he could say "please pass the bread," and I've learned that the three most dangerous words in the English language are "Follow me, Mommy."

As one fellow local says, "Deer Valley has a

ton of powder in the glades, but it's dwindling because we're not keeping our mouths shut about it." So don't ask me to tell you where the unlisted tree shots are—shots like "Wheatie's Trees" (named for a longtime employee who in Deer Valley's early days hosted Aloha Fridays wearing a Hawaiian shirt and passing out blender drinks), or "Two Idiots and a Liftie" (for three perpetrators who must remain nameless). To earn glade-skiing rights at Deer Valley, you simply need to poke around and discover your own hidden stashes. It is all there for the taking.

All of this is why I chose Deer Valley for my decadent Wednesday morning powder fest.

My brother—an ex-racer weaned on the blue ice of Vermont, now a Manhattan doctor who doesn't get nearly enough ski turns annually—was skiing with me. The powder on Orient Express was knee-deep. After five or six runs, we still hadn't seen another soul. We kept looking over our shoulders, expecting to see a throng emerge behind us, but they never came. We grinned at each other when we stopped by a stand of aspens to catch our breath. My brother is a man of few words. He simply looked at me and said, "Unbelievable."

Then we returned to reality with a little bit of Nirvana tucked inside our pockets. 🌲

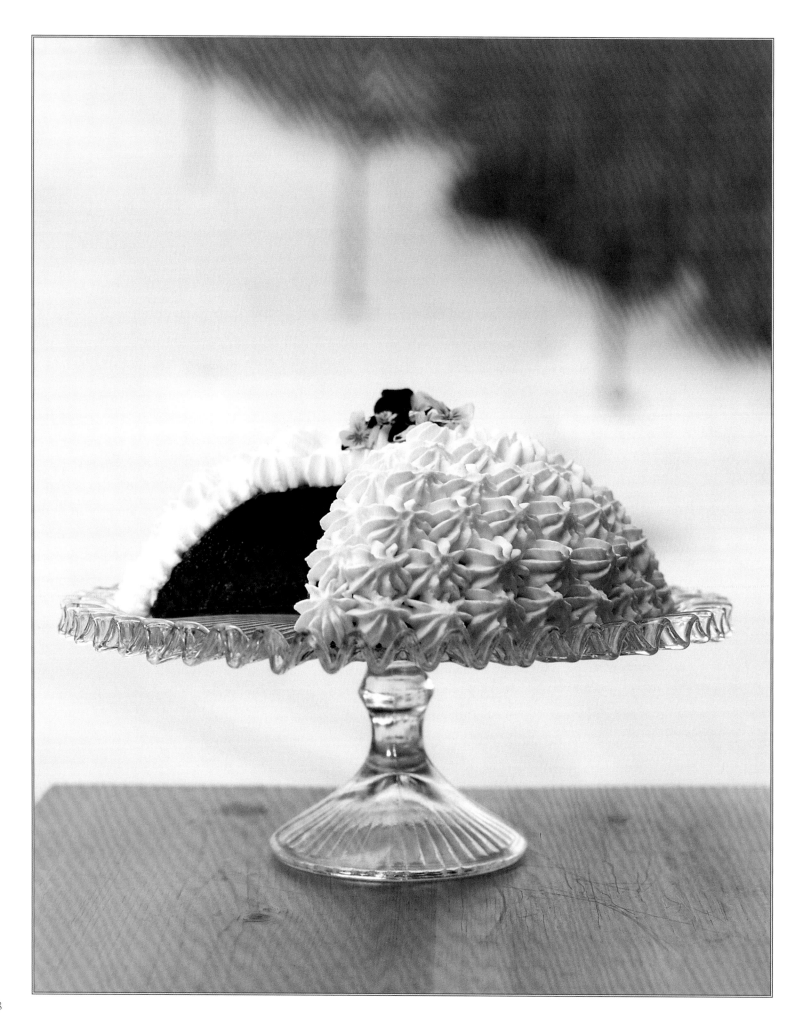

Chapter 6

From the time Deer Valley Resort was conceived, its founders set out to redefine ski resort food and its presentation. They have succeeded. Food has always been a priority at Deer Valley. "The truly unique thing about Deer Valley is that it's the first ski resort created by hospitality people," says Steve Dering, who was the resort's first marketing director from 1979 to 1983. "Everybody else running ski resorts was in the uphill transportation business, and 'oh, by the way, here's a five-dollar hamburger, try to digest it.' Food and beverage and service were always fundamental to Deer Valley. The skiing is really good, but they set a whole new standard, that no one to this day has ever equaled, with the food and beverage operation."

When people talk about Deer Valley, many will talk about the food before they talk about the skiing. Meals are the centerpiece of the day. People don't indulge themselves merely because they've skied off a few calories. They indulge because of the food itself. As a matter of fact, you'll find many business people having lunch at Deer Valley's day lodges even when they're not skiing. Park City residents meet at McHenry's Beach on sunny spring afternoons to enjoy locally brewed beer and a specialty pizza—maybe the one topped with walnuts, caramelized onions, roasted garlic and herbed cream cheese.

In the morning at Snow Park Lodge, you can see guests stop in their tracks at the breakfast buffet, eyeing slices of fruit-covered brioche sprinkled with toasted almonds. Looks of astonishment spread over newcomers' faces as they realize they can request a cooked-to-order breakfast such as huevos rancheros or an egg-white omelet with sautéed mushrooms and onions, fresh

THE CHOCOLATE SNOWBALL, AN ORIGINAL MARIPOSA DESSERT, ADAPTED FROM A RECIPE JULIE WILSON BROUGHT FROM LA VARENNE COOKING SCHOOL. *CHOCOLATE SNOWBALL* IS THE TITLE OF LETTY FLATT'S COOKBOOK

Left: Avocado and grilled
vegetable pizzette from
Royal Street Café. Above:
Letty's housemade vanilla
bean ice cream with choco-
late-espresso cookies.
Opposite: Refreshing
Summer Pudding, made with
multitudes of fresh berries.

basil and aged goat cheese. A uniformed young man at the griddle soothes a harried young mother with his question, "A little whipped cream and fresh berries on your cinnamon French toast, ma'am?" "Sure," she sighs with a growing smile, as she relaxes into the unanticipated pleasure of the moment. *This* is the way to start a ski day.

Deer Valley's first menus were created by world-renowned hotelier Jim Nassikas, his son, Bill (Deer Valley's first food and beverage director) and Julie Wilson, the current food and beverage director who was then Silver Lake Lodge manager. In the culinary world, these people are known as "foodies" because of their passion for the ritual of cooking and the sharing of exquisite meals and good conversation with friends. In their home kitchens, these are people who use freshly picked ingredients as inspiration for new

culinary creations, and who would rather read a cookbook or a food magazine than a novel. This is why the food at Deer Valley is so good. The people who create it do so with efforts that come from the heart as well as from the palate and the stomach.

Your mouth will water as you listen to Julie Wilson talk about sautéing grouse prepared with "apples, calvados [apple brandy], leeks, shiitake mushrooms, chicken stock, a dash of cream and fresh thyme." As she plans a luncheon menu for a group of visiting mountain bikers, she'll croon

enthusiastically as an idea comes to her: "Ice-cream sandwiches! They're so fun—they'll love that." The fat-tire enthusiasts do indeed love it. Deer Valley's ice-cream sandwiches are made with thick circles of housemade vanilla bean ice cream between two jumbo chocolate chip cookies.

Wilson relies on resort founder Polly Stern's input when she and the chefs are creating Deer Valley menus. "Polly's food knowledge is very astute," says Wilson. "I trust her taste buds and her opinions. If she says there should be more color on a plate, she's right." Polly and Edgar Stern (along with Bob Wheaton, Deer Valley's president and general manager, and Gil Williams, the president of Royal Street Corporation), serve as the first official "tasters" for proposed new selections. Polly is a foodie herself. "I first realized I loved food when I was four years old, visiting my aunt in Canada," she says. "She was a bread maker, and fresh bread was always rising or baking. The aroma was

wonderful. She also made the best steamed chocolate pudding I've ever had." Polly owns a library of cookbooks numbering in the hundreds, which she plans to donate someday to the resort.

Jim Nassikas likes to quote an old Chinese proverb that says, "If we know well the beginning, the end will take care of itself." He set up the resort's food and beverage operation for long-lasting success, with a professional hotel-style kitchen designed to handle large crowds. His meticulous attention to detail resulted in such elements as preheated soup tureens and coffee cups. Nassikas also chose the traditional

Left: A Mariposa top seller, baby
spinach salad with grilled Gala apples,
caramelized cashews and sheep feta
from France. Above: The Natural Buffet,
a skier's healthful lunch bounty.

black-and-white-checked pants and white toques worn by Deer Valley chefs, and the attractive corduroy pants, collared shirts and vests worn by the servers.

While other ski resorts were serving only grilled cheese sandwiches, hamburgers and hot dogs on plastic or paper plates, Deer Valley opened in 1981 with cafeterias featuring separate, well-signed stations for the various types of fare—the "Carvery" with roast barons of beef and roast turkey; the "Natural Buffet," a cornucopia of salads, steamed artichokes, artisan cheeses, fruits, vegetables and breads that to

this day is consistently more popular than burgers; "Sandwiches," made to order; the "Grill" for hamburgers, bratwursts and the like; "Specials," for soups, stews, chilies and hot entrées; and "Desserts." The architectural details in the lodges, along with brass railings, tray slides, carts for flatware, and other amenities such as china plates, created a fine ambience for Deer Valley guests. In the beginning, lunch was also served at the Café Mariposa, but that was discontinued when it became evident that skiers were more than content with the foods being offered in the cafeterias. Café Mariposa, therefore, became a dinner-only restaurant.

Says Julie Wilson, "Our success all has to do with the food and beverage team we work with and the fact that we've been together for so long. We all have a common goal: to exceed the guests' expectations. We've lived with that goal since we started at Deer Valley." Wilson has been with the

THE DEER VALLEY DIFFERENCE
Edibles at Altitude

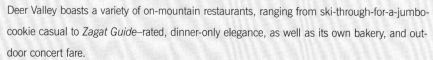

Deer Valley boasts a variety of on-mountain restaurants, ranging from ski-through-for-a-jumbo-cookie casual to *Zagat Guide*–rated, dinner-only elegance, as well as its own bakery, and outdoor concert fare.

Opened initially as the Snuggery and Huggery because the lodges were "snugged" and "hugged" into their respective valleys, these two day-lodge eateries are now known simply as Snow Park Restaurant and Silver Lake Restaurant. Breakfast and lunch are served daily during the ski season at both lodges. Though cafeteria-like in style, you'd never think to call these timbered environs "cafeterias." The breakfast buffet at Snow Park Lodge features fare that includes, among other choices, cooked-to-order egg dishes (a house-smoked salmon omelet, for instance), Belgian waffles with fresh blueberries, strawberries and whipped cream, and pecan challah French toast with real maple syrup. (Come on! You deserve it! You're skiing!) Abundant lower-fat choices on the Natural Breakfast Buffet include Irish oatmeal with dried fruit, fresh fruit with yogurt-mint sauce and housemade granola. A selection of fresh pastries is also available. Silver Lake Lodge serves a continental-style breakfast with fresh pastries, housemade granola, Irish oatmeal, and beverages.

Lunches at Silver Lake and Snow Park restaurants include one of Deer Valley's most famous food items, the Turkey Chili. Deer Valley guests consume 825 bowls of Turkey Chili each winter day, with a selection of toppings that include fresh salsa, scallions, jalapeños, grated cheddar cheese and sour cream. The Turkey Chili was celebrated during the 2002 Olympic Winter Games by the creation of an Olympic "Turkey Chili" pin.

Other lunch items include carved roasts, hot daily specials, gourmet pizzas, a variety of deli and grilled sandwiches, stews and soups, and beef, turkey or vegetarian burgers. Guests may find an offering of such unusual fare as a butternut squash and shiitake mushroom enchilada, or soups of smoked tomato and fresh basil or curried chicken and grilled leek. At the Carvery you may find marinated New York strip with wild mushroom sauce or turkey with sage-lemon sauce. The Natural Buffet is so much more than a salad bar, offering such items as fresh mozzarella and grilled vegetables, fresh artichokes with saffron aioli, five different salads composé, housemade salad dressings and freshly baked breads. At Bald Mountain Pizza in Silver Lake Lodge guests will find please-the-kids pizzas such as the Four-Cheese (mozzarella, Romano, fontina and Parmesan) and a daily-changing variety of specialty pizzas such as the New Orleans muffuletta with green olive tapenade, salami, ham

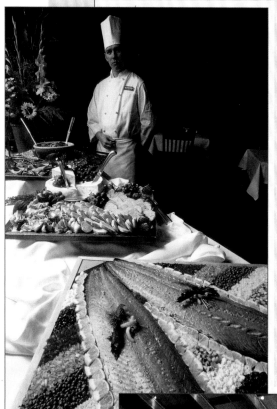

ABOVE LEFT: BANQUET FARE MADE WITH THE SAME QUALITY AND CARE AS GUESTS EXPERIENCE IN DEER VALLEY'S FINE DINING RESTAURANTS, THE MARIPOSA AND ROYAL STREET CAFÉ. ABOVE: GUESTS ENJOYING LUNCH IN THE BALD MOUNTAIN ROOM OF SILVER LAKE LODGE.

and provolone. Bald Mountain Pizza also serves Caesar salad, minestrone soup, and pasta with a choice of sauces: grilled vegetable marinara, wild mushroom and basil, or traditional Bolognese.

The upper level of Snow Park Lodge and its deck become a cocktail and appetizer lounge during the après-ski hours, offering soft live music and a no-smoking, child-friendly environment.

First open for the 2001–02 season, Empire Canyon Lodge is Deer Valley's third and newest day lodge, serving lunch daily and dinner on Thursday nights during the ski season. Lunch fare is similar to that found at the Snow Park and Silver Lake restaurants, although Empire Canyon Lodge has its own unique offerings, including panini (an Italian sandwich warmed on an iron griddle) such as the popular reuben or the smoked turkey, blue cheese and spinach; and from the Gourmet Grill, grilled sandwiches such as portabello mushroom and eggplant with roasted garlic on a Parmesan focaccia bun with mixed baby greens. Any item offered at the Gourmet Grill can also be served as a salad; you only have to ask. Available only at Empire Canyon Lodge are the coveted housemade potato chips cradled in little white paper bags, and snickerdoodle cookies. Thursday nights, Empire Canyon Lodge is the intimate setting for Fireside Dinners cooked in three of the lodge's fireplaces. Guests will find warm raclette cheese at the Empire Fireplace, dripping slowly onto plates. Accompanying trimmings include steamed new potatoes, pearl onions, cornichons, cured Italian and Swiss meats and freshly baked baguettes. At the North Fireplace, diners are offered bubbling veal and wild mushroom stew, beef Bourguignonne and vegetarian

LEFT: LUNCH AND LIBATIONS AT
ROYAL STREET CAFÉ. LOWER LEFT:
DUCK CONFIT AND BUTTERLEAF
WRAPS FROM ROYAL STREET CAFÉ.

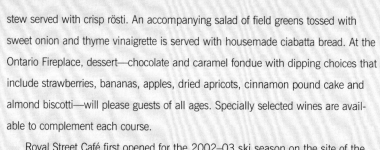

stew served with crisp rösti. An accompanying salad of field greens tossed with sweet onion and thyme vinaigrette is served with housemade ciabatta bread. At the Ontario Fireplace, dessert—chocolate and caramel fondue with dipping choices that include strawberries, bananas, apples, dried apricots, cinnamon pound cake and almond biscotti—will please guests of all ages. Specially selected wines are available to complement each course.

Royal Street Café first opened for the 2002–03 ski season on the site of the former McHenry's restaurant in Silver Lake Lodge. Hip yet sophisticated, casual but elegant, this restaurant has become a lively spot for a sit-down (reservations available) lunch during the ski day or an après-ski dinner. Not-to-be-missed standbys retained from the McHenry's days are the Vermont cheddar burger and the oriental chicken salad with orange glazed grilled chicken, Napa cabbage, tatsoi and crisp vegetables in sesame, soy and fresh ginger vinaigrette. New items quickly gaining star status are the sautéed pink snapper on udon noodles with lemongrass, and the house-smoked pulled pork sandwich—tender, slow-roasted pork simmered in Polygamy Porter barbecue sauce, served with coleslaw on a mini baguette with beer-battered onion rings. Do not miss the housemade brownie, so gooey it's served warm in a bowl, topped with malt ice cream and almond brittle.

The Mariposa, rated #1 in the *Zagat Restaurant Guide*, is the most sophisticated of Deer Valley's restaurants, open during the ski season for dinner only. The name derives from Utah's state flower, the sego lily, which early Spanish explorers called "mariposa" because of its resemblance to a butterfly. This is the restaurant that brought fame to the Deer Valley signature dish of Chilean sea bass with honey soy roasted-ginger sauce. Deer Valley guests will attest to the fact that it simply melted in the mouth. However, when Deer Valley became aware in 2000 that Chilean sea bass was on the endangered species list, it was taken off the menu. You should have heard the uproar. Resort chefs tried using scallops and other fish varieties as the replacement for this incredible fish, but none of the substitutes was as popular as the sea bass. Finally, the chefs found another variety of sea bass, Japanese mero, and the winning combination is back on the menu. The Mariposa is also famous for its twists on the mixed-grill theme, serving such variations as lamb chops, venison filets and wild-boar sausages. The mushroom risotto cakes are satisfyingly creamy. The Mariposa tasting menu allows guests to sample a "little bit of this, and a little bit of that" and includes a vegetarian option. Many a marriage proposal has occurred in this intimate restaurant tucked away in Silver Lake Lodge. Its setting is one of Park City's most romantic. Gaining the *Wine Spectator* Award of Excellence in 1999 and every year since, Mariposa cellars 150 different wines.

ABOVE: THE MARIPOSA'S GRADE-A SASHIMI.
LEFT: MOUNTAINS OF TIGER SHRIMP AND
SNOW CRAB AT THE SEAFOOD BUFFET.

Winter evenings, Monday through Saturday, Snow Park Lodge becomes the stage for the true extravagance of the Seafood Buffet. Some diners find it difficult to progress beyond the Natural Buffet with its oysters, tiger shrimp, fresh Dungeness crab, and house-smoked salmon, Caesar and spinach salads, herring in red wine vinaigrette, cheeses and housemade breads. The sushi bar features California, eel and yellowfin rolls. The Hot Appetizers station features selections in unique combinations that may include Cajun crab cakes, baby back ribs with cilantro lime glaze, New Zealand clams steamed with a sauce of smoked tomato, fresh herbs and white wine, a Napoleon of crab and avocado with lemon wasabi cream, and Thai seafood chowder. Entrées comprise such delights as roast prime rib of beef, mango-glazed Muscovy duck breast, yellowfin tuna with green olive pesto, and roasted butternut squash ravioli in a sage buerre noisette with fresh tomato basil concassé. The fun atmosphere at Seafood Buffet makes it the best choice for large groups. The dessert bar, with a baker's dozen choices and a white-toqued chef available to describe the selections, could become the site of nightlong conversations. "Oh I couldn't! Oh my! What are these? Oh, well, just a little bit of this…I'm eating for two…these are for my friends…."

Skiers can grab quick slopeside sustenance in the form of Turkey Chili, juices, hot chocolate and housemade cookies and bars at Snowshoe Tommy's (named for a miner who used to wander these mountains) atop Bald Mountain, or at Cushing's Cabin (named for Joe Cushing, who cut many of the initial ski runs at Deer Valley) at the Flagstaff Mountain summit. Sunset Cabin, set just off the Sunset ski run in the trees, offers an intimate mountain setting for privately catered fondue and smoked salmon lunches, for parties of two to 16.

Among the many things that have made Deer Valley unique is Deer Valley Bakery, a bakery that not only provides fresh baked goods to all the resort's restaurants and catered events, but also fills special orders for consumption elsewhere. Three pastry chefs

Below: Famous Deer Valley Jumbo Cookies, served hot from the ovens all day. Right: Executive Pastry Chef Letty Flatt at the Mariposa dessert table.

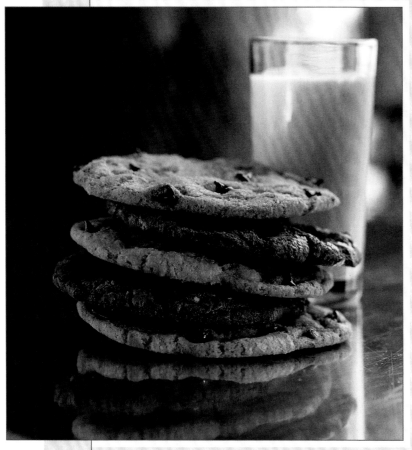

supervise a staff of 30. On a busy winter day, they are elbow to elbow, rolling out dough on marble pastry boards and whipping meringues in 60-quart mixers, surrounded by shelves laden with parfait cups, tartlet shells, panna cotta molds and flour sifters. Deer Valley Bakery also makes wedding cakes and other desserts for sale outside the resort. It has supplied carrot cake to a local brewpub for 10 years, and created a gingerbread stout cake using the pub's own brew.

At Deer Valley Bakery, bread making begins at midnight. Bakers produce varieties that include baguettes, brioche, challah for French toast, and white and seeded whole-wheat sourdough born from the sourdough starter that Jim Nassikas hand-carried from San Francisco's Stanford Court Hotel in 1985. The white-aproned crew creates many other delights—raspberry cream cheese Danish, blueberry corn muffins, oatmeal rosemary scones and banana maple nut coffee cake, just to name a few, and such unique adornments as the whimsical bread "mice" for banquet displays.

A fresh wave of bakers arrives at 4 A.M. to mix up 200 pounds of cookie dough (using 20 pounds of butter), resulting in 1,700 jumbo cookies that will be consumed that day. Every four-inch cookie is molded with an ice-cream scoop to keep the size consistent, yet each cookie is pleasingly individual due to the quirks of handcraftsmanship.

Most of Deer Valley's standard bakery recipes, such as the signature Chocolate Snowball or the Deep Powder Carrot Cake, are archived on notebook paper in a three-ring binder. "Someday I'll get them on a computer," laments Letty Flatt, Deer Valley's executive pastry chef. But the creativity of the pastry chefs continues, with bakers who constantly experiment with new ideas. "What we're looking for is, how do we make it taste 'wow,' how do we make it look 'wow'?" says Flatt. "'Great' isn't necessarily what we want to hear."

Flatt is a graduate of New York's French Culinary Institute, a member of Bakers Dozen (a national network of bakers) and the author of a cookbook, *Chocolate Snowball: And Other Fabulous Pastries from Deer Valley Bakery*. She writes in her book of one of her most inspired creations: "Several times a year, Deer Valley's food and beverage team designs a multi-course banquet for local

food and wine enthusiasts. I take the time to perfect new menu ideas for these parties; they are a wellspring of my best and favorite desserts. I made individual Caramel and Blood Orange Dacquoise for one of these parties—with caramel buttercream and blood orange curd encased in hazelnut meringues."

Flatt describes her desserts as if they were her children. Just listening to her talk about them, you can imagine her torching the crust on a crème brûlée to a tap-of-the-fingernail crispness, or whipping the filling for a smooth chocolate silk pie. She is a vegetarian, a skier, a windsurfer and a student of yoga, and has the boyishly lean physique of a teenager. So it's a relief to see her dipping into a massive bin of Ghirardelli chocolate coins and professing that she eats several handfuls a day. Chocolate, as it should be, is a resounding theme in the bakery. A large white banner reading GOT CHOCOLATE? hangs over racks of sheet pans. A photograph taped to a walk-in cooler shows the baking team in their whites, each member wearing a chocolate moustache.

Though she's a master chocolatier, Flatt's specialties are low-fat confections whose sinfully delicious flavors belie their minimal calories. Try the Almost Sinless Brownies or one of Letty's low-fat Black Forest mousse cakes. You won't miss any of the fat, or the flavor. (The secret? Puréed prune instead of oil; egg whites and cocoa powder instead of cream and chocolate; and 100 percent black-cherry juice without added sugar.)

During the summer months, guests can order Gourmet Picnic Baskets for concerts at Deer Valley's grassy amphitheater. The baskets contain such edibles as chilled petit filet of beef on a bed of caramelized onions, served with horseradish chive cream; or roasted game hen marinated with rosemary, cumin and maple; with fresh baguettes, Cambozola cheese and Letty's incredible chocolate fresh-raspberry brownie.

Deer Valley also operates a Concert Concession at the outdoor concerts, where guests who don't wish to carry bags and coolers up the hill can partake of a grilled chicken foccacia sandwich with sautéed onions and mushrooms and sundried tomato aeoli, or the popular Turkey Chili dog with a Caesar salad, as well as burgers, cookies, ice-cream sandwiches, beer, soft drinks and Deer Valley's signature Minted Lemonade.

The Deer Valley Signatures stores, located at the resort and on Park City's Main Street, have sold take-home fare since 1998, offering Deer Valley specialties such as sherry pecan vinaigrette dressing or lime cilantro grilling glaze. Anyone with a hankering for a bowl of Deer Valley's Turkey Chili can buy the mix in a Signatures store or order it online and cook it up at home.

Even employees are treated to the best of fine cuisine at Deer Valley. Three employee dining rooms—The Silver Spoon, The Daly Bowl and The Grotto—serve complimentary breakfast pastries and delectable lunch fare. Where else do employees get fresh sushi or roasted garlic and baby beets on the salad bar? ☾

ABOVE: SILVER LAKE LODGE
EXECUTIVE CHEF CLARK
NORRIS. RIGHT: SNOW PARK
LODGE AND EMPIRE CANYON
LODGE EXECUTIVE CHEF
JODIE BEROS.

company since 1981. Silver Lake Lodge's executive chef, Clark Norris, started in 1984 and was the first Utah chef to be invited to cook at New York's famed James Beard House. Executive pastry chef Letty Flatt worked as a Deer Valley ski patroller in 1981 and 1982 before shifting to the bakery. Snow Park Lodge's manager and the resort's wine buyer, Kris Anderson, has worked at Deer Valley since 1982. Clint Strohl, the manager of the Silver Lake and Empire Canyon lodges, has worked at Deer Valley since 1984. The team's newest member is Jodie Beros, whose fresh energy inspires all who work with her. Jodie started at Deer Valley in 1998 as a chef in the employee cafeterias; the next year she became a sous chef. In 2000 Jodie took over as executive chef for Snow Park Lodge, and in 2001 as executive chef for Empire Canyon Lodge as well. Wilson and the rest of Deer Valley's executive food and beverage staff enjoy a wide range of outdoor

activities—hiking, mountain biking, fly-fishing, hunting—that keep them connected to nature and appreciative of its edible gifts.

The chefs make it a priority to innovate so they don't get burned out. "The Deer Valley staff never rests on its laurels," says food and wine writer Virginia Rainey. "They're always looking to improve, move, change, test themselves and deliver the best they can in food." Last year Julie Wilson introduced the concept of fireside dinners at Empire Canyon Lodge, featuring raclette devices, designed by Wilson and executive chef Jodie Beros, that rotate a half wheel of raclette in

ABOVE: A DECADENT GUEST LUNCH OFFERING, CHOCOLATE SILK PIE. RIGHT: FRESHLY BAKED RASPBERRY AND BLUE-BERRY MUFFINS FOR BREAKFAST.

and out of the fireplace. The management team takes annual "food finding" trips to such inspirational locales as Napa, California, and New York City, where they engage in a whirlwind of restaurant tours and chef interviews to keep up on the latest trends. "We have two lunches and two dinners a day," says Letty Flatt. "We walk between the restaurants—that's the only way to get any exercise. You get to the last restaurant and you think, 'I can't do it!' Then we all look at the menu, and all of a sudden we're eating again!"

The food and beverage team's talents and passions shine most brightly at weddings, par-

ties and banquets. The resort's memorable 10th-anniversary celebration had a New Orleans theme to honor founders Edgar and Polly Stern. Snow Park Lodge was transformed into a bayou, with Spanish moss hanging from the ceilings, a fog machine lending an eerie cast and alligator-costumed actors crawling around the floor at the guests' feet. The Louisiana fare included regional specialties such as fresh, flown-in crayfish, roasted venison, Cajun coleslaw, jambalaya, corn-bread oysters, and red beans and rice. Sheets of a New Orleans newspaper served as table covers. A regional beer, Dixie, was also flown in to accompany the meal.

At one Cigar Dinner, resort bakers created a cigar-shaped dessert by rolling up chocolate crepes and filling them with red cinnamon ice cream. Each cigar was presented in a chocolate ashtray with chocolate shavings as ashes and thinly spun caramel threads curling from the cigar like smoke.

ABOVE: THE BALD MOUNTAIN
ROOM AT SILVER LAKE LODGE,
READY FOR ONE OF THE MANY
WEDDINGS CATERED BY DEER
VALLEY. RIGHT: BRIDE AND
GROOM WEDDING CAKES FROM
DEER VALLEY BAKERY.

Matchbooks were fashioned from shortbread cookies.

One of the staff's favorite dinners on record was a reception for La Chaîne des Rotîsseurs (an esteemed international food and wine society, of which Edgar Stern and Julie Wilson are members). The staff decided to base the entire dinner on passages from the work of Ernest Hemingway. They pored through his novels and short stories, selecting quotes to inspire the menu. A fishing boat and antique typewriters were displayed as decorations. The first course, Belon oysters flown in from France, was accompanied by a quote from *A Moveable Feast* left at each place setting: "As I ate the oysters with their strong taste of the sea and their faint metallic taste that the cold white wine washed away, leaving only the sea taste and the succulent texture, and as I drank their cold liquid from each shell and washed it down with the crisp taste of the wine, I lost the empty feeling and began to be happy and to make plans."

Other courses, each presented with an appropriate quote, included head-on shrimp, prawns, smoked trout, marinated wild mushrooms and new potatoes, and celery remoulade and radishes, with wine pairings for each. Dessert was a trio of fresh-fruit tartlets of red and yellow plums and pears, with matching eau-de-vies.

Julie Wilson portrays the food and beverage team as a family. "It's not just the people who

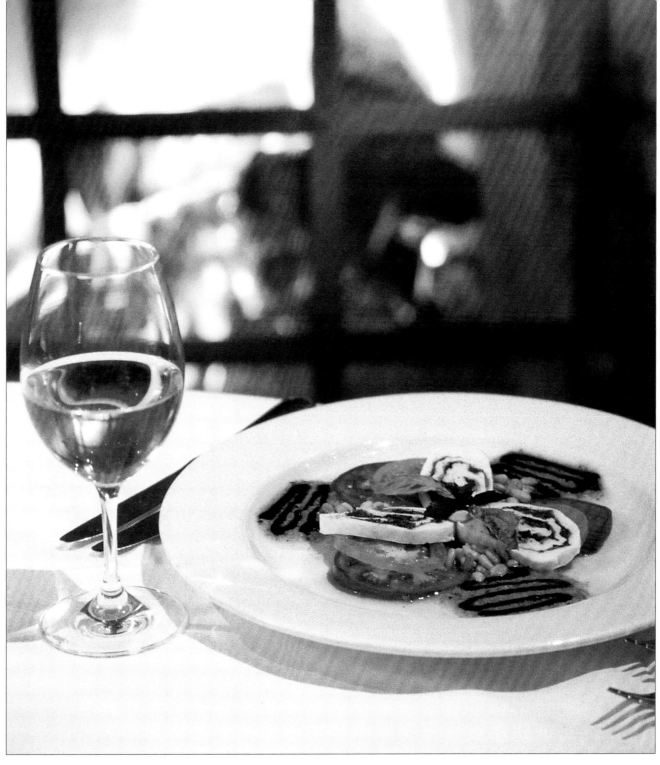

Housemade mozzarella roulade with fresh basil and red and golden tomatoes, a Mariposa vegetarian appetizer.

work here, though," she says. "It's the interaction with the guests. They're part of the family too." Fifteen-year employee Cynthia Smith, the bright-eyed manager for Seafood Buffet, is like a daughter to many Deer Valley guests, and now her own daughter works at the Buffet as well. Snow Park Lodge cashier Teresa Henshaw's melodic Irish accent and cheery personality are cherished by guests, and when her husband died last year and the guests found out about it, Henshaw was flooded with cards and flowers. Second-home owner David Weinburger skis

Deer Valley every single day of the season. He says if he didn't come here every morning, his life wouldn't be the same. While he sits chatting with Wilson, 12-year restaurant attendant Kevin Mahoney pours coffee for them without being asked. "Kevin is such a big part of Snow Park Lodge—guests expect to see him every year, have him talk to their kids. If Kevin isn't there, guests notice and ask why," says Wilson. "It's the sort of neighborhood feeling you'd get in a little corner cafe in the city, but it's a ski resort."

Once a year, a winter menu tasting is held for local food writers, invited like family into the kitchen at Silver Lake Lodge. A long table is beautifully set with linens and bouquets of fresh alstrœmeria amid gleaming pots and pans and labeled bins cradling ramekins, coffee spoons, water pitchers, and stacks of white plates of all sizes. Chefs move like dancers between cutting

DEER VALLEY PEOPLE
Food and Beverage Director Julie Wilson

Julie Wilson believes that the best dishes contain a harmonious blend of salt, acid and sugar. Wilson herself is equally well balanced. She oversees 10 restaurants and 600 employees at a ski resort renowned for its mouth-watering cuisine, and through it all she remains earthy yet elegant, driven yet sweet, spicy but mellow.

Wilson is a familiar sight in Deer Valley restaurants, moving from place to place checking that things are running smoothly. Every day, Wilson "tastes the line," sampling soups, sauces and specials. Then she advises chefs about what needs "a little more of this, or a little less of that." You may find her behind the line at Snow Park Lodge describing the ingredients of the housemade soup, working the panini iron at Empire Canyon Lodge, ladling Turkey Chili at Silver Lake Lodge, or greeting guests at the door of the Royal Street Café.

Wilson's go-getter nature is organic. "My parents never told me I had to do this or do that. They let me try what I wanted," she explains. At age 17, the Chicago native declared her desire to spend the summer with her cousins on Nantucket. Her mother told her she could go but only on one condition. "I couldn't just hang around. I had to get a job," Wilson says. "But I wasn't old enough to serve liquor in a restaurant, and they didn't want teenagers selling dresses." While hitchhiking Nantucket's sandy roads (hitchhiking was safe on the island at that time), a "grandfather in a big, gold Cadillac" gave her a ride. They discussed her job search. He asked Wilson if she could cook. Wilson and her father had cooked together frequently, so she felt confident that she could wing it, and she said "yes." She worked as the family chef for the next two summers. She purchased *Joy of Cooking* and searched page by page for great ideas and creative concepts, training herself.

While she was attending the University of Vermont, where she was studying special education, she spent a summer cooking for several families in East Hampton, Long Island. One of those jobs proved intolerable for the no-nonsense Wilson. "I cooked for an elderly couple. They made me wear a maid's uniform. I had to feed their fluffy little dog a perfectly cooked soft-boiled egg every morning and serve it to him on a doily on the floor. For dinner, I had to feed the dog Häagen-Dazs in a crystal bowl. I lasted about three weeks before I quit." Undaunted, Wilson found more satisfying employment with another family, training a Mexican cook in the ways of American cuisine and serving as a fourth in tennis matches on the manicured grass courts of East Hampton's Maidstone Club. "I taught the cook how to cook, played tennis, had a free room and got paid. It didn't get much better than that," she says.

Realizing that special education was possibly the wrong career choice, Wilson wrote a letter to the editors of *Gourmet* magazine, asking where she should attend culinary school. Someone wrote back. After working a summer at the Say Fromage cheese shop in Aspen, Colorado, Wilson went to Paris, where she studied for a year at the renowned La Varenne cooking school and celebrated her 21st birthday.

Wilson's plan to work for a catering business in New York City changed when her father, a banker who had done business with many ranchers in the Northwest, moved to Elko, Nevada, to operate a ranch of which he was part owner. Wilson worked as a ranch hand for four months during the late fall and early winter of 1979, helping to move cattle from summer to winter ranges, and separating pregnant cows from the herd before inoculations. The image of Wilson shooing a pregnant heifer into a holding pen by waving her arms wildly at the oncoming animal always makes her Deer Valley coworkers laugh.

In early 1980 Wilson moved to Salt Lake City and opened Le Dejeuner restaurant with a friend from La Varenne. (Le Dejeuner

THE MARIPOSA'S SIGNATURE ENTRÉE, JAPANESE MERO WITH A HONEY
TAMARI GLAZE AND FRESH GINGER SAUCE.

received the local Five Spoon Award.) Wilson later moved to Park City, where she opened her own catering business, Bouquet Garni. While backcountry skiing in Park City one moonlit night, Wilson learned that the land she was skiing was slated to become a luxury ski resort. Her interest was piqued. The next day, she telephoned Deer Valley's corporate offices to inquire about restaurant positions and was instructed to contact James Nassikas, president of San Francisco's Stanford Court Hotel. In her down-to-earth manner, she called the Stanford Court and casually asked to speak with "Jim." There was astonished silence on the other end of the line. "Uh..." the receptionist stammered in disbelief. "You mean, Mr. Nassikas?"

Jim Nassikas was intrigued by Wilson's courageous spirit. He flew to Salt Lake City and dined at her restaurant. "I sat down with him and we talked for hours," said Wilson. "It was wonderful. We talked about our dreams. We clicked." Wilson was hired as Silver Lake Lodge manager, promoted to the resort's assistant food and beverage director two years later, and within five years, at age 27, became Deer Valley's food and beverage director.

Though Deer Valley's restaurants have garnered numerous awards, sometimes life in the kitchen can be decidedly less than elegant. Wilson encounters her share of pressures, which she handles gracefully. One of her worst memories is of the day Jim and Bill Nassikas hosted a prestigious wine dinner. "We had some butter boil over on the hot plate and the whole kitchen went up in smoke. We had to use the fire extinguishers, and while this highly respected group is sitting in the Caribou Room waiting for dinner, there's white flame-retardant powder all over everything in the kitchen." Other challenges include banquets when someone miscounts, "and you have to cook 40 filet mignons 'à la minute' while people in the dining room are screaming at you." And there are lost tempers. "I once had a skier throw a blueberry pie across the room," says Wilson. How does she handle such situations? "You just keep your nose

ABOVE: ZINFANDEL PEAR TART WITH MAYTAG
BLUE CHEESE CRUST. LEFT: ROYAL STREET CAFÉ'S
GRILLED CHICKEN QUESADILLA WITH CILANTRO
SOUR CREAM AND FRESH AVOCADO SALSA.

down and keep working and try to solve the problem. You offer to buy him a new blueberry pie."

Wilson's penchant for digging in and getting the job done comes naturally. Pretty enough to be a fashion model, she hunts, fly-fishes, snowshoes, smokes the occasional cigar and, like any self-respecting member of a kitchen crew, is not afraid to share an earthy joke.

Eating holds as much importance to Wilson as cooking, and she adores "putting the bounty to the table." "There's nothing better than hunting by a river on a rainy, snowy November day, jump-shooting and then plucking, roasting and eating ducks," she says. Camping with her family is important. "One of my favorite things in life is getting into our drift boat with my husband and children and spending the night on the river when there's nobody around. We bring racks of lamb with cilantro pecan pesto to roast on the open fire."

"Blending nature with food," she muses, "that's how I love to cook, with wonderful, earthy flavors, whether it be fresh herbs or wild mushrooms." (The *New York Times* former food critic Craig Claiborne was so enamoured of Wilson's wild rice and mushroom soup he wrote an article about it and published the recipe in the *Revised New York Times Cookbook*.) Recently, on a mule pack trip to Oregon's Wallowa Mountains, Wilson happily discovered a patch of wild leeks, which prompted a cooking frenzy. "We put them in scrambled eggs, we made wild-leek quesadillas, we made wild-leek everything," she beams.

She works daily in some pretty impressive-looking lodges but, she says, "Little cabins are my favorite thing." The Wilsons enjoy the annual ritual of visiting a 100-year-old Wisconsin cabin, where Julie shoots grouse and woodcock. "My father started going to this cabin when he was 12. We hunt until we have enough birds for a feast. We have a certain way we cook our birds. Woodcock, we season with salt and pepper alone. They're very fatty, so they sear up beautifully on a charcoal fire. Then we pick out the perfect Petite Syrah. And we always eat them with bratwurst. You get these Wisconsin brats on the fire with the woodcock—you can't believe the flavor sensation."

Wilson's favorite meals are "simple and flavorful." It seems her life follows the same recipe. Every spring after Deer Valley closes, the Wilsons spend a night at the resort's fifteen-square-foot Sunset Cabin. "Snowshoeing to the top of Bald Mountain in the spring and having a picnic with my family, with fresh bread and roasted tomatoes and fresh mozzarella, sitting with my husband in a snow pit, the kids ski or snowboard, we play backgammon…It's a pretty wonderful thing." ☽

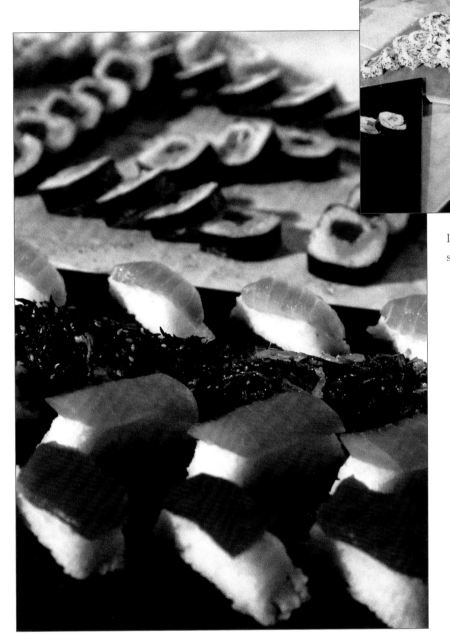

boards and stovetops, sautéing prawns in butter, or stirring a caramelized shallot sauce. Chefs from each of the resort's evening restaurants present items they'll add to their respective menus. They hover over the dishes with anticipation, adjusting garnishes, ladling steaming sauces over plates, cupping beggar's purses into form with their hands or waiting for soufflés to rise. Wine is poured freely with each course. The Seafood Buffet chef tempts with grilled blue nose bass with a Thai curry glaze and lemongrass beurre blanc. The Royal Street Café chef serves shrimp and lobster "margaritas" in glasses with layers of papaya salsa and guacamole, and wonderfully seasoned gold corn tortilla strips for dipping. A seared veal chop from The Mariposa is presented with balsamic glaze, green and yellow beans, roasted shiitake mushrooms and mashed red bliss potatoes. Dessert is a caramel apple tart served with cider sauce and crème fraîche. A golden apple is carved like the center of a rose and surrounded by a sweet cookie crust. One might display it as a piece of art rather than consume it. (Alas, the desire to consume wins out.) The vin de glacier that accompanies the dessert enlightens the flavors and brings color to cheeks.

This is a ski resort? One couldn't do better in San Francisco or New York. Here in the warmth of a Deer Valley restaurant, guests nibble their way to gastronomical contentment as snowcats groom the slopes for skiing it all off tomorrow. Life is good. And it tastes delicious. 🏔

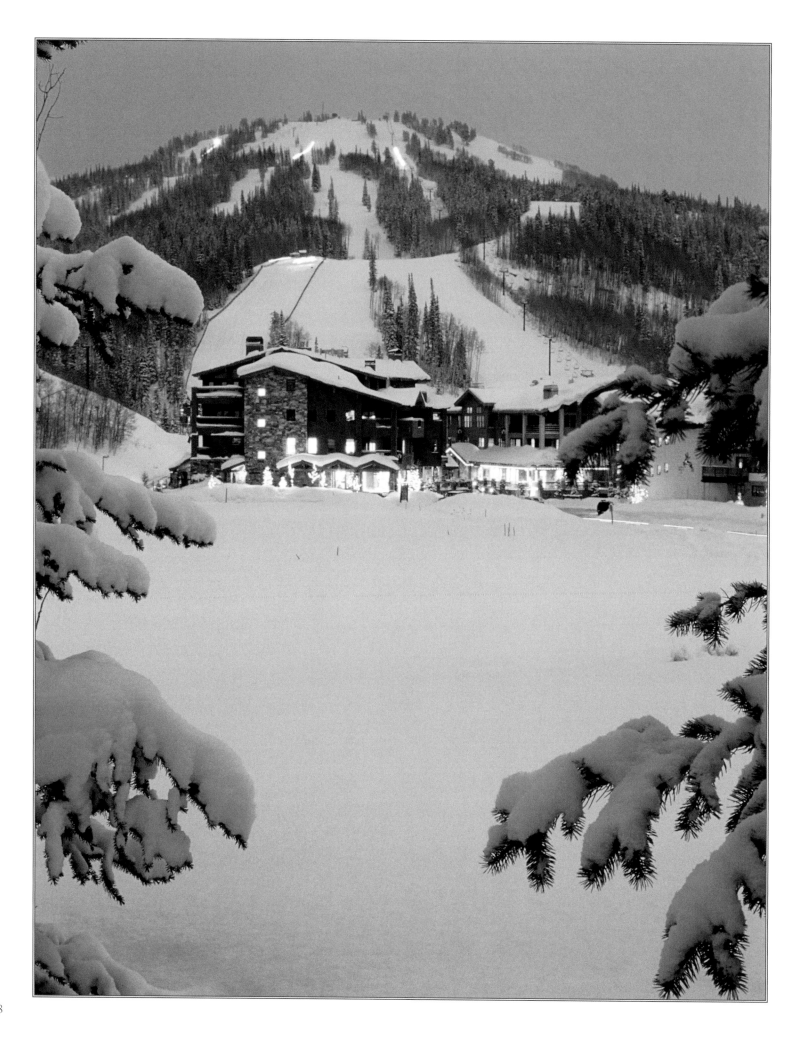

Chapter 7

ARCHITECTURE

The "Deer Valley look" originated with the resort's first two day lodges, Snow Park and Silver Lake, both of which opened for Deer Valley's inaugural season in 1981. These lodges set the standard for the private real estate development that has flourished throughout Deer Valley. The lodges incorporate certain design elements found in National Park lodges built during 1930s by the Works Progress Administration (a style sometimes referred to as "parkitechture") without copying the exact design of any of those lodges.

"Snow Park and Silver Lake lodges are masterpieces of mountain architecture in a North American sense," says Jim Nassikas, former Deer Valley president. "They're not Swiss or Austrian [and] there's nothing Disneyland about them."

The San Francisco architectural firm of Esherick, Homsey, Dodge and Davis designed the original lodges, assisted by Salt Lake-based architect Bill Selvage. Both lodges have been remodeled and expanded over the years by WPA Architecture of Provo, Utah.

The designers' intent was to create a sense of mass with large, open spaces, beams, fireplaces and rectangular wall openings. An abundant use of wood and stone gives the lodges substance. Roof slopes lend to the effect and assist in reducing snow buildup. "The result is a natural look that fits with the mountains and the heavy vegetation and evergreens around us," says Deer Valley's vice president of real estate, Bob Wells.

Interior designer Andrew Delfino (who had worked with Jim Nassikas at San Francisco's award-winning Stanford Court Hotel) assisted

THE DEER VALLEY ARCHITECTURAL STYLE INCORPORATES A SENSE OF MASS THAT BEFITS ITS MOUNTAIN SURROUNDINGS.

Left: Deer Valley's midmountain Silver Lake Lodge features interior areas that are both spacious and intimate. Below: The original Silver Lake Lodge, pictured here, was badly damaged in a 1984 fire. Renovations included expansion of the lodge.

with furniture selections for Deer Valley's first two lodges. It was Delfino's idea to use oversized Douglas fir timbers from Oregon as columns in the lodges.

The floors of the day lodges are made partially of Alaskan cedar and the walls are western red cedar. The cedar quiets the clatter of ski boots. There are large seating areas as well as small nooks and dining rooms, providing both spaciousness and intimacy. Deer Valley enthusiast and homebuilder Howard Kadwit refers to the style of the lodges as "simplistic mass," simple in design, yet large and open. That "feel" appeals to skiers for both practical and aesthetic reasons. "Having the ability to move freely in a larger space is wonderful for skiers, who are often carrying equipment and dressed in several layers of clothing," says Kadwit. Aesthetically, Kadwit appreciates the sturdy oak tables and chairs in the lodge dining areas. "It's not like sitting on

a wobbly bench. When you sit down at a Deer Valley lodge table, you feel like you're going to settle in and have something good to eat. It feels like a second home."

The rectangular windows, set deeply into stone surrounds, are reminiscent of castle windows. Fires burning in the oversized stone fireplaces warm skiers, and attendants keep the fires stoked to a mellow crackle. "Sensible, practical and enjoyable" is how resort founder Edgar Stern describes Deer Valley's architectural style. Polly Stern calls it "comfortable and welcoming."

Leather couches abound for the ski weary. Oriental carpets, overstuffed chairs upholstered in warm, earth-tone fabrics, and flagstone fireplaces warm the spirit. Antique "settles" (high-backed wooden benches) are placed around the lodges as well.

No detail for the guests' convenience has been overlooked. Daily newspapers hang from wooden scrolls throughout the dining areas, so guests can peruse them while attendants wander about refilling coffee cups. Phone booths in the lower levels of the lodges are equipped with notepads and sharpened pencils. Lockers and a personalized ski basket check are available for storing street shoes or extra clothing. First-time guests at Deer Valley do a double take when they enter the restrooms, not expecting granite countertops, brass fixtures, slate floors, elegant wash bowls and fresh flower arrangements.

"Some ski lodges are more ornate, but that's not comfortable for skiers," says Stern. "Deep carpets, for instance, make it difficult to walk when wearing ski boots, plus the boots will destroy them." No recorded music is played in Deer Valley Resort buildings (or at the chairlifts or in the restaurants, for that matter), so visitors are able to enjoy the quiet.

When the original lodges opened in 1981, there was no space for a ski school office or a children's center. Deer Valley's former director of skier

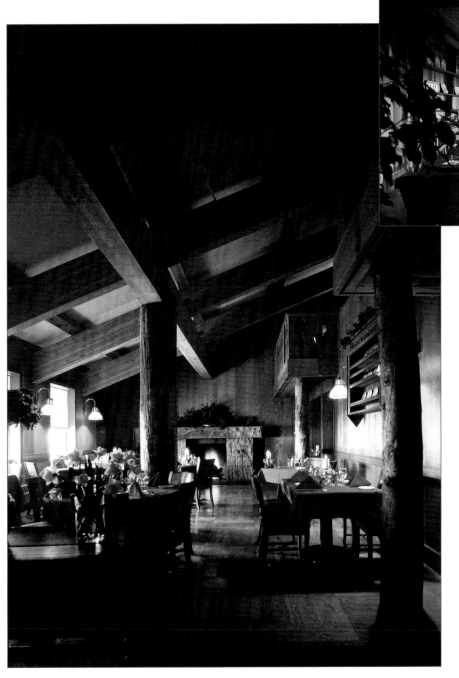

OPPOSITE: MANY OF THE PRIVATE
HOMES AT DEER VALLEY PROVIDE
AMPLE ROOM FOR VISITORS.
ABOVE: THE LOUNGE, UPSTAIRS
IN SNOW PARK LODGE, IS AN
INTIMATE SPOT FOR APRÈS-SKI
LIBATION, SNACKS AND LIVE
MUSIC. LEFT: THE COZY
MARIPOSA IN SILVER LAKE
LODGE IS ONE OF PARK CITY'S
MOST ROMANTIC RESTAURANTS.

services, Sal Raio (who worked at the resort for 20 years), "took over space originally earmarked for a restaurant at Snow Park Lodge and turned it into a day care center," says the current skier services director, John Guay. "And he took over a little broom closet to [use as] a ski school office. Sal understood the customer-service side of ski school, the need for guests to be able to walk into an office to talk about their needs, whether it was kids' ski school or a private lesson. And he saw the need for a licensed day care center. I think that's been our niche—taking care of the children so

that parents can enjoy all of the amenities Deer Valley has to offer, whether it be a private lesson or a leisurely lunch. I think the children's center and ski school have been more successful than anyone could have imagined."

One expansion at Silver Lake Lodge came about after a fire in April 1984. "Silver Lake Lodge practically burned down," recalls Letty Flatt, Deer Valley's executive pastry chef, who in 1984 was a ski patroller and also served on the town's volunteer fire department. The fire started along the south side of the lodge and burned for 36 hours. Firefighters had to bring in a backhoe to rip the roof off to get to the fire. Flatt remembers, "We had staffers taking the chairs and antiques, such as a 17th century hutch and collector plates, out of The Mariposa restaurant by hand. Luckily, every- thing made it out." Three feet of water collected in the basement of the

153

THIS DEER CREST HOME IS STUNNING
FROM EITHER THE INSIDE (BELOW) OR
THE OUTSIDE (LEFT).

building, where ski school uniforms were found floating in black water.

During reconstruction the building was expanded and altered to fit changing needs. As building maintenance manager at the time, Bob Wheaton was in charge. "That's when [Bob's] management and organizational skills really shone through," says Chuck English, the resort's director of mountain operations. "I believe [that job] put him in the spotlight that he deserved."

The resort's third day lodge, the 35,000-square-foot Empire Canyon Lodge, designed by WPA Architecture, was completed in December 2001. Created to offer more lunchtime seating capacity and guest space during the ski day, the new lodge is immensely popular with Deer Valley visitors. Though the wood in Empire Canyon Lodge is also cedar, it hasn't yet dark-

ened as cedar does with age, so it has a lighter look. The lodge has an open-air design, heavy roof beams and large windows. The main entry, with double glass doors opening onto a massive fireplace, leather couch, comfortable upholstered chairs and Oriental carpet, is one of the resort's most inviting.

The simple yet homey style of the lodges extends to the private homes and condominiums in Deer Valley as well. Written design guidelines have been part of Deer Valley's real estate planning from day one. The prologue to

THIS HOME WAS ONE OF THE FIRST
IN DEER VALLEY'S BALD EAGLE
NEIGHBORHOOD AND HAS BEEN
FEATURED IN *ARCHITECTURAL DIGEST*.
LEFT: NOTE THE RECTANGULAR
WINDOWS AND STONEWORK,
WHICH ARE ENCOURAGED BY DEER
VALLEY'S ARCHITECTURAL
GUIDELINES.

the Deer Valley design guidelines says it all: "If everyone tries to get everyone else's attention, no one will get anyone's attention; if, on the other hand, the atmosphere is calmer and more pleasant, one has the leisure to notice everybody." Another part of the guidelines says, "Deer Valley is an area of remarkable natural beauty. Its housing and facilities are intended to reinforce this quality to ensure that the 'spirit' of Deer Valley isn't undermined by arbitrary, unthoughtful design."

When Deer Valley Resort sold parcels of land surrounding the new ski area to developers, it recorded covenants, conditions and restrictions requiring that the land be developed in compliance with Deer Valley's master plan, city permits and Deer Valley's design guidelines. "It really worked," says Bob Wells, "because the design guidelines were not at all inconsistent with what people wanted in a mountain community. Plus we had cooperation from developers and architects and it all came together. They're called 'guidelines' for a reason. You don't want them to be so absolute that you take away the talent and creativity of the designer or architect. It's resulted in something that's referred to now as the 'Deer Valley look.'"

The design guidelines were written at a time when the architectural style known as "mine shaft," so named because of no roof overhangs, was popular. However, this particular style was inappropriate for snow conditions. The

DEER VALLEY PEOPLE
Vice President of Resort Planning and Real Estate Development Bob Wells

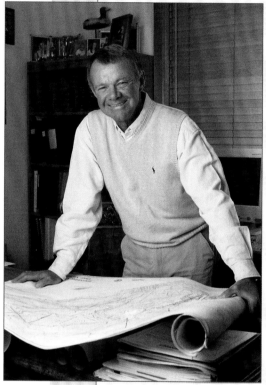

Bob Wells is one of the people behind the development planning that has come to be described nationwide as the "Deer Valley look." Though he's lived in the Wasatch mountains for over 30 years, the Mississippi native still carries the hint of a drawl. Frenetic and complicated real estate transactions don't seem to shake his relaxed demeanor.

A CPA with a degree in accounting from Mississippi State, Wells was introduced to Edgar and Polly Stern and Royal Street Corporation's many business ventures while working as a tax specialist for the Arthur Andersen accounting firm in New Orleans. In 1970, he got a taste of the skiing life when he accompanied friends to Colorado for a week. "It was my first time ever skiing," says Wells. "I basically rolled down the slopes for seven days. I recall sitting out in front of the bar at the end of the day with my ski boots off and watching other people walking down the street in their ski boots and wondering how they were possibly doing that. My feet were covered in blisters." However, Wells was hooked. Within days of his return to New Orleans, he was in a meeting at Royal Street Corporation's office where he joked with executive Dwight Martin that since he had become a ski expert, his billing rates were going up. "He offered me a job in Park City. I'd been working on Royal Street's acquisition of the Treasure Mountain Resort and was familiar with the project. I pretended that it took me a day to decide to accept the offer. It actually took me about five minutes." Wells visited Park City within the week and moved to the mountain community with his family in February 1971.

Hired as the financial officer for Greater Park City Company, Wells became a self-taught real estate expert. "I converted from a tax CPA to a real estate developer just because I had to. In the early days, we had a staff of architects and engineers and pretty much designed all of the development that Greater Park City Company did between 1971 and 1975." Wells dealt with banks and construction lenders, worked with architects and procured planning approvals and licenses. He calls the experience "a bath of fire."

Wells worked as escrow officer for the 1974–75 restructuring of Greater Park City Company, serving as disseminator of records for the very complicated transactions. "That whole deal was very difficult to put together [and was even challenged in a 1989 lawsuit by the mining company, which was settled in the early '90s]; but 25 years later, when you look back, it really worked. Everybody is happy," says Wells.

Between 1974 and 1977, Wells worked for Moana Corporation, a property management company that took over some of the existing Greater Park City Company rental pool operations. He then started his own property management company with his wife, Patti. "She had been in the property management business for years. We were a real mom-and-pop operation. We did a lot of the housekeeping, and I remember spending several Christmases cleaning ovens in condos."

Wells sold his property management company in 1979 and went to work for Deer Valley again, handling initial land sales to developers. He left Deer Valley once more in 1981, spent five years trying to develop a resort at Nevada's Mt. Rose, and developed Stag Lodge, a ski-in/ski-out lodge midmountain at Deer Valley.

In late 1986, when Deer Valley terminated discussions with Trammel Crow relating to the potential sale of an interest in the

BELOW: BOB WELLS IS PROUD OF HIS INVOLVEMENT WITH DEVELOPING THE STAG LODGE, PICTURED HERE. RIGHT: A ROOM AT THE STAG LODGE. LARGE WINDOWS AND NATURAL DESIGN ELEMENTS ARE A FOUNDATION OF MOUNTAIN-STYLE ARCHITECTURE.

resort, John Miiller, then Deer Valley executive vice president, offered Wells the job of managing real estate for the resort. "It was absolutely perfect timing. I was broke. On January 1, 1987, I went back to work at Deer Valley and have been here ever since."

During his time in Park City, Wells has fully immersed himself in the community. He helped raise three children and has been active in skiing, golf and fly-fishing. He served on the Park City Planning Commission for four years and on the City Council for eight. He was twice the president of the Convention and Visitors Bureau, as well as president of the Park City Lodging Association.

"All of that involvement was like having multiple educations," says Wells. "Those [early days] were fun days. It was a very exciting time." Wells is most proud of having helped to start the free public bus system in Park City. "We bought eight used buses from San Mateo, California," recounts Wells. "They had to be driven here, and they barely made it. This was 1980 or so. It was hard to get parts for those vehicles, but we ran them for two or three years and that was the start of Park City's free transportation system."

Did Wells ever imagine in 1971 what the Park City area might look like 30 years later? "I imagined that there would be growth, but never on the value scale that has occurred." ☾

guidelines call for homes to blend with the site. Exterior walls must be solid all the way to the ground, providing a sense of "solidity and repose." Masonry must extend far enough above the ground (depending on location) to prevent deterioration from snow build-up, which in some places has exceeded eight feet. "[From the beginning] we discouraged gimmicks like curved walls or round windows," says Wells. "Roof shapes were expected to be medium, so no flat roofs and no steep roofs. Building materials were expected to exhibit a natural and sim-

ple look with a combination of wood and stone. Two different materials on a facade are great, a third one introduced as an accent is okay, but never more than three," says Wells. "And don't show us any carvings. Except for bears," he says, referring to the home facing Last Chance trail that guests refer to as "the bear house" due to the family of carved whimsical bears on the home's rooflines and deck railings.

A favorite end-of-day activity at Deer Valley is to carve slow turns down Last Chance, Success, Kimberly, Rising Star or Silver Dollar, and occasionally stop to admire the exquisite homes along the way. It's like flipping through the pages of *Architectural Digest* on skis. The homes bordering Last Chance are of particular interest. In addition to the previously mentioned "bear house," there are now a "raccoon house" and a "totem pole" house. No

other ski resort in the world offers this kind of home tour on skis.

Mark Prothro, president of Bellecorp, has developed housing communities in Deer Valley's north Silver Lake area, including Belleterre, Belleview, Bellemont and BelleArbor. "One of the most important reasons people buy here at Deer Valley is the ability to have ski-in/ski-out property, which a lot of ski areas don't offer." Prothro believes homeowners are buying more than just houses when they buy at Deer Valley. "What they're really buying is an experience with their families," he says. "Whether it's winter or summer, Deer Valley continues to offer activities for everyone. That, coupled with the ease of getting to Deer Valley, has made many of my buyers choose Deer Valley over other resort areas."

The first subdivision developed in the Deer Valley area was American

Flag; that development was soon followed by Solamere and then Evergreen. Homes in the earlier subdivisions were built much smaller than those built later. There was actually a concern in the early days that people were just going to build little cabins, and so guidelines for the earlier subdivisions specified a minimum square footage. Homes in American Flag initially topped out at about 4,000 square feet, so when Evergreen was designed (one of the few communities in which Deer Valley sold lots to individuals rather than to developers)

ABOVE: THE CHATEAUX,
MIDMOUNTAIN AT DEER VALLEY,
OFFERS SPACIOUSNESS APPEALING
TO SKIERS WITH ALL THEIR
EQUIPMENT IN TOW. LEFT: THE
SEDUCTIVE LOBBIES IN THE
CHATEAUX ARE ENOUGH TO KEEP
SOME GUESTS INSIDE ALL DAY.

planners thought that 4,000 square feet would suffice there as well. "We were wrong," says Wells. "They wanted bigger building pads and didn't want their houses right next to the street. We had designed the lots to have easy driveway access from the road, but that's not what people wanted. The end result was homes in the 7,500-square-foot range. The largest houses today are in the Bald Eagle community, which was developed after Evergreen, probably averaging about 10,000 square feet per home." Park City officials became concerned that Deer

Valley homes were being built too big for the lot sizes. (The names "trophy home" and "starter castle" came into use.) In the late 1980s the city placed restraints on home sizes. Therefore, guidelines for the newer subdivisions specify a maximum size. This is just one of the ironies that grew out of Deer Valley's success.

Today, roughly 80 different projects, encompassing almost 2,000 units, have been completed in Deer Valley. You'd never know there were so many, as they are artfully hidden amidst trees or set discreetly low on the hillside.

Don Resnick, one of the managing partners of Silver Lake Associates, was involved in developing The Chateaux in Silver Lake Village. A long-time skier and ski instructor, he says he fell in love with Deer Valley the day

Above: The Lodges near Deer Valley's base boasts an enticing entry. Left: The lobby in The Lodges, near Deer Valley's base area, features a massive floor-to-ceiling rock fireplace. Opposite: The Goldener Hirsch in Silver Lake Village is built in the Austrian mountain style. The ski-in/ski-out access is unbeatable.

he set foot on the slopes. "Then I understood that some land at Silver Lake might become available, and the vision we had was the same vision that Edgar Stern had for that site: a first-class hotel facility with a restaurant." Resnick, who also owns a home in Deer Valley, calls the "Deer Valley look" an "American alpine" look. "It's cedar shake roofs, stone and wood. It's browns, beiges and tans. It's unique in North American skiing. I don't think anyone has a concept like Deer Valley. Edgar Stern absolutely created Deer Valley in his own image, which is one of beauty and class."

Expansion of Deer Valley development is now being done by Deer Crest Associates to the east on Little Baldy Mountain, and by United Park City Mines Company to the west on Flagstaff Mountain. Both of these developments are additions to the original plans for Deer Valley Resort.

In the end, of course, it's not the wood, stone or mortar that makes the difference—it's the people. "The second-home owners are a huge part of why Deer Valley has been successful," says John Guay. "The ski-in/ski-out homes bring families to Deer Valley. They provide the resort a customer base that's very supportive of ski school, the restaurants and the children's center. These people become part of the Deer Valley family—back several times each winter for a week at a time. The real estate connection is really good for us."

163

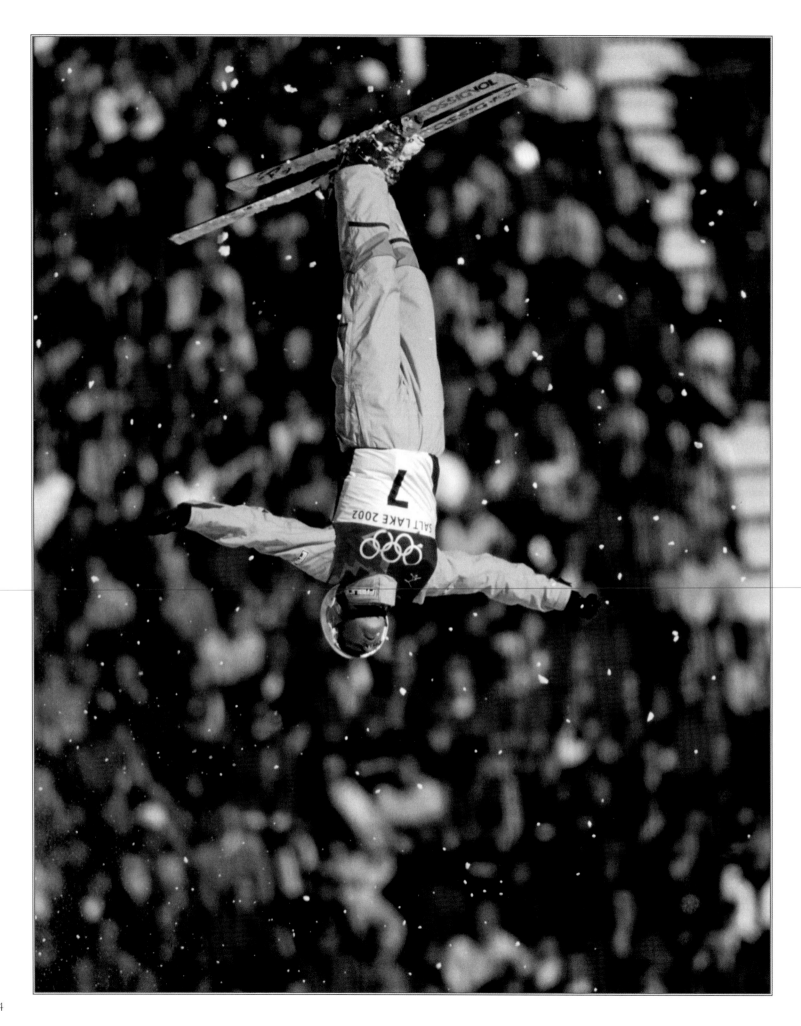

Chapter 8

COMPETITION

Resort founder Edgar Stern was less than thrilled about the prospect of Deer Valley hosting events for the 2002 Olympic Winter Games. "To be honest," Stern had said, "I'm scared to death of it, because we'll have six times as many people here as we ever have. There's so much that could go wrong in that situation. I'm concerned that the service our guests have come to expect could be diminished. We'll work through it, I guess." Deer Valley did much more than "work through" the challenges of the Olympics. As host to the 2002 alpine slalom and freestyle aerials and moguls events, Deer Valley came through with flying colors.

Deer Valley's upscale reputation did not, at first glance, appear to be a match with adrenaline-producing freestyle skiing. Nonetheless, resort management made a decision to commit an all-out effort to hosting these exciting Olympic events, recognizing that they would enhance the resort's image and expand the public's understanding of what the resort truly has to offer. "I was excited when we got the freestyle events," says resort guest services manager Terry Bouman. "It was something new. The Deer Valley crew is used to being flexible and adapting to whatever comes along. We thought, 'Okay, we're going to do aerials? Great. How do we do that?' We sat down and figured out how to do it. And we did it well."

Advocates of bringing the Olympic Winter Games to Utah had been trying to do so since 1965, when a group led by then-Governor Calvin Rampton made a pitch for the 1972 Games. (The 1972 Games went to Sapporo, Japan.) Deer Valley became involved in the process in 1990 when, as resort president and general manager Bob Wheaton tells it, "We supported

FREESTYLE ATHLETES REACH HEIGHTS UP TO 60 FEET ON DEER VALLEY'S AERIALS COURSE.

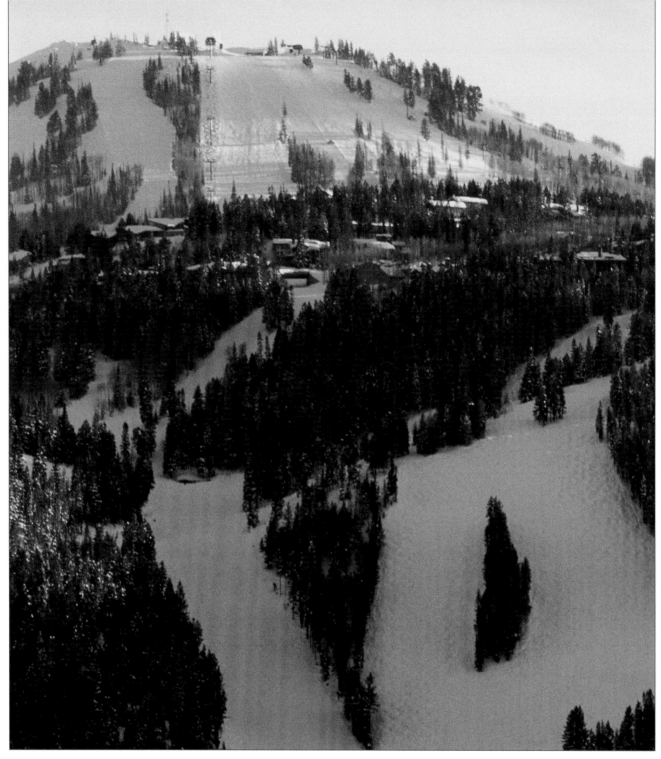

THE NATURAL CONVERGENCE OF CHAMPION (CENTER), KNOW YOU DON'T (RIGHT) AND WHITE OWL RUNS (FAR RIGHT)
MADE THE WIDE AREA AT THEIR BASE IDEAL FOR AN OLYMPIC STADIUM.

the Olympic movement because it made sense. We were looking for skier days. ["Skier days" is an industry term that reflects the number of skiers at the resort.] We put our hands up in the air at a meeting, and suddenly we were in." An eight-foot sign was erected at the top of Deer Valley's Big Stick run—prematurely, as it turned out—reading, "America's Choice for the 1998 Olympics: Deer Valley: giant slalom and moguls." Salt Lake City lost the 1998 Games to Nagano, Japan, by four votes. "It was one of those off-the-wall things with no sense of reality attached," says Chuck English, the resort's director of mountain operations. "Mountain employees would walk by the sign and chuckle."

Then in 1995, the Salt Lake Organizing Committee for the Olympic Winter Games of 2002 (SLOC) won the bid for Utah. As 50,000 Utahns celebrated victory on the lawn of Salt Lake's City and County Building,

English was thinking, "Oh my God! What have we done now? We don't have an aerials hill or a moguls course."

Before it could host Olympic competition, Deer Valley was required to produce two "test" World Cup events as dress rehearsals for February 2002. International Olympic Committee and U.S. Olympic Committee members were called in to help. Deer Valley hired course experts and ex-athletes, including Chris Haslock, Jeff Chumas, Timmy Meagher, Konrad Rotermund, Kris "Fuzzy" Feddersen

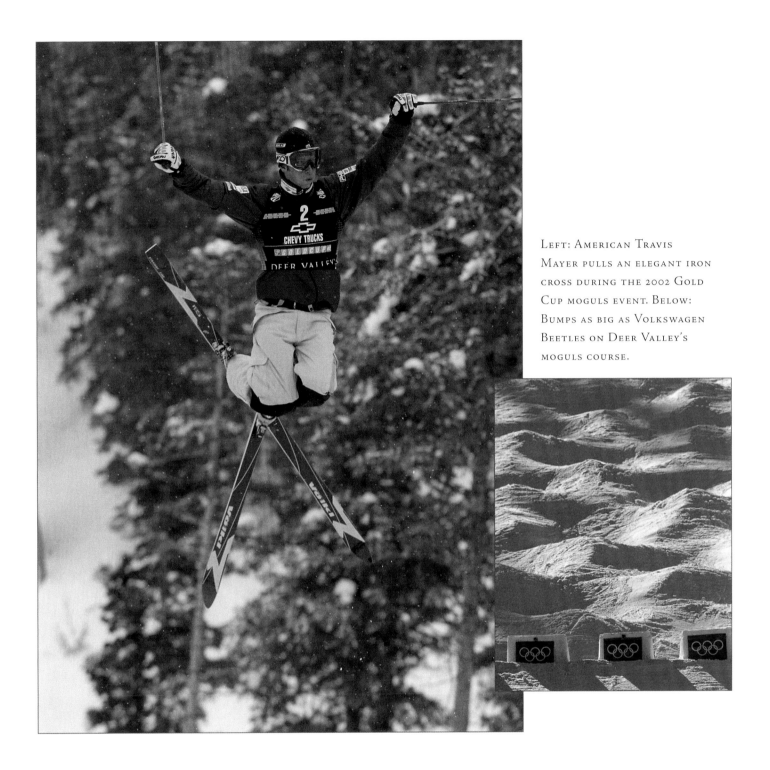

LEFT: AMERICAN TRAVIS MAYER PULLS AN ELEGANT IRON CROSS DURING THE 2002 GOLD CUP MOGULS EVENT. BELOW: BUMPS AS BIG AS VOLKSWAGEN BEETLES ON DEER VALLEY'S MOGULS COURSE.

and Jim Clifford, to serve as consultants and chiefs of course for the World Cup events that would precede the Olympics. Evergreen Engineering was hired by Deer Valley to design an Olympic amphitheater, including a stadium where slalom, moguls and aerials events could all be observed from one spot. (Designers would ultimately submit 30 different renderings before plans were approved.)

Deer Valley's existing Know You Don't run would serve well for the slalom course. But moguls and aerials courses had to be built from

scratch. "The thing was," says English, "freestyle brought to mind randomness and freeness, but specifications for moguls and aerials courses are highly technical. We were thinking, 'Where's the freestyle part of this whole thing?' I don't think any of us understood the scope of what was required."

The creation of freestyle venues that would look perfect draped in winter white began by moving tons of dirt. Construction of the Champion run for moguls actually started in 1997. First, a steep, forested pitch on Bald Eagle Mountain had to be cleared. Then 20,000 yards of fill dirt were added to contour the fall line. (At the time, construction was booming in Park City and contractors were looking to get rid of dirt, making Deer Valley a veritable dirt broker.) Two thousand loads of fill were brought in by dump trucks that summer.

ABOVE: PIG-TAILED ALISA CAMPLIN
OF AUSTRALIA BROKE A WORLD
RECORD (AND WON THE GOLD
MEDAL) DURING DEER VALLEY'S
2003 FIS FREESTYLE WORLD
CHAMPIONSHIPS. RIGHT: AT 265
METERS, DEER VALLEY'S CHAMPION
IS THE LONGEST—AND MOST
CHALLENGING—MOGULS COURSE
ON THE INTERNATIONAL CIRCUIT.

Mogul creation is a sophisticated art. At the 1992 Albertville Olympics—the first time mogul skiing was a medal event—the moguls were sculpted by hand. At the Lillehammer Games of 1994, the moguls were so perfectly spaced that machines had obviously been at work. Today, it takes two days for Deer Valley's grooming crew to create a moguls course for elite competition. The chief of moguls sets poles in a pattern down the slope, indicating where the bumps should be. Grooming crews deposit huge piles of snow in appropriate places on the slope. Then groomer Tom Macintosh, who has become a master mogul builder, breaks the massive piles of snow into thirds and alternates them in a checkerboard pattern, while his snowcat hangs from a winch on the 27-degree slope. Observing the process one day, Edgar Stern reportedly said, "We bought all these snowcats

for you all to make smooth and effortless corduroy, and you're using them to build moguls!"

Once the piles of snow have been evenly spaced, 20 volunteers spend several days skiing and shoveling the moguls until they are smooth and free of ice chunks. Then the competitors begin training, molding the bumps with their skis. Jumps are built a third of the way and two-thirds of the way down the course. Mogulists reach heights of 20 feet pulling "daffys," "iron crosses," "helicopters" and "backscratchers" from these abrupt launch pads while skiing 15–20 miles an

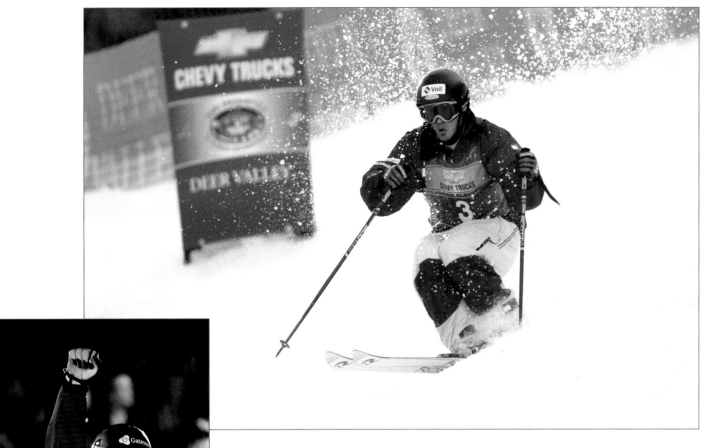

DEER VALLEY HAS WELCOMED THE
WORLD'S BEST ATHLETES TO ITS MOUN-
TAIN. ABOVE: DURING THE 2003 WORLD
CHAMPIONSHIPS, AMERICAN TOBY
DAWSON DEMONSTRATES SUPERB MOGUL
SKIING THAT EARNED HIM TWO BRONZE
MEDALS. LEFT: PARK CITY TRANSPLANT
AND 1998 OLYMPIC AERIALS GOLD
MEDALIST ERIC BERGOUST RALLIES
WITH THE SELLOUT CROWD.

hour down the 265-meter course covered with moguls that are three feet or more deep—the longest on the international competition circuit.

"The strong athletes love Champion," says English. "You can see our course taking its toll on them. The last third of the course, they're just rag dolls coming down that thing, all on man-made snow that's intentionally hard. It's so impressive to watch these kids. You don't see a lot of mogul skiers over 25. There's a reason for it."

"Deer Valley's moguls course is the most challenging out there," says U.S. Ski Team pub-

lic relations director, Juliann Fritz. "That's what all the athletes talk about. That course makes them or breaks them. It's the longest course ever on the moguls circuit. It's not as steep as some, but it's so long that the endurance factor is significant."

Construction of the White Owl aerials course began during the summer of 1998. Curiously, White Owl had been a Nordic jumping site at Snow Park ski area in the late 1940s. This time, course workers encountered rock while trying to terrace the run, and nearly three-quarters of a ton of dynamite was needed to remove it.

Aerialists perform highly technical and potentially dangerous gymnastic maneuvers 50 feet above the snow. The course must be perfectly precise. "Aerials courses are regulated like a gymnastics competition would be," says

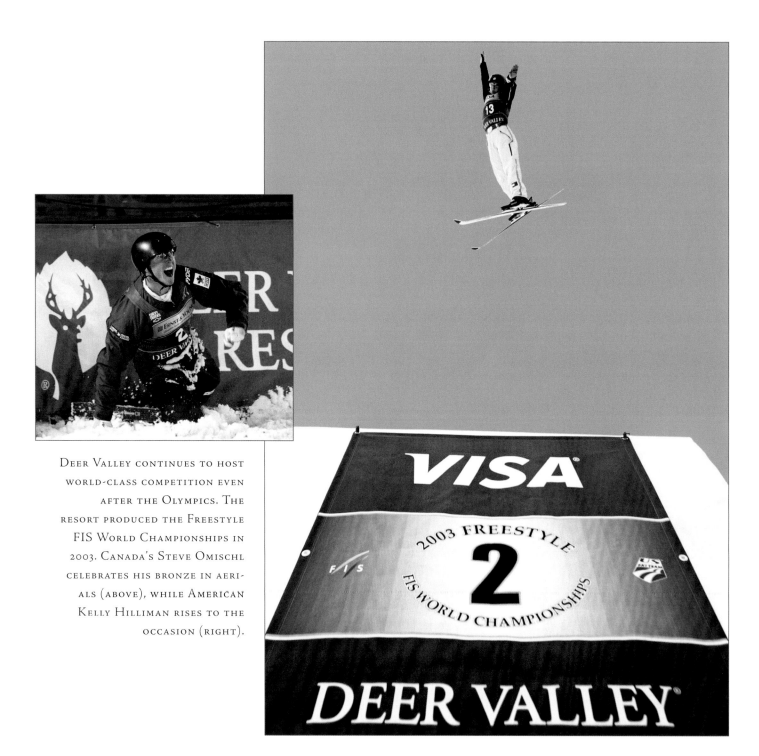

DEER VALLEY CONTINUES TO HOST WORLD-CLASS COMPETITION EVEN AFTER THE OLYMPICS. THE RESORT PRODUCED THE FREESTYLE FIS WORLD CHAMPIONSHIPS IN 2003. CANADA'S STEVE OMISCHL CELEBRATES HIS BRONZE IN AERIALS (ABOVE), WHILE AMERICAN KELLY HILLIMAN RISES TO THE OCCASION (RIGHT).

English. "The parallel bars at the University of Utah, for instance, need to be the same height and dimensions as parallel bars in Nebraska, so the athletes know what to expect. Aerials venues have to have a certain amount of predictability, right down to angles of curves throughout the jumps." An aerials site starts with a very steep section called the "in run," followed by a 60-foot flat area, or "table." "Kickers," the jump launches, are built of snow. Coaches and athletes create the kickers, 12-foot-high ramps that propel jumpers straight up into the sky to heights up to 60 feet.

The most labor-intensive section of an aerials course is the landing hill, which has a pitch of about 38 degrees. Twenty to 30 volunteers, called "choppers," walk up the incline shoulder to shoulder, with shovels, chopping grooves into the surface, aerating the snow and making it soft for landing.

At least an hour's chopping is needed before each competition, and variables such as adverse weather, humidity and freezing temperatures can make the job all the more difficult.

Chopping is hard work, and by midday most of the crew has stripped to T-shirts, even in 20-degree temperatures. The entire group is made up of volunteers, most of whom have worked Deer Valley's aerials hill since the first World Cup event in 2000. They call themselves "Team Chop." Competition to be included in the group is fierce despite the demands of the job,

because it also offers the best view of the aerials course during competitions. From directly underneath the kickers, choppers can feel the rush of air and hear the aerialists' clothing flapping against their bodies as they fly overhead.

The landing hill is sprinkled with tiny bits of pine boughs that Deer Valley staffers and volunteers cut from recycled Christmas trees—30 trash bags full are scattered over the snow during a typical event. The needles provide depth perception for the jumpers who, if the light is flat, may have trouble distinguishing sky from snow.

One hundred thousand yards of fill dirt were used to prepare the Olympic stadium area and the finish areas for the freestyle and slalom courses. Temporary roads were cut right across the Know You Don't run to make a thoroughfare for dump trucks. By 2000 the venue was ready for the Olympic test events in 2001.

Deer Valley had little experience hosting big competitions, though it had hosted small local events like Masters races and the Utah Winter Games. In 1997, before Champion was built, a moguls event was held on Big Stick. Just before the NorAm competition began, high winds upset a 12-foot judging stand and four people were injured. Thankfully, all recovered, but the incident was a wake-up call not only to USSA and Deer Valley, but to Park City itself. "A number of people probably cursed us

171

THE DEER VALLEY DIFFERENCE
Grooming

If Deer Valley had a bumper sticker, it might read, THE SKIING'S FAST 'CAUSE THE GROOMING'S SLOW. Every night a fleet of 13 snowcats and two winch cats groom 60 runs. You would think they would be racing the clock to get the job done, but the "product" is better, they say, if they take their time. "If something's not satisfactory, we'll go back and keep working until it's done right," says 23-year employee and lead groomer Dave Smith.

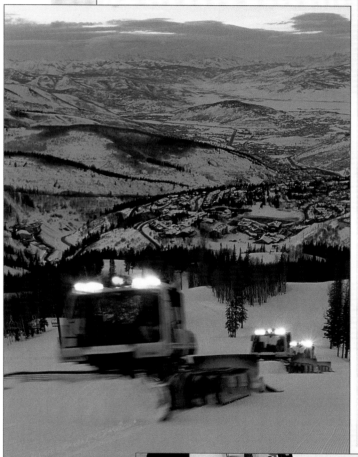

Smith spends his nights "laying out the glass," "mowing the lawn," and "filling the dish" in a Bombardier snowcat. As he drives, the beat of reggae music wafts through the cab. "We want a nice, smooth, even surface, no surprises out there for skiers, no big chunks of ice lying around," he says. "We strive to do that on a nightly basis." Tonight he steps out of his cat to inspect a spot of oil that has leaked onto a moonlit slope. "I'll need to clean that up," he says.

Smith's boss, self-described perfectionist and grooming supervisor Dave Anderson, says his department's bottom line is "making sure the quality of product lives up to expectations." He looks for three things on Deer Valley's slopes: snow distribution, consistent snow density and a defect-free surface.

"During the day, skiers move more snow than you could imagine down the hill and out to the edges of a run because of [their] skis' edging action. Part of our job is to move that snow back into place ["filling the dish"] and get a nice, even distribution so the snowpack will sustain another day's worth of skiing.

"Snow's like cement. It cures and sets up over time. Something you groom early in the evening will have longer to set up before a skier's on it the next day, so it will be firmer. We like soft snow, but it has to be hard enough to hold up too. And we don't want snow hard in one spot and soft in another. That would make it feel irregular."

Anderson tours the mountain each morning on his snowmobile looking for seamless passes. "If everything blends and you can't tell where one cat made a pass and the next one came in, that's what you're looking for. You want wall-to-wall 'corduroy.'"

Smith's barometers of grooming success come from

TOP: DEER VALLEY GROOMERS "LAYING OUT THE GLASS" ON RESORT SKI SLOPES. LEFT: DEER VALLEY INVESTS IN STATE OF THE ART EQUIPMENT TO ENSURE STATE OF THE ART GROOMING.

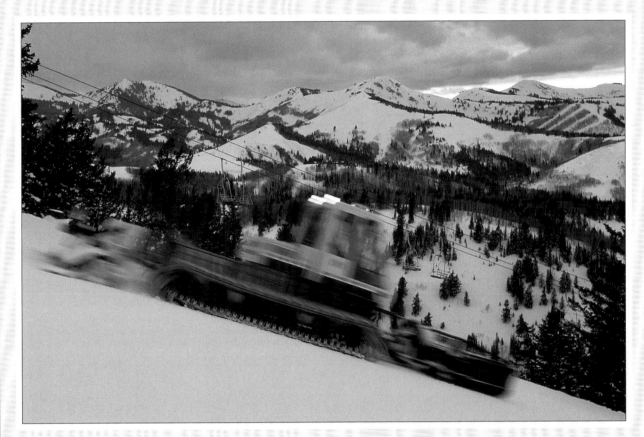

DEER VALLEY GROOMERS WORK IN TWO SHIFTS: FROM 4:30 P.M. TO MIDNIGHT AND MIDNIGHT TO 10 A.M.

reviewing runs in his snowcat's headlights ("the lights enhance any imperfections") and the "Stein test." If a groomer creates "kitty litter" (improper snow consistency) or "spills out a berm" (spitting snow out to the side that's not getting processed), Smith simply asks his crew, "Would Stein complain about skiing over it tomorrow?" If the answer is yes, he tells them, "You'd better go chase it."

To ensure safety, Deer Valley's groomers don't work the mountain during skier hours. Groomers work in two shifts, from 4:30 P.M. to midnight, and midnight to 10 A.M. "Skiers and snowcats don't mix," says Smith. "The possibility of having an incident is too great. If somebody rails out on his skis and flies into your cat, that's something you have no control over. We just don't ever put the two together."

Why has Smith chosen to work these crazy hours all these years? "We all just take a lot of pride in our work. We go the extra mile to make sure everything's good. If you go out and ace a project, like repairing a rough spot or filling in avalanche-bomb holes, there's definitely a sense of gratification." And enjoyment. "I just like driving cats. It's a blast. Plowing through the monster snowmaking piles—that's big fun. It's not like work."

Though groomers' hours are long, their unique work environment makes for sometimes surreal scenes. Beams of light from snowcat headlights illuminate snow-covered forests. Groomers often see owls, ring-tailed weasels and white rabbits "darting around like crazy." Storms are "pretty cool," says Smith, who knows the mountain so intimately that he identifies specific trees as landmarks during whiteout blizzards. And the stargazing is unbeatable. "Working graveyard [shift] in the springtime, the sky's outrageous. You get a different feel for the constellations, being out there from midnight to dawn." Several years ago the grooming crew saw a space shuttle reenter the earth's atmosphere. "We all rallied on Birdseye at 5:30 A.M. to watch it," says Smith. "The shuttle was moving at 26,000 miles an hour. It went north to south, horizon to horizon, just a ball of flame. It was wild."

Does Smith ever get spooked working on the mountain in the dark of night? "Naw. I've been waiting to see an alien spaceship, though, and I haven't seen it. That kind of bums me out." ☾

after that," says Chuck English, "because the city now has strict permitting rules for temporary structures. Park City Mountain Resort had been producing events like this for 10 years, and suddenly their race department was being questioned about how they were attaching TV cameras to scaffolding without a permit. When you think how, by 2002, we were all hosting crowds of 10,000 people in our stadiums, it was a good thing we got our ducks in a row when we did."

Deer Valley had tasted its first big-time competition when it hosted the moguls and slalom events for the 1998–99 National Championships. Resort staffers got a crash course in International Ski Federation protocol, venue preparation, communications—the works. In 2000 and 2001 Deer Valley held its two pre-Olympic World Cup events. The hard work paid

off. "People were skeptical until they saw our first World Cup," says Ginger Ries, the resort's event manager. We did it better than anyone had ever done it. They were blown away by what we could do. After that, we had the reputation of being the place to go for freestyle events."

Olympic stadium construction began in 2001, during a dry summer. One of the first tasks at hand was to build a paved road underneath the Burns chairlift so that 76 semi truckloads of scaffolding could be brought in. Bob

Wheaton likened it to "a huge erector set." Chuck English had traveled to the Nagano Games in 1998 to inspect its aerials stadium, an eight-story structure that prompted him to think, "My God, this thing's overbuilt. We're not going to build anything this big." Little did he know.

Deer Valley's stadium ended up being 12 stories tall, 300 feet across, 150 feet deep and 130 feet high at the back, with seating for 10,000 spectators. Two levels of stacked single-wide trailers sat on top of the structure, creating 40

press boxes. The certificate of occupancy for the stadium bleachers was procured on December 30, 2001.

The very next night, Deer Valley hosted USSA's Gold Cup event, a "wild card" competition whose purpose was to select U.S. Olympic Team members for the Games, now a mere five weeks away. The Gold Cup event was trend-setting. Deer Valley threw the very first nighttime aerials event, with jumpers flying off the kickers under the lights. It was an extravaganza of white snow against black sky, moonlight and spotlights, foot-tapping music, spectators' *oohs* and *aahs* held aloft in clouds of cold air, and a finale that included fireworks. For the ten thousand spectators there had never been a New Year's Eve like this. For many locals who were unable to get tickets to Olympic events, attending the Gold Cup was

175

probably even better—getting to watch the Olympic athletes strut their stuff up close and personal.

Deer Valley was ready to "welcome the world," as the Olympic advertising campaign said. For three years, Deer Valley managers had been meeting with military and FBI SWAT teams to discuss security. Every inch of Snow Park Lodge had been videotaped and inventoried by FBI personnel. They knew the width and number of hinges on every door, in case they had to blow one off during a hostage situation. Stories have been told of backcountry skiers who strayed onto land between Deer Valley and Park City Mountain Resort or Brighton and were surprised by SWAT team members in white popping up out of the snow and asking them politely to move their ridgetop picnics elsewhere. A radar station was installed on top of Deer Valley's 9,400-foot Bald Mountain to monitor air space over all of Park City, the Soldier Hollow cross-country venue, Park City Mountain Resort and Snowbasin, where Olympic events were taking place. "We started thinking, 'This is maybe a little bit bigger than we thought,'" says Chuck English.

After the terrorist attacks of September 11, 2001, security concerns climbed to an all-time high. Deer Valley staffers who had been preparing for the Games for years now faced the possibility that the whole thing might be

TOP: AN ATHLETE'S VIEW OF THE DEER
VALLEY VENUE FROM THE TOP OF
CHAMPION. NOTE THE TENTS IN DEER
VALLEY'S PARKING LOTS, WHICH
SERVED AS SECURITY OFFICES AND
OPERATIONS HEADQUARTERS FOR THE
2002 GAMES. RIGHT: AN EXUBERANT
CROWD ENCOURAGES HOMETOWN HERO
JOE PACK DURING THE 2002 GAMES.
JOE WENT ON TO WIN THE SILVER
MEDAL IN AERIALS.

canceled. However, the Games went on as scheduled, accompanied by magnetometer and bag searches ("mag and bag"), wand checks, car searches, armed guards and patrol sheds every 100 yards along a perimeter of fence that surrounded Deer Valley's entire base area. Though such invasive security measures might not have been well received before the events of 9-11, now they were welcomed. Some feared that the 2002 Olympic Winter Games would be remembered as "military games," but as spectators passed through security check points, they thanked the guards for their efforts. One Deer Valley guest was stopped at a chairlift magnetometer because he kept setting off the metal-detector alarm. It turned out he had left a coat hanger in the back of his ski jacket—and had been skiing with it all day!

Aside from safety concerns, Deer Valley's number-one priority during the Games was to prevent interruption of the experience of the regular Deer Valley guests. It took an effort of Olympic proportion. The massive Olympic stadium banner depicting an inverted aerialist served as metaphor for the situation at the resort: everything was topsy-turvy. Deer Valley's lower parking lots were taken over by SLOC for approximately two months, and were filled with "technical" trailers, staff and volunteer check-in buildings, security headquarters and more. Parking shuttles and

LEFT: TRAVIS MAYER OF THE USA
CELEBRATES HIS 2002 OLYMPIC
GAMES SILVER MEDAL IN MOGULS.
MAYER SAID THE OVERWHELMING
SOUND OF THE CHEERING CROWD
LED HIM TO VICTORY. BELOW:
FEBRUARY 12, 2002: AMERICAN
JONNY MOSELEY PERFORMS HIS
"DINNER ROLL" MANEUVER DURING
HIS MOGULS RUN. MOSELEY
PLACED FOURTH BUT WON THE
CROWD'S APPROVAL.

city buses were used to transport guests to the mid-mountain area. Snow Park Lodge was completely taken over by Olympics-related activity, so the nightly Seafood Buffet was discontinued for six weeks, and ski school and ski rental operations were relocated to a 100-foot by 60-foot heated tent at Silver Lake Village. The paved road that normally served as a parking-lot tram turnaround just under Snow Park Lodge was transformed into a tented, heated and wired press center for 300 members of the international press.

Even before spectators arrived, Deer Valley's population swelled. Hundreds of law enforcement officers from all around the country broke bread with staffers in the employee dining rooms, becoming almost like family. In addition to Deer Valley's own staffers, 900 volunteers and 1,000

SLOC employees entered the base area daily through security check points.

Wide West ski run became a village of food booths, sponsor dining, self-contained ATMs and portable toilets. Several miles of fencing were installed. Several hundred miles of television cable were hung from trees or buried under the snow. Four Deer Valley snowcats with drivers were assigned to Olympic course needs for three weeks, to prepare the courses for the seven days the events actually took place.

Despite the circumstances, nearly everything

on the mountain was fully operational for Deer Valley's regular guests. Seventeen of its 19 lifts and two of its three day lodges were open to the public. Grooming and snowmaking were running at full speed. To ensure that skiers could cross the paved emergency and handicapped access road that led from the lower mountain to Olympic Stadium, two Deer Valley employees did nothing all day but shovel snow over a small section of that road. Whether there were 5,000 skiers on the mountain or 500, the Deer Valley product had to be the same.

Everything done by Deer Valley for the Olympics showed the Deer Valley touch. Since advertising banners are not allowed during Olympic competition, even the manufacturer's labels on 30 snow guns had to be covered; Deer Valley did it with tape that matched the hunter green of the snow gun towers. At the first Olympic event, the food and beverage concession stands arranged by SLOC proved inadequate to handle the crowds, and Deer Valley regulars who were there just to attend the Games expressed dismay at not being able to get the Healthy Heart muffin for breakfast or Turkey Chili for lunch. Deer Valley management was understandably troubled by this situation, because the lack of service was so out of character for Deer Valley and could reflect badly on the resort. So Deer Valley stepped in. On the second day and subsequent days of competition,

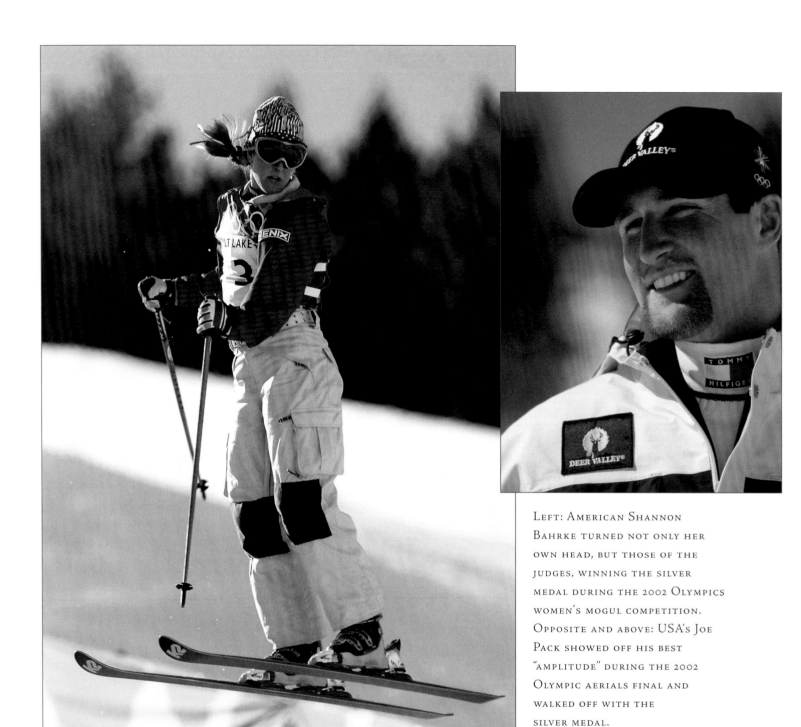

LEFT: AMERICAN SHANNON BAHRKE TURNED NOT ONLY HER OWN HEAD, BUT THOSE OF THE JUDGES, WINNING THE SILVER MEDAL DURING THE 2002 OLYMPICS WOMEN'S MOGUL COMPETITION. OPPOSITE AND ABOVE: USA'S JOE PACK SHOWED OFF HIS BEST "AMPLITUDE" DURING THE 2002 OLYMPIC AERIALS FINAL AND WALKED OFF WITH THE SILVER MEDAL.

staffers set up a concession in Snow Park Lodge, offering Deer Valley's continental breakfast fare, Caesar salads and Turkey Chili.

"Deer Valley maintained its standards even during the Games," says USSA's Tom Kelly. "And it goes to show the [reputation] that Deer Valley has. No [other] ski area can say they have a food item so adored that people demand it!"

The Olympic event announcers unfailingly characterized the resort as "beautiful Deer Valley," calling the attention of three billion television viewers worldwide to Deer Valley's groomed slopes, vivid blue skies, snow-covered firs and breathtaking vistas.

Deer Valley hosted six medal events, kicking off the first day of the Games, February 9, 2002, with women's moguls. Fourteen thousand people

arrived on a brilliant bluebird day to watch American Shannon Bahrke, with her sparkly red, white and blue eye makeup and face paint, golden braids flopping, win the silver medal— the first American medal of the 2002 Games.

The weather was equally spectacular for men's moguls on February 12. Jonny Moseley performed his "dinner roll" maneuver to an appreciative crowd and then was embraced by a sea of cheering well-wishers. Although Moseley, the 1998 gold medalist in moguls, didn't end his day on the podium, fellow

American Travis Mayer did, placing second after being inspired by the chanting of the crowd.

In men's aerials, Czech competitor Ales Valenta landed a quint-twisting-triple jump, only the second time such a maneuver had been completed in competition, gaining him the gold medal. To the delight of the crowd, hometown boy and Deer Valley "Big Air Ambassador" Joe Pack took the silver. The former Park City High School football player earned it in front of his hometown crowd, playing "air guitar" with a ski in the finish corral to celebrate. Fellow American and Park City local Brian "Curr Dog" Currutt placed sixth. Perhaps the quintessential Olympic moment at Deer Valley, showing both the thrill of victory and the agony of defeat, was watching Park City local Eric Bergoust, the 1998 Nagano gold medalist, fall on his

second jump and end up in last place. "I don't regret going for it," he said afterward. "I wanted to be either first or last. Nothing else would do."

The women's aerials event marked two firsts: Pig-tailed Alisa Camplin won the first Winter Games gold medal ever for Australia, and Switzerland's Evelyne Leu set a world-record aerials score of 203.16.

Women's slalom took place on a snowy day, giving spectators a winter-wonderland experience but slowing the competitors down a bit. Croatian Janica Kostelic won the event, the

third of a record-breaking four gold medals she would eventually earn at the Games. Jean-Pierre Vidal of France captured the men's slalom title. Deer Valley's director of skiing, Stein Eriksen, was honored in a ceremony before the race, on the 50th anniversary of his having won the silver medal in slalom at the 1952 Oslo Olympics. (He was also honored in a 50th anniversary ceremony at Park City Mountain Resort for his Oslo gold medal in the Giant Slalom.)

The crowds dispersed, the confetti was swept away, the fences were dismantled. The spirit of good-hearted athletic competition, however, and perhaps more focus on freestyle skiing, remain as the Olympics' legacy to Deer Valley. Twelve months after the Olympics, Deer Valley hosted the largest freestyle World Championships in the history of the sport, with another spectacular nighttime aerials event.

Deer Valley has embraced the full range of freestyle activities, donating moguls course time on weekends to teenagers training with the Wasatch Freestyle Association. Deer Valley guests of all ages can test their stamina on either Champion or Know You Don't, and they can stop on the Olympic site, look up at the hill, and imagine the sound of a cheering crowd.

"It was spectacular to be associated with an event of the caliber of the Olympics," says Chuck English. "It was such an honor."

185

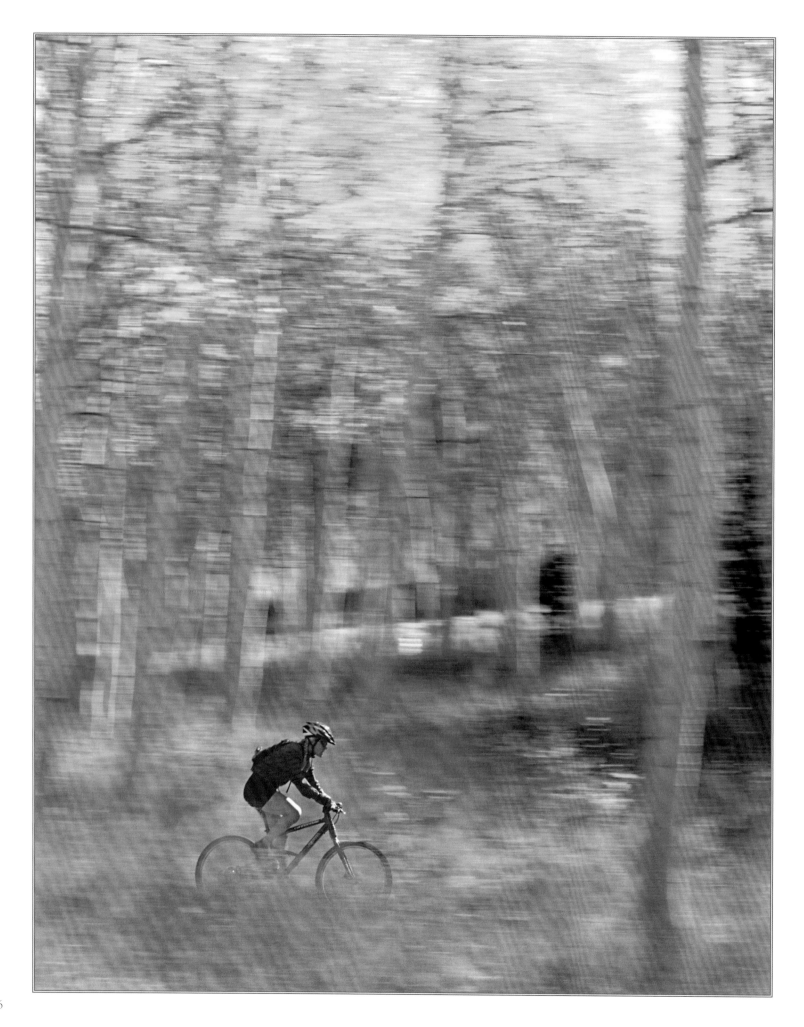

Chapter 9

SUMMER

S ummer at Deer Valley Resort has its own special character, and the brevity of this mountain season makes guests savor it all the more. The boulders and rocks over which Deer Valley guests have skied all winter become visible in summer, and the snow-free slopes are truly impressive adorned in green. Daytime temperatures in midsummer can reach 85 degrees, but at night often fall to a cool 50. The mood of Deer Valley summers is relaxed and even-paced, with activities revolving around mountain biking, hiking and scenic chairlift rides, a popular Summer Adventure Camp for children, outdoor summer concerts and lunch at the mid-mountain Royal Street Café. Nature itself provides the most satisfying entertainment, with melodious birdsong and what seems an ever-present breeze blowing through the tiny leaves of abundant quaking aspen.

From mid mountain at Silver Lake Village, guests can take the Sterling chairlift for scenic rides or easy access to 50 miles of hiking and mountain biking trails. The quarter-mile Scenic Overlook loop trail on Bald Mountain gives guests of all ages and abilities the chance to take in spectacular views in every direction. Occasionally a hang glider or paraglider can be seen riding the high mountain wind currents alongside red-tailed hawks. Picnic tables near the viewpoint provide a place to rest.

In the summer of 1992, Deer Valley attached bike-carrying hooks to the Sterling lift chairs and began offering lift-accessed hiking and mountain biking as well as scenic rides. It was the first ski resort in Park City to do so. In the usual Deer Valley way, mountain biking is presented with first-class service, from groomed trails with banked turns and comfortable, tire-cradling

IN SUMMER, DEER VALLEY'S 50 MILES OF MOUNTAIN BIKING AND HIKING TRAILS ARE UNCROWDED.

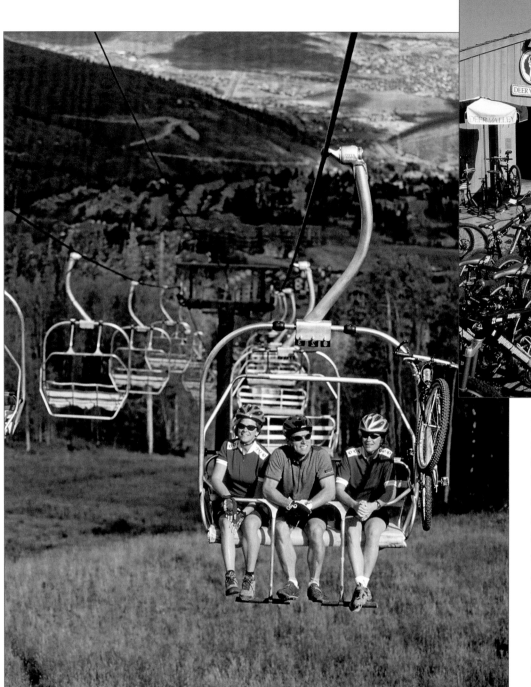

Left: Deer Valley was the first ski resort in Park City, and one of the first in Utah, to offer lift-served mountain biking and hiking. Above: The Bike Corral at Silver Lake Village offers bike rentals, tours, clinics and lessons. Opposite: As the mountain biking season closes, aspen groves turned stunning gold provide a mesmerizing backdrop for a scenic chairlift ride on the Sterling Lift.

berms, to the mountain bike patrol—a staff of seven who monitor the trails, making sure no one has lost his or her way or needs extra water on a hot day. At the Silver Lake Bike Corral at the base of Sterling lift, guests can rent mountain bikes that come with complimentary helmets and water bottles. Mountain biking lessons and clinics are offered as well.

Mountain Bike Action magazine consistently rates Deer Valley among the top 10 mountain biking destinations in the country. The mountain biking at Deer Valley has been the subject of many articles in national magazines, and Deer Valley was named "Best Place to Bike" by the Citysearch Web site in 2002. "Mountain biking is one of the things that help keep Deer Valley fresh," says Bob Wheaton, resort president and general manager. "When we first got into the sport, mountain bikers had the reputation of being the

scourge of the earth. But we opened our chairs and trails to them. People were surprised. We still maintain the core values of what Deer Valley is about, but also have some fun with it and offer some alternative experiences, whether it be the skiercross course for the public, the freestyle ski events, or the mountain biking."

The sound of fat tires crunching on gravel under hot summer sun evokes adventure in the backcountry and the fun of exploring places unreachable during the winter months. From Deer Valley Resort's network of trails, bikers

Opposite: Daring downhiller in a padded suit during Deer Valley's 2001 NORBA races. Above: Deer Valley held its first NORBA competition in 1990. Left: Racers get used to mud-speckled faces.

can access the Mid-Mountain Trail, which runs for 22 miles at an elevation of 8,000 feet through Park City Mountain Resort, ending in the Canyons Resort.

Some of Deer Valley's trails, such as The Meadow or Deer Camp, wind their way through high alpine meadows dotted with Indian paintbrush, yarrow, columbine, lupine, mountain bluebell and other wildflowers. Other trails, Thieves Forest and Fire Swamp among them, shoot straight down the fall line. Pockets of loose rock rattle handlebars as downhill riders dressed in protective pads soar down at high speeds.

Riders thirsting for a technical challenge navigate the switchbacks of Twist and Shout, Aspen Slalom or Team Big Bear (named for the California mountain biking team that cut the trail). The six-mile Tour des Suds trail gets its name from an annual locals' bike race to the top of 9,100-foot Flagstaff Mountain. At the end of the race, riders are rewarded with beer from the local brewpub. Due to certain quirks in Utah's liquor laws, race organizers cannot use the word "beer" in their advertisements, so event posters humorously promote "frothy beverages."

Deer Valley has hosted a number of national and local mountain biking races, including the region's first NORBA race in 1990. (NORBA is the National Off-Road Bicycling Association, the mountain biking arm of the United States Cycling Federation.) Deer Valley has hosted eight NORBA events as well as the national finals and a mountain biking World Cup.

This Deer Valley guest finds solitude as fat tires softly roll on a pine needle–covered trail.

Opposite: Mountain columbine, lupine and other wildflowers are abundant on Deer Valley's mountains. Above: Summer hiking and biking trails are available to every ability level, from novice to expert. Left: The aspen leaf, seen here in autumn gold, forms the background of Deer Valley's famous logo.

Deer Valley not only offers opportunities for summer sports, but also caters to special occasions. Deer Valley's splendid alpine setting and its mountain lodges, exquisite cuisine and attention-to-detail service make it a desired location for weddings. There is something about wedding vows taken in a church of trees and sky that makes them all the more poignant. Deer Valley first began catering to brides' needs after receiving an unexpected phone call. "I remember getting a phone call in February 1982, our first season open," says Karen Gibbs, Deer Valley's banquet and conference manager. "It was a young woman

asking for information about having her wedding at Deer Valley that summer. We all looked at each other in the office and said, 'My gosh!' We hadn't been focused on anything beyond getting this first-class ski resort up and running. We suddenly realized we needed a banquet manager."

Deer Valley's bakers create a multitude of wedding cakes for both on-site and off-site weddings, from the most elegant fondant to the colorful "whimsy" cakes that have become popular in recent years. The banquet crew often faces its biggest challenges in catering weddings. They have been asked to provide kosher kitchens. They have created some over-the-top settings. One wedding reception was held in a crystal-clear tent so the guests could enjoy the views of aspen and wildflowers. On another occasion, telephones were placed and wired at each table so guests could call each other from across the tent to ask for dances. "We treat every event,

THE DEER VALLEY DIFFERENCE
The Utah Symphony

The Utah Symphony Orchestra was founded in 1940. Maurice Abravanel, the music director from 1947 to 1979, put the Utah Symphony on the musical map. The orchestra performs for 70,000 school children each year through a grant from the Utah State Office of Education. The orchestra's home is the beautiful Abravanel Hall in downtown Salt Lake City.

The Utah Symphony has been pleasing summer audiences at Deer Valley since 1985. Spending Saturday evenings in July and August at outdoor Utah Symphony concerts has become a tradition for locals and visitors, who enjoy picnics on the grassy slopes behind Snow Park Lodge while they listen to the music. Utah Symphony CEO and Opera General Director, Anne Ewers, says, "We have

ABOVE: THOUSANDS OF
ENTHUSIASTS ENJOY THE UTAH
SYMPHONY AT DEER VALLEY'S
OUTDOOR AMPHITHEATER. RIGHT:
THE SUN SETS OVER A UTAH
SYMPHONY CONCERT.

TOP: SPACIOUS SEATING, EITHER ON BLANKETS OR CHAIRS, IS A GREAT FEATURE OF DEER VALLEY'S CONCERT AMPHITHEATER. BOTTOM: THE CANNONS FIRE DURING THE ANNUAL PERFORMANCE OF TCHAIKOVSKY'S *1812 OVERTURE*.

a wonderful long-term relationship with our patrons at Deer Valley, which has continued to develop beautifully over the years. The support of these patrons, along with the chance to create music in a glorious mountain setting, has made Deer Valley an ideal venue. This is certainly our second home."

The program varies each year, with performances of the classics as well as some unique pairings of the orchestra with other performers, such as pop-icon Don McLean, traditional harmony makers The Kingston Trio, western music's Michael Martin Murphy and piano artist Marvin Hamlisch. Other evenings center on musical themes, like "Bravo Broadway" and "Italian Opera Arias." The annual performance of Tchaikovsky's *1812 Overture* is everyone's favorite, with cannons firing during the final movement. This is the social scene of the weekend, where neighbors visit over picnic baskets and children run from blanket to blanket looking for treats from various friends. ☾

DEER VALLEY'S SUMMER MOUNTAIN
BIKING AND HIKING SEASON RUNS
FROM THE FIRST PART OF JUNE
THROUGH LABOR DAY. THE LIFT
IS OPEN WEDNESDAYS THROUGH
SUNDAYS DURING THE SEASON.
TRAILS ARE ALSO OPEN DURING
THE SEASON WHEN THE LIFTS ARE
NOT RUNNING AND BEFORE AND
AFTER THE OFFICIAL SEASON,
WEATHER PERMITTING. OPPOSITE:
THE FULL MOON SHINES ON
AUTUMN COLORS IN THE DEER
CREST AREA OF THE RESORT.

every wedding, as if it were our own," says Kathy Nosek, banquet and conference coordinator. "We want every couple to go away saying, 'That was the most wonderful day of our lives.' We take personal responsibility for that." At a recent wedding, the florist failed to deliver bouquets, so at the eleventh hour, Nosek plucked flowers from table settings, wrapped them at the base and calmly handed them to a grateful bride.

All of Deer Valley's summertime guests can enjoy first-class service and delicious cuisine in the comfort of the Royal Street Café in Silver Lake Lodge. Those seated on the deck are shaded by a green and white awning, while they enjoy the mountain breeze and watch the activities going on around them. Comfortable booths are available for those who prefer being indoors. The Royal Street Café offers an eclectic menu appealing to virtually every taste, with a tempting variety of appetizers, soups, salads, sandwiches,

hot dishes and desserts. Beverages, including Deer Valley's signature non-alcoholic lemonade Refreshers, wine, spirits and locally brewed beers help keep guests cool. A favorite of locals is the Mojito, a concoction of silver rum, freshly squeezed lemonade, muddled mint and a floater of dark rum.

Deer Valley's Summer Adventure Camp, held in the Children's Center at Snow Park Lodge, takes youngsters from ages 18 months through 12 years and provides them a camp experience that both teaches and entertains. Divided into three age groups, the children are led by

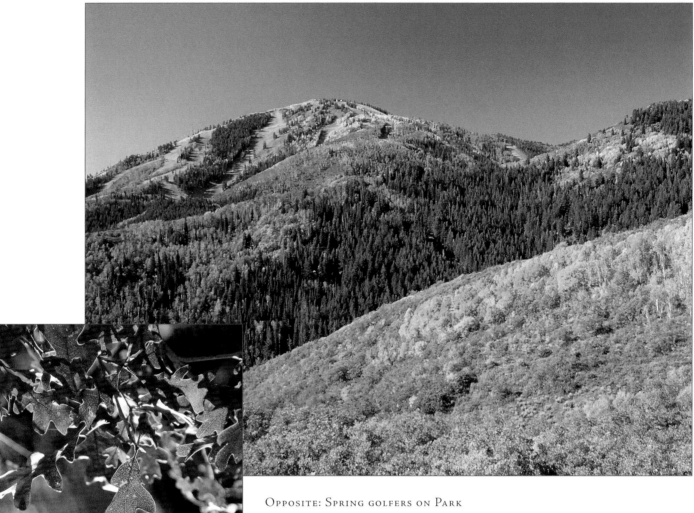

Opposite: Spring golfers on Park City Golf Course still spy snow on Deer Valley's Bald Mountain. Left: Deer Valley's terrain is home to shrubby Gambel oak that turns red in fall.

enthusiastic counselors in well-organized activities appropriate to each group. The Jamboree group (ages 18 months to three years) enjoys playtime, music and movement, art and other activities designed for toddlers. The Explorers (ages four through kindergarten) are introduced to team-building games and events, and taken on field trips to hike and explore the mountain environment. The Mountaineers (first grade through age 12) participate in nature-discovery studies and team-oriented sports as well as the hiking and exploration field trips. Mountaineers are also introduced to mountain biking and taught basic biking skills. Explorers and Mountaineers alike are offered the opportunity to participate in swimming, biking, inline skating, scavenger hunts and creative arts and crafts, with free play time and R&R (read and relax) time between activities. For the last several years, 7- to 12-year-olds at Summer Adventure Camp have participated in a program called S.A.V.E., the Summer Adventure Volunteer Experience. The children, along with their counselors, develop a project (car washes for the last two years) in which they raise money for a local cause. The theme of activities for the project week is related to the selected cause. The beneficiary of the 2003 project was Wasatch Back Country Rescue; in 2002 it was Peace House, a local women's and children's shelter.

Deer Valley visitors may attend a variety of concerts at the grassy amphitheater behind Snow Park Lodge, a popular spot for live musical entertainment. Concert goers know that there isn't a bad seat in the house at

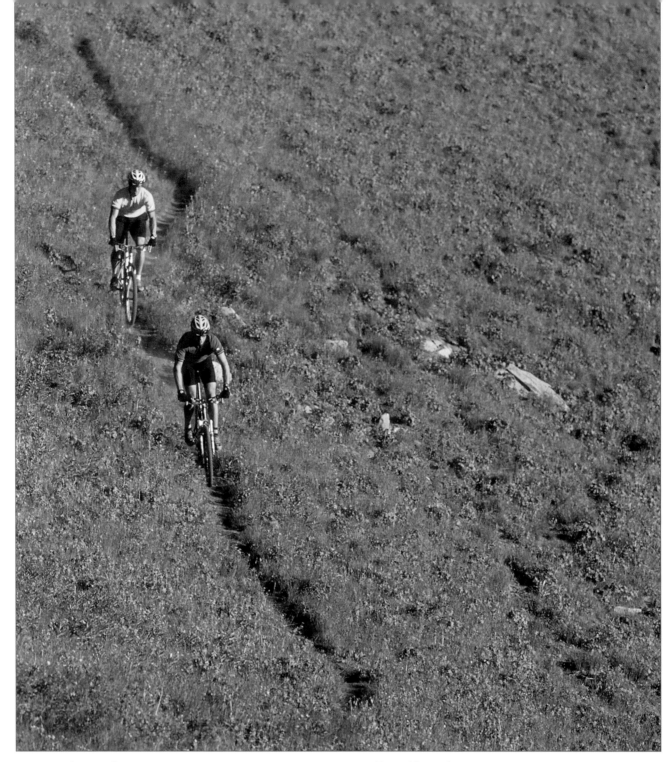

ABOVE: SINGLE TRACK TRAILS ARE HIGHLY APPEALING TO DEER VALLEY'S SUMMER MOUNTAIN BIKERS.
OPPOSITE: GOODBYE SUMMER, HELLO FALL.

a Deer Valley summer concert. Grass, not dust, is guaranteed, and the audience settles on chairs or blankets to watch the show. The Deer Valley barbecues are fired up, and grilled chicken sandwiches, brats and burgers are sold at the concert site. Picnickers may order in advance a gourmet picnic basket with a bottle of wine from Deer Valley's kitchen, or may bring their own food and beverages.

Deer Valley had hosted an annual bluegrass festival for 14 years, until 2003. Popular acts enjoyed at Deer Valley over the years have included Ani DeFranco, Indigo Girls, Lyle Lovett, Little Feat, Peter, Paul and Mary, Bob Dylan and many more. Since 1985, the Utah Symphony has played at Deer Valley on Saturday nights in July and August. As the concert proceeds, the setting sun soaks the sky in purple, gold and red, and the silhouetted moun-

tains become a backdrop like no other. The temperature drops quickly when the sun goes down, and seasoned spectators pull out blankets and fleece jackets. Children snuggle close and take in the music as they watch the stars emerge. In the meadow above the amphitheater, deer delicately pick their way across the slope. One of the last concerts each season features Tchaikovsky's *1812 Overture*. Children and adults wave miniature American flags in time to the music, as anticipation builds for the blast of cannons that comes in the final movement.

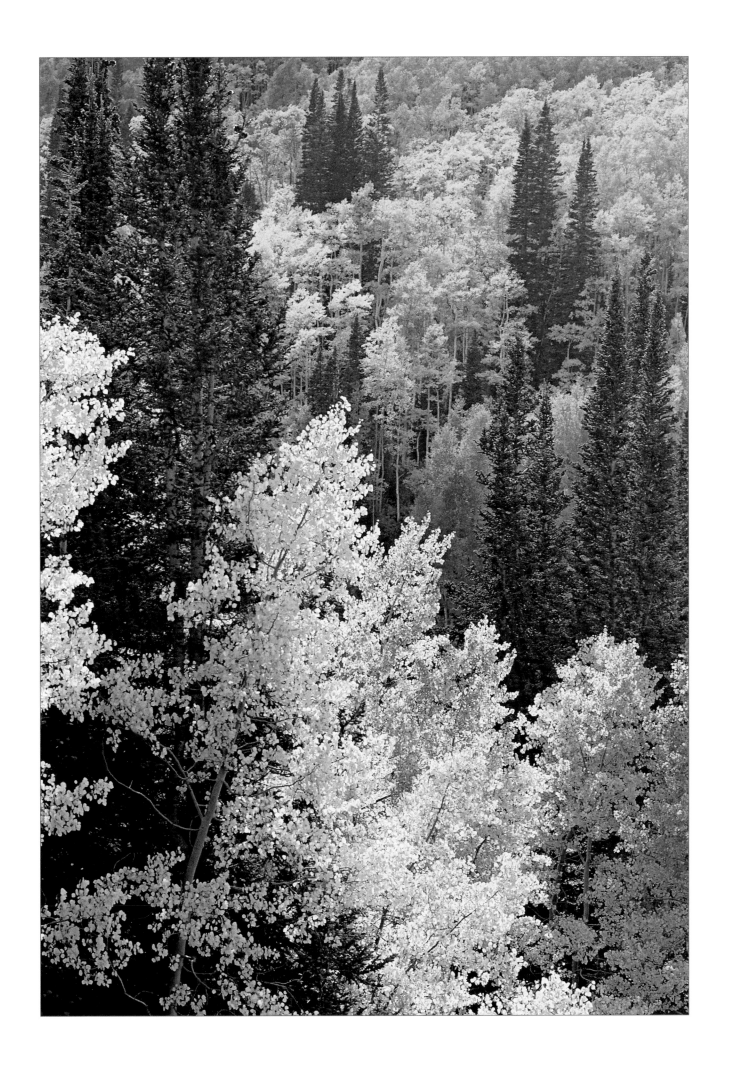

ACKNOWLEDGMENTS

Quite a few tears were shed during the writing of this book. I was taken aback by how many Deer Valley employees and guests, men and women alike, got emotional while talking with me about their roles, dreams, experiences, memories or relationships at Deer Valley. I too shed some tears during the birthing of this book. Emotions came to the surface because everyone involved with Deer Valley truly seems to care about the place and the people. Those who spend time here, as residents, employees, or guests, appreciate how fortunate they are to enjoy such a beautiful and peaceful spot, where recreation, and not turmoil, is a way of life. Granted, Deer Valley Resort is a tiny corner of a planet fraught with problems. Yet I see everyday nobility in how much people here care about what they do and strive to be their best, whether at carving a turn, bussing a table or loading a chairlift. That makes a positive statement to the world, in a small but touching way.

Thanks to my husband, Mark, and my sons Caleb Edward and Jesse MacLean, for your sublime patience while sharing me with the deadlines of this project. I want Caleb and Jesse to know this: Even when Mommy's working very hard, nothing is more important than you two are. You bring me endless joy.

Thank you, Dad, for hauling me out of bed at our Vermont house when I was seven (despite the howling wind) and teaching me to ski. Thank you, Tondo, for taking me on my first Utah ski vacation and introducing me to the pleasures of Deer Valley.

Thanks to all of those who spent countless hours talking to me, answering questions and correcting all the facts I didn't get right the first, or even the second, time around. That list includes Mr. and Mrs. Edgar Stern, Bob Wheaton, Chuck English, Julie Wilson, Bob Wells, Letty Flatt, Scott Enos, Dave Anderson, Dave Smith, Terry Bouman, Roger Burns, Stein Eriksen, Francoise Eriksen, Heidi Voelker, Steve Graff, Jim Nassikas, Roger Penske, Scott Guthrie, Kathy Nosek, Karen Gibbs, Steve Dering and Howard Kadwit. To the rest of the Deer Valley staff and guests with whom I've talked, thanks for your thoughts, stories, suggestions and openness. Many of your stories never made it into this book, but I relish them all.

To Jean Herndon, for the unexpected and countless editing hours. I'd like to bestow upon you my English grandfather's favorite phrase: "Bless Your Little Heart." Mrs. Stern's meticulous and thorough editing was truly remarkable. Thanks to Bill Grout of Mountain Sports Press for taking a chance on a first-time book writer and for urging me to "just keep going." My wish for you? Mushroom risotto cakes at the Mariposa. I'm telling you: They will change your life. Thanks to Michelle Schrantz, Scott Kronberg, Paul Prince and the rest of the crew at Mountain Sports Press for making the book look so lovely and read so well. My hat is off to all of the talented local photographers who provided images for this book. Thank you.

To Deer Valley's Coleen Reardon, Christa Graff, Erin Grady and Chris Carlson for support, assurance, encouragement and venting sessions. Thanks, women. You're truly the best. And special thanks to Gil Williams, who got me into this in the first place, for understanding, support, motivation and answers to my questions.

To Sally Elliott, Marianne Cone, Hal Compton and Sandra Morrison: I'm so impressed with your knowledge of and passion for local history, and your willingness to share it. One of the gifts to come out of working on this project is a new fascination for local lore. You sparked that fire. Thank you.

To my cherished writing friends, Bon Bon, Markman, Dana, Cheryl, Andy, Joe, Karri and Kurt, as well as Sister Kate, Susan and Dorothy of WWW. To my river divas, Virginia and Lesley, for keeping me alive via email during this process. To Les Gals (Abby, Abby, Juan and Laura) and Ardys, for the same reason. To Mom, Kathi and Kimmy, and the rest of the Gould and Case clans, my friends and neighbors, for keeping the faith and putting up with eight months of hearing about this book. I'm done now. I promise.

Most of all, I'd like to thank the Deer Valley employees, those I know and those I don't, for working so hard that every time I'm at Deer Valley skiing, mountain biking, hiking or dining, I find myself thinking, "This is a magical place." I know that takes a lot of behind-the-scenes effort. Thank you.

Cheers to the happiness that skiing and dining in the mountains has brought me, and to the fact that I've been lucky enough to enjoy those things with all my heart.

—Kristen Gould Case, September 2003

BIBLIOGRAPHY

BOOKS

2002 Salt Lake City
The *Deseret News* Staff

Treasure Mountain Home, Park City Revisited
George A. Thompson and Fraser Buck

Come Ski With Me
Stein Eriksen

Park City Trails
Raye Carleson Ringholz

Walking Through Historic Park City
Raye Carleson Ringholz and Bea Kummer

First Tracks, A Century of Skiing in Utah
Alan K. Engen and Gregory C. Thompson

For the Love of Skiing: A Visual History
Alan K. Engen

In Pursuit of Perfection: Team Penske Indy Car
Hazleton Publishing, 1994–95

ARTICLES

"Riding the Rails" and "Livin' on the Line"
David Hampshire, as published in *Park City* magazine

"The One and Only Stein,"
Morten Lund, as published in *Skiing Heritage*

"For the Corporate Penske, No Fear of Sharp Turns"
Edward Wyatt, *The New York Times*, 1996

"Taking Care of Business"
Leon Mandel with Donald Davidson, *Autoweek*, 1993

"The Story of Aspen"
Mary Hayes

SKI magazine archives

INTERVIEWS

Tom Kelly and Juliann Fritz from the United States
Ski and Snowboard Association

Sally Elliott, Marianne Cone, Sandra Morrison
and Hal Compton from the Park City Historical Society

Edgar and Polly Stern, Roger Penske, Bob Wheaton,
Chuck English, Stein and Francoise Eriksen, Heidi Voelker,
Gil Williams, Cindy Williams, Chris Sprecher, Cheryl Fox,
Dave Staley, Kathy Nosek, Scott Guthrie, Karen Gibbs,
Julie Wilson, Letty Flatt, Scott Enos, Dave Anderson,
Dave Smith, Roger Burns, Terry Bouman, Bob Wells,
John Guay, Maca Leontic and Steve Graff from
Deer Valley Resort.

Steve Dering

Jan Wilking

Howard Kadwit

Jim Nassikas

TRANSCRIPTS

Mel Fletcher Oral History Interview
Anji Buckner, May 10–June 28, 2000,
courtesy of the Park City Historical Society

VIDEOS

The Legendary Skier: The Stein Eriksen Story
White Wing Visions, 2001

Skiing with Edgar, Stein and Bob, 3.14.01
Manitou Productions video

"Stein, Edgar and Jim" fireside chat video

Silver and Snow, The Park City Story
Park City Historical Society, 2002

The Greatest Snow on Earth: Utah's Skiing Story
Working Title Productions

OTHER

Park City Museum and Historical Society

Alf Engen Ski Museum

The notebook of letters from Edgar Stern's 80th birthday party

PHOTO CREDITS

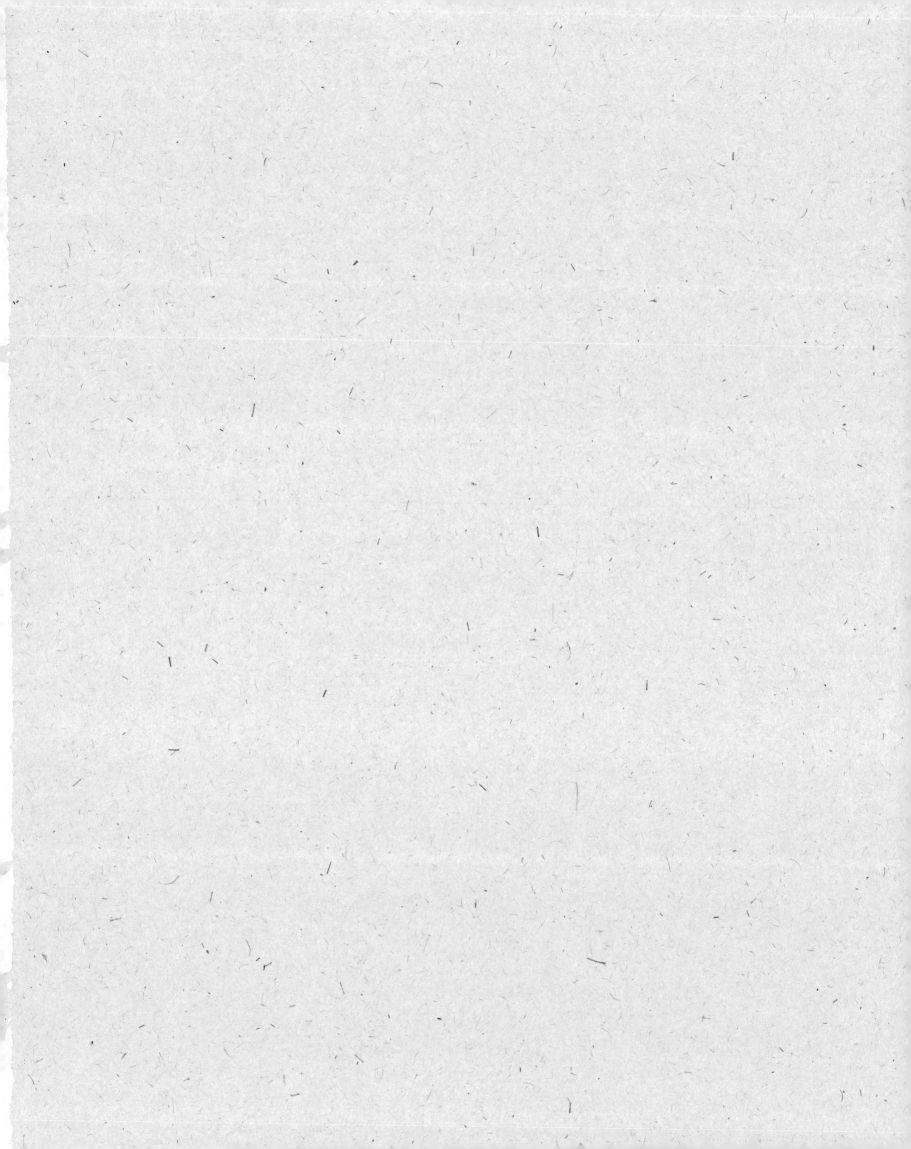